Quest

Second Edition

2

 **Reading and Writing**

Pamela Hartmann

 **McGraw-Hill**

Quest 2 Reading and Writing, 2nd Edition

Published by McGraw-Hill ESL/ELT, a business unit of The McGraw-Hill Companies, Inc. 1221 Avenue of the Americas, New York, NY 10020. Copyright © 2007 by The McGraw-Hill Companies, Inc. All rights reserved. No part of this publication may be reproduced or distributed in any form or by any means, or stored in a database or retrieval system, without the prior written consent of The McGraw-Hill Companies, Inc., including, but not limited to, in any network or other electronic storage or transmission, or broadcast for distance learning.

ISBN 13: 978-0-07-325302-2
ISBN 10: 0-07-325302-2
1 2 3 4 5 6 7 8 9 VNH/VNH 12 11 10 09 08 07 06

ISBN 13: 978-0-07-110335-0 (INTERNATIONAL STUDENT BOOK)
ISBN 10: 0-07-110335-X
1 2 3 4 5 6 7 8 9 VNH/VNH 12 11 10 09 08 07 06

Editorial director: Erik Gundersen
Series editor: Linda O'Roke
Development editor: Jennifer Bixby
Production manager: Juanita Thompson
Production coordinator: MaryRose Malley
Cover designer: David Averbach, Anthology
Interior designer: Martini Graphic Services, Inc.
Artists: Jonathan Massie, Ron Mahoney
Photo researchers: David Averbach, Tobi Zausner, Poyee Oster

INTERNATIONAL EDITION ISBN 0-07-110335-X
Copyright © 2007. Exclusive rights by The McGraw-Hill Companies, Inc., for manufacture and export. This book cannot be re-exported from the country to which it is sold by McGraw-Hill. The International Edition is not available in North America.

 **McGraw-Hill**

www.esl-elt.mcgraw-hill.com

The *McGraw-Hill* Companies

● ● ● ● ● ACKNOWLEDGEMENTS

The publisher and author would like to thank the following education professionals whose comments, reviews, and assistance were instrumental in the development of the Quest series.

- **Roberta Alexander,** San Diego Community College District
- **David Dahnke,** North Harris College (Houston, TX)
- **Mary Díaz,** Broward Community College (Davie, FL)
- **Judith García,** Miami-Dade College
- **Elizabeth Giles,** The School District of Hillsborough County, Florida
- **Patricia Heiser,** University of Washington, Seattle
- **Yoshiko Matsubayashi,** Kokusai Junior College, Tokyo
- **Ahmed Motala,** University of Sharjah, United Arab Emirates
- **Dee Parker and Andy Harris,** AUA, Bangkok
- **Alison Rice,** Hunter College, City University of New York
- **Alice Savage,** North Harris College (Houston, TX)
- **Katharine Sherak,** San Francisco State University
- **Leslie Eloise Somers,** Miami-Dade County Public Schools
- **Karen Stanley,** Central Piedmont Community College (Charlotte, NC)
- **Diane Urairat,** Mahidol Language Services, Bangkok
- **Pamela Vittorio,** The New School (New York, NY)
- **Anne Marie Walters,** California State University, Long Beach
- **Lynne Wilkins,** Mills College (Oakland, CA)
- **Sean Wray, Elizabeth Watson, and Mariko Yokota,** Waseda International University, Tokyo

Many, many thanks go to Marguerite Ann Snow, who provided the initial inspiration for the entire series. Heartfelt thanks also to Erik Gundersen, Linda O'Roke, and Jennifer Bixby for their help in the development of the second edition. I would also like to thank Dylan Bryan-Dolman, Susannah MacKay, Kristin Sherman, and Kristin Thalheimer, whose opinions were invaluable. I thank Keith Folse for the four-section grid on page 45 and Eli Hinkel for the ideas on hedging on pages 252–253.

TABLE OF CONTENTS

TO THE TEACHER

Quest: The Series

Quest Second Edition prepares students for academic success. The series features two complementary strands—*Reading and Writing* and *Listening and Speaking*—each with four levels. The integrated Quest program provides robust scaffolding to support and accelerate each student's journey from exploring general interest topics to mastering academic content.

Quest parallels and accelerates the process native-speaking students go through when they prepare for success in a variety of academic subjects. By previewing typical college course material, *Quest* helps students get "up to speed" in terms of both academic content and language skills.

In addition, *Quest* prepares students for the daunting amount and type of reading, writing, listening, and speaking required for college success. The four *Reading and Writing* books combine high-interest material from newspapers and magazines with readings from academic textbooks. Reading passages increase in length and difficulty across the four levels. The *Listening and Speaking* books in the *Quest* series contain listening strategies and practice activities based on authentic audio and video recordings from "person on the street" interviews, radio programs, and college lectures. Similar to the *Reading and Writing* books, the four *Listening and Speaking* books increase in difficulty with each level.

Quest Second Edition Features

- New *Intro* level providing on-ramp to Books 1-3
- Redesigned, larger format with captivating photos
- Expanded focus on critical thinking and test-taking strategies
- Addition of research paper to *Reading and Writing* strand
- New unit-ending *Vocabulary Workshops* and end-of-book academic word lists
- Expanded video program (VHS and DVD) with new lecture and updated social language footage
- EZ Test® CD-ROM-based test generator for all *Reading and Writing* titles
- Teacher's Editions with activity-by-activity procedural notes, expansion activities, and tests
- Test-taking strategy boxes that highlight skills needed for success on the new TOEFL® iBT test

Quest Reading and Writing

Quest Reading and Writing includes three or four distinct units, each focusing on a different area of college study—sociology, biology, business, history, psychology, art history, anthropology, literature, or economics. Each unit contains two thematically-related chapters.

TOEFL is a registered trademark of Educational Testing Service (ETS). This publication is not endorsed or approved by ETS.

Chapter Structure

Each chapter of *Quest 2 Reading and Writing* contains five parts that blend reading and writing skills within the context of a particular academic area of study. Readings and activities build upon one another and increase in difficulty as students work through the five sections of each chapter.

Part 1: Introduction
- Before Reading – discussion activities on photos introduce the chapter topic
- Reading – a high-interest reading captures students' attention
- After Reading – activities check students' understanding and allow for further discussion

Part 2: General Interest Reading
- Before Reading – prediction and vocabulary activities prepare students for reading
- Reading – a high-interest reading at a slightly higher level than the reading in Part 1 allows students to explore the chapter topic in more depth
- After Reading – comprehension, discussion, and vocabulary activities check understanding

Part 3: Academic Reading
- Before Reading – prediction and vocabulary activities prepare students for reading
- Reading – a textbook selection prepares students for academic reading
- After Reading – strategies (such as skimming for main ideas, using a dictionary, and synthesizing) and activities give students the opportunity to use academic skills

Part 4: The Mechanics of Writing
- Chapter-specific writing, grammar, lexical, and punctuation boxes equip students to express their ideas.
- Content-driven grammar boxes are followed by contextualized practice activities that prepare students for independent writing assignments.

Part 5: Academic Writing
- A step-by-step model leads students through the writing process which may include brainstorming, narrowing the topic, writing topic sentences, planning the writing, and developing ideas into a paragraph.
- Writing assignments focus on a variety of rhetorical styles: chronological, description, analysis, persuasive, and process.
- Writing assignments ask students to use the writing mechanics taught.

Teacher's Editions

The *Quest Teacher's Editions* provide instructors with activity-by-activity teaching suggestions, cultural and background notes, Internet links to more information on the unit themes, expansion black-line master activities, chapter tests, and a complete answer key.

The *Quest Teacher's Editions* also provide test-taking boxes that highlight skills found in *Quest* that are needed for success on the new TOEFL® iBT test.

Video Program

For the *Quest Listening and Speaking* books, a newly expanded video program on DVD or VHS incorporates authentic classroom lectures with social language vignettes.

Lectures

The lecture portion of each video features college and university professors delivering high-interest mini-lectures on topics as diverse as animal communication, personal finance, and Greek art. The mini-lectures run from two minutes at the *Intro* level to six minutes by Book 3. As students listen to the lectures they complete structured outlines to model accurate note taking. Well-organized post-listening activities teach students how to use and refer to their notes in order to answer questions about the lecture and to review for a test.

Social Language

The social language portion of the videos gives students the chance to hear authentic conversations on topics relevant to the chapter topic and academic life. A series of scenes shot on or around an urban college campus features nine engaging students participating in a host of curricular and extracurricular activities. The social language portion of the video is designed to help English language students join study groups, interact with professors, and make friends.

Audio Program

Each reading selection on the audio CD or audiocassette program allows students to hear new vocabulary words, listen for intonation cues, and increase their reading speed. Each reading is recorded at an appropriate rate while remaining authentic.

Test Generator

For the *Quest Reading and Writing* books, an EZ Test® CD-ROM test generator allows teachers to create customized tests in a matter of minutes. EZ Test® is a flexible and easy-to-use desktop test generator. It allows teachers to create tests from unit-specific test banks or to write their own questions.

SCOPE AND SEQUENCE

Chapter	Reading Strategies	Writing Strategies
UNIT 1 BUSINESS		
Chapter 1 **Doing Business Internationally** • Introduction: *International Marketing Mistakes* • General Interest Reading: *International Culture* • Academic Reading: *Improving CQ: Understanding Cultural Values*	• Understanding New Words • Dealing with New Words • Guessing the Meaning from Context: Punctuation • Predicting • Finding the Main Idea • Finding Details • Thinking Ahead • Guessing the Meaning from Context: Using Logic • Using Graphic Organizers: Venn Diagrams and Charts	• Focus: Writing an Expository Paragraph • Strategy: Making Inferences
Chapter 2 **The Global Economy** • Introduction: *The Exchange of Material Goods* • General Interest Reading: *Excerpt from Lawrence Durrell's* Bitter Lemons • Academic Reading: *Economic Systems*	• Previewing for Topics • Guessing the Meaning from Context: Accepting Incomplete Knowledge • Understanding Parts of Speech • Guessing the Meaning from Context • Keeping a Word Journal • Guessing the Meaning from Context: Using the Next Sentence • Marking a Textbook • Finding the Topic Sentence • Using Graphic Organizers: Charts	• Focus: Writing a Paragraph of Analysis • Strategy: Writing a Topic Sentence

The Mechanics of Writing	Critical Thinking Strategies	Test-Taking Strategies
UNIT 1 BUSINESS		
• Simple Present and Simple Past • Modals of Advice • The Subject *You* • Adjective Clauses • Transitional Expressions: Coordinating Conjunctions	• Thinking Ahead • Making Inferences	• Finding Details • Guessing the Meaning from Context: Using Logic • Finding Errors • Editing a Test Essay
• The Passive Voice • Transitional Expressions: Adverbial Conjunctions • Recognizing and Repairing Run-Ons and Comma Splices	• Synthesizing and Applying Information • Using Graphic Organizers: Charts	• Understanding Parts of Speech • Guessing the Meaning from Context

Chapter	Reading Strategies	Writing Strategies
UNIT 2 ART HISTORY		
Chapter 3 **Themes and Purposes** • Introduction: *Looking at Art: What's the Story?* • General Interest Reading: *The Sacred Realm of Art* • Academic Reading: *Art as the Mirror of Everyday Life*	• Determining Point of View • Guessing the Meaning from Context: Pictures and Captions • Finding Main Ideas: Major Sub-Topics • Understanding Italics	• Focus: Writing a Paragraph of Comparison-Contrast • Strategy: Gathering Supporting Material
Chapter 4 **The Ancient World: Egypt** • Introduction: *The Rules of Egyptian Art* • General Interest Reading: *Finds Reveal Much of Life at Pyramids* • Academic Reading: *Egyptian Civilization: A Brief History*	• Guessing the Meaning from Context: Using Opposites • Recognizing Style: Newspaper Feature Stories • Guessing the Meaning from Context: *in other words, that is, i.e.* • Finding Evidence	• Focus: Writing a Paragraph of Cause and Effect
UNIT 3 PSYCHOLOGY		
Chapter 5 **States of Consciousness** • Introduction: *Lucid Dreaming* • General Interest Reading: *Dreaming Across Cultures* • Academic Reading: *The Function and Meaning of Dreaming*	• Understanding Ellipses • Having Questions in Mind • Finding the Topic Sentence • Choosing the Correct Dictionary Definition	• Focus: Writing a Paragraph of Analysis • Strategy: Writing about Symbols • Strategy: Gathering and Organizing Ideas • Strategy: Using Graphic Organizers: Idea Maps

The Mechanics of Writing	Critical Thinking Strategies	Test-Taking Strategies
UNIT 2 ART HISTORY		
• Appositives • Adjective Clauses • Participial Phrases • Prepositional Phrases • Adjectives • Order of Adjectives • Transitional Expressions: Comparison-Contrast	• Comparing and Contrasting Two Works of Art • Determining Point of View	• Understanding Pronouns
• Infinitives of Purpose • Transitional Expressions of Cause and Effect: Subordinating Conjunctions • Transitional Expressions and Phrases • Conjunctions of Cause and Effect: Review	• Identifying Causes and Effects • Finding Evidence	• Applying Information
UNIT 3 PSYCHOLOGY		
• Transitional Words of Time • Verbs in Narration • Writing about Symbols	• Determining Point of View • Having Questions in Mind	• Answering Questions about Details

Chapter	Reading Strategies	Writing Strategies
Chapter 6 **Abnormal Psychology** • Introduction: *Culture and Mental Illness* • General Interest Reading: *What is Abnormal?* • Academic Reading: *Approaches to Psychological Therapy*	• Understanding Connotation • Finding an Implied Main Idea	• Focus: Writing a Summary Paragraph • Strategy: Paraphrasing and Citing Your Sources
UNIT 4 HEALTH		
Chapter 7 **Medicine and Drugs: Addictive Substances** • Introduction: *Consequences of Addiction* • General Interest Reading: *Drug Use and Abuse Worldwide* • Academic Reading: *Addiction: What Can Be Done About It?*	• Understanding Metaphors • Noticing British English	• Focus: Writing a Persuasive Paragraph • Strategy: Writing a Good Proposition
Chapter 8 **The Mind-Body Relationship** • Introduction: *What Does New Research Tell Us?* • General Interest Reading: *The New Science of Mind and Body* • Academic Reading: *A Skeptical Look: Placebo Effect*	• Scanning for Specific Information • Guessing the Meaning from Context: Review of Dictionary Use	• Focus: Writing a Persuasive Paragraph • Strategy: Hedging

The Mechanics of Writing	Critical Thinking Strategies	Test-Taking Strategies
• Passive Voice • Writing Definitions with Adjective Clauses • Writing about Advantages and Disadvantages • Adverbial Conjunctions	• Using a T-Chart to Analyze Advantages and Disadvantages • Finding an Implied Main Idea	• Understanding Stems and Affixes
UNIT 4 HEALTH		
• Subordinating Conjunctions • Identifying and Repairing Fragments • Present Unreal Conditional	• Predicting Opposing Arguments • Understanding Metaphors	• Finding Sentences with Similar Meaning
• Expressing Possibility • Review of Conjunctions • Italics and Quotation Marks	• Seeing Two Sides of an Issue • Hedging	• Determining Topic, Main Point, Purpose, and Tone

Welcome

Quest Second Edition prepares students for academic success. The series features two complementary strands—*Reading and Writing* and *Listening and Speaking*—each with four levels. The integrated Quest program provides robust scaffolding to support and accelerate each student's journey from exploring general interest topics to mastering academic content.

New second edition features

- New *Intro* level providing on-ramp to Books 1-3

- Redesigned, larger format with captivating photos

- Expanded focus on critical thinking skills

- Addition of research paper to *Reading and Writing* strand

- New unit-ending *Vocabulary Workshops* and end-of-book Academic Word List (AWL)

- Expanded video program (VHS/DVD) with new lecture and updated social language footage

- EZ Test® CD-ROM test generator for all *Reading and Writing* titles

- Test-Taking strategy boxes that highlight skills needed for success on the new TOEFL® iBT

- Teacher's Editions with activity-by-activity procedural notes, expansion activities, and tests

Captivating photos and graphics capture students' attention while introducing each academic topic.

U N I T 2

ART

Chapter 3
Themes and Purposes

Chapter 4
The Ancient World: Egypt

Test-Taking Strategy

Understanding Pronouns

On reading tests and when reading in general, it's important to understand the meaning of subject pronouns (such as *he, she, it, they*) and object pronouns (such as *him, her, it, them*). Each pronoun refers to a noun or **noun phrase** (small group of words) that comes before it. Writers use pronouns because they want to avoid repeating a noun.

Examples: People without much experience in art often do not know what to look for in a work of art. They might glance quickly at a painting or sculpture and decide immediately if they like it or not.

D. UNDERSTANDING PRONOUNS What do the pronouns in green mean in the sentences below? Highlight the noun or noun phrase that the pronoun refers to.

1. Art attempts to take something spiritual and make it visible.

2. The creature's catlike eyes identify him as the infant man-jaguar.

3. Masks do not appear casually in the community. Rather, people call on them during difficult times.

4. An image from Tibet shows the Buddha sitting in meditation. He is the largest figure and faces front.

5. The *bodhisattvas* have postponed their goal of Nirvana because they want to help other people to reach that goal.

Critical Thinking Strategy

Comparing and Contrasting Two Works of Art

When reading, students often need to compare and contrast two things–in other words, look for similarities and differences between two or more things. This frequently happens in an art history class because it is often necessary to compare and contrast works of art.

One way to compare two things is to make a **simple list.**

Example: In both the Olmec and Bwa cultures:
• art is evidence of the religion.
• communication with the spirit realm is important.
• the art involves animals.

The best way to contrast two things is with a specific graphic organizer called a **T-chart.** It's called a T-chart because of its shape, like the letter T.

Example:

Olmec	Bwa
ancient	present-day
figures	masks
purpose unclear	purpose is to manifest nature spirits

Strategy-based approach develops reading, writing, critical thinking, and test-taking skills needed for academic success.

Three high-interest reading selections in each chapter introduce students to the course content most frequently required by universities.

Read about marketing mistakes. As you read, think about this question:
• What mistake did these companies make?

International Marketing Mistakes

Chicken in China

The slogan for KFC (Kentucky Fried Chicken) used to be "finger-lickin' good."
5 This meant that the chicken tasted good—*so* good that you would want to lick your fingers that held a
10 piece of it. The unfortunate translation of this slogan into Chinese was "eat your fingers off."

A Kentucky Fried Chicken restaurant in China

Mineral Water

15 One brand of Italian mineral water is Traficante. There was no problem with this in Italy. However, there *was* a problem when the company wanted to sell its product in some other countries. Unfortunately, in Spanish, *traficante* means "drug dealer"—someone who sells drugs illegally.

Nike Shoes

20 Nike once filmed a TV commercial in Kenya. The camera closed in on a tribesman who spoke in his language, Maa. The famous Nike slogan appeared on the TV screen: "Just Do It." However, in his own language, the Kenyan was actually saying something different: "I don't want these. Give me big shoes." The commercial was intended for TV in the United States, so the company didn't change it.

Samarin for Upset Stomachs

25 Samarin is a Swedish medicine for stomach problems. Several years ago, the company had a magazine ad in three sections, like a comic strip. It showed a man on the left. He was holding his stomach and looked sick. In the middle section, he was drinking a glass of Samarin. In the section on the right, the man was smiling. The company probably wishes that it had asked for the opinion of Arabic speakers before it began this advertising program in the Middle East. People read Arabic from right to left. Therefore, many
30 potential customers saw the ad and thought, "This product will make me sick."

Art as the Mirror of Everyday Life

When children start to draw and paint, they deal with the images that they know best: mother and father, sisters and brothers, the teacher, the house, the dog. Many artists never lose their interest in everyday things, so much of our finest art depicts subjects that are close to the artist's personal world.

5 Art that depicts the moments of everyday life and its surroundings is known as *genre*. Often, its purpose is a simple one—to record, to please the eye, to make us smile. Images like this
10 occur in all periods of the history of art, in all cultures and parts of the world. A charming example from China is *Court Ladies Preparing Newly Woven Silk*. No grand political or
15 social issues are presented here. Instead, the artist has depicted a delightful scene of daily activity: Three women and a girl stretch and

Figure 1: *Court Ladies Preparing Newly Woven Silk*, from China, 12th century

iron a piece of silk, while a little girl
20 peeks underneath to see what is going on. The women's pastel kimonos, their quiet gestures, and the atmosphere of pleasant shared work give us a gentle masterpiece of Chinese genre.

Equally charming genre pieces occur in an early French manuscript, one page of which we shall study here. During the Middle Ages (about
30 1100–1500 A.D.), wealthy people paid artists to illuminate (hand-paint) books, especially prayer books. In the early 15th century, the Limbourg Brothers illuminated one of the most
35 famous books in the history of art, *Les Très Riches Heures* ("the very rich book of hours"). It contains a calendar, with each month's painting showing a seasonal activity.
40 The *February* page, shown here, depicts a small hut with three people around a fire. They have pulled their clothes back to get maximum

Figure 2: *February* page from *Les Tres Riches Heures du Duc de Berry*. Illumination. Musee Conde, Chantilly

Gradual curve in each chapter from general interest to academic content supports students as they engage in increasingly more difficult material.

Discussion, pair-work, and group-work activities **scaffold the learning process** as students move from general interest to academic content.

Finding the Topic Sentence

As you know, you can find the main idea of a paragraph in the **topic sentence**. Usually, this is the first sentence of the paragraph. However, sometimes the first sentence is either too general or too specific to be the topic sentence. Instead, you will find the main idea in another sentence. When this happens, look for an "umbrella" sentence that covers all of the details in the paragraph.

C. FINDING THE TOPIC SENTENCE In the reading on pages 145–147, the topic sentence was the first sentence in only two of the paragraphs. Which ones? In the other paragraphs, where was the topic sentence? Highlight it.

In small groups, compare your highlighted sentences. Did everyone highlight the same sentences?

D. IDENTIFYING GENERAL AND SPECIFIC IDEAS Look back at the topic sentences you highlighted in the reading on pages 145–147. Write how the groups of people in the chart below use or understand dreams. Then write examples or details from the reading that support your answers.

Group of People	How They Use or Understand Dreams (general ideas)	Examples or Details (specific ideas)
Artists		
Egyptians		
Greeks/Medieval Christians		
Senoi		
Native Americans		

Compare your answers with a partner's answers.

E. VOCABULARY CHECK Look back at the reading on pages 145–147 to find the words for these definitions. Line numbers are in parentheses. Write the correct words on the lines.

1. magic words (40–45) _____

2. experiencing (a dream) (55–60) _____

3. fear, anger, or hatred toward another person (80–85) _____

UNIT ① VOCABULARY WORKSHOP

Review vocabulary that you learned in Chapters 1 and 2.

A. MATCHING Match the words to the definitions. Write the correct letters on the lines.

Words

___f___ **1.** acquaintance

_____ **2.** acquire

_____ **3.** behavior

_____ **4.** costly

_____ **5.** determine

_____ **6.** edible

_____ **7.** enterprise

_____ **8.** hierarchy

_____ **9.** ignore

_____**10.** synthesize

Definitions

a. way of acting

b. expensive

c. decide

d. business

e. put together information from different sources

f. someone whom you know—but not a close friend

g. get

h. pay no attention to (something or someone)

i. something you can eat

j. organization into a system of ranks from lowest to highest

B. WORDS IN PHRASES: PREPOSITIONS It will help your vocabulary and grammar to begin to notice words in phrases. In this exercise, fill in each blank with the correct preposition that belongs in the phrase. To check your answers, turn back to pages 19–20.

A knowledge ___of___ cultural values is essential for cultural intelligence.

Thomas and Inkson give two ways to look _____ cultural values. The first

is from Geert Hofstede, a Dutch social scientist . . . Statistical analysis of the country differences showed

these to fall into four separate areas ("dimensions"):

Individualism. In individualistic cultures, people think _____ themselves

as individuals and prefer _____ work alone or to do activities in small

Unit-Ending *Vocabulary Workshops* reinforce key **unit vocabulary** that appears on the Academic Word List (AWL).

Expanded video program for the *Listening and Speaking* titles now includes mini-lectures to build comprehension and note-taking skills, and updated social language scenes to develop conversation skills.

Audio program selections are indicated with this icon 🎧 and include recordings of all lectures, conversations, pronunciation and intonation activities, and reading selections.

Teacher's Edition provides activity-by-activity teaching suggestions, expansion activities, tests, and special TOEFL® iBT preparation notes

EZ Test® CD-ROM test generator for the *Reading and Writing* titles allows teachers to create customized tests in a matter of minutes.

UNIT 1

BUSINESS

Chapter 1
Doing Business Internationally

Chapter 2
The Global Economy

Doing Business Internationally

Discuss these questions:
- Look at the picture. What are some things you can buy in this building?
- What country do you think the building is in?
- What do you know about Starbucks Coffee?

PART ① INTRODUCTION International Marketing Mistakes

BEFORE READING

A Tide ad

A Coca-Cola ad

👥 **THINKING AHEAD** Look at the advertisements (ads) above. Discuss these questions with a partner.

1. Which country produces these products?

2. What languages are in the ads? In which countries might you see these ads?

3. Which of these products have you seen or used?

READING

Read about marketing mistakes. As you read, think about this question:
• What mistake did these companies make?

International Marketing Mistakes

Chicken in China

The slogan for KFC (Kentucky Fried Chicken) used to be "finger-lickin' good."
5 This meant that the chicken tasted good— *so* good that you would want to lick your fingers that held a
10 piece of it. The unfortunate translation of this slogan into Chinese was "eat your fingers off."

A Kentucky Fried Chicken restaurant in China

Mineral Water

15 One brand of Italian mineral water is Traficante. There was no problem with this in Italy. However, there *was* a problem when the company wanted to sell its product in some other countries. Unfortunately, in Spanish, *traficante* means "drug dealer"—someone who sells drugs illegally.

Nike Shoes

Nike once filmed a TV commercial in Kenya. The camera closed in on a tribesman
20 who spoke in his language, Maa. The famous Nike slogan appeared on the TV screen: "Just Do It." However, in his own language, the Kenyan was actually saying something different: "I don't want these. Give me big shoes." The commercial was intended for TV in the United States, so the company didn't change it.

Samarin for Upset Stomachs

Samarin is a Swedish medicine for stomach problems. Several years ago, the company
25 had a magazine ad in three sections, like a comic strip. It showed a man on the left. He was holding his stomach and looked sick. In the middle section, he was drinking a glass of Samarin. In the section on the right, the man was smiling. The company probably wishes that it had asked for the opinion of Arabic speakers before it began this advertising program in the Middle East. People read Arabic from right to left. Therefore, many
30 potential customers saw the ad and thought, "This product will make me sick."

Gerber Baby Food

For many years, there has been a picture of a cute baby on every jar of Gerber baby food. However, this
35 was a problem when Gerber began to sell its product in Africa. There are people who cannot read in some areas of Africa. For this reason, it is the custom to put pictures on the labels to show what product is inside. Imagine the horror of people there when they saw their first jar.

Source: Marketing Translation Mistakes (http://www.i18nguy.com/translations.html)

AFTER READING

A. CHECK YOUR UNDERSTANDING With a partner, discuss the mistakes that each of these companies made.

- KFC
- Traficante
- Samarin
- Gerber
- Nike

Example: KFC didn't check the translation of its slogan into Chinese.

Critical Thinking Strategy

Making Inferences

Sometimes writers don't **state** (say) something directly. Readers have to **infer** (guess or figure out) the meaning. In other words, they have to **make an inference**.

Example: **You read:** "The unfortunate translation of this slogan into Chinese was 'eat your fingers off.'"
You infer: The company didn't understand the meaning of its own slogan in Chinese.

B. MAKING INFERENCES Infer the answers to the questions in the chart below. Write your answers in the boxes. Then compare your answers with a partner's answers.

Company	Information	Inference
Traficante	There was a problem when the company wanted to sell its product in some other countries. Unfortunately, in Spanish, *traficante* means "drug dealer" (someone who sells drugs illegally).	Why was this a problem?
Nike	In his own language, the Kenyan was actually saying something different: "I don't want these. Give me big shoes." The commercial was intended for TV in the United States, so the company didn't change it.	What did the company think about the TV audience (viewers) in the United States?
Samarin	The company probably wishes that it had asked for the opinion of Arabic speakers before it began this advertising program in the Middle East.	What didn't the company do?

Reading Strategy

Understanding New Words

When you're learning a new language, you find many words that you don't know. At first, you might want to use the dictionary every time you see a new word, but really there are so many new words that it is almost impossible to look them all up. You will save time and enjoy the language more if you learn to guess the meaning of many new words without using a dictionary.

C. UNDERSTANDING NEW WORDS Read the made-up words in the ads below. In your opinion, what is the question on the left? What is the answer on the right? What is the company advertising?

BEFORE READING

In what cultures do people **bow**?

Where might this **marketplace** be?

Why is this man hitting his elbow?
What might this gesture mean?

👥 **A. THINKING AHEAD** In small groups, discuss these questions about the pictures.

1. Where are the people in each picture? What are they doing? Discuss the question below each picture.

2. Can you think of some possible problems for people who do business in different countries?

3. Before you travel to another country, what information is helpful to have about the **culture** (common social practices) in that country?

Dealing with New Words

You will often find new words when you read in English. It's important not to use a dictionary for every new word. Instead, follow these steps.

1. Try to guess the meaning of a new word from the **context**. The context is the sentence or paragraph that the word is in.

2. If you can guess the meaning, don't use a dictionary (even if you don't understand the exact meaning).

3. Sometimes the context is too **limited** (short, not helpful), or there are too many new words, so you can't guess the meaning. What should you do? First, decide how important the word is.

4. If the word isn't **essential** (absolutely necessary), don't worry about it. Just keep reading.

5. If the word is essential and you can't understand the sentence or paragraph without it, you'll need to use a monolingual (English-English) dictionary. Your teacher can suggest one.

B. DEALING WITH NEW WORDS Read the sentences below. Using the steps from the box above, try to guess the meaning of the green words. Circle your answers and write your guesses on the lines. (**Note:** These are just made-up words.)

1. This is one of the largest **ebbists** in the country but not one of the largest companies in the world.

Is it possible to guess the meaning?　　(Yes)　　No　　Yes, but not exactly

If yes, my guess: _companies_ _____

If no, is the word important?　　　　Yes　　No

2. It's especially important to **mebegle**.

Is it possible to guess the meaning?　　Yes　　No　　Yes, but not exactly

If yes, my guess: _____

If no, is the word important?　　　　Yes　　No

3. It's important to avoid decisions based on **lazzapilts**—mistaken ideas.

Is it possible to guess the meaning?　　Yes　　No　　Yes, but not exactly

If yes, my guess: _____

If no, is the word important?　　　　Yes　　No

4. We need to think about the **tubblies**—for example, the health and education systems.

Is it possible to guess the meaning?　　Yes　　No　　Yes, but not exactly

If yes, my guess: _____

If no, is the word important?　　　　Yes　　No

5. An understanding of the language allows you to notice the **gished** meanings and other information that is not said directly.

Is it possible to guess the meaning?   Yes   No   Yes, but not exactly

If yes, my guess: _____

If no, is the word important?   Yes   No

6. In some cultures, it is polite to arrive at a party very **merwat**.

Is it possible to guess the meaning?   Yes   No   Yes, but not exactly

If yes, my guess: _____

If no, is the word important?   Yes   No

 Now, compare your answers with a partner's answers.

Reading Strategy

Guessing the Meaning from Context: Punctuation

Sometimes it's easy to guess the meaning of a new word from the context because there's a definition or synonym after a comma (,) or dash (–) or in parentheses.

Examples: He's not a close friend, just an **acquaintance**, a person whom I know but not very well.

It's a highly successful **enterprise**–business–in our country.

This company does business **globally** (internationally).

C. GUESSING THE MEANING FROM CONTEXT: PUNCTUATION As you read, look for meanings of new words after commas or dashes or in parentheses.

READING

Read about the elements of culture. As you read, think about this question:

• How can a knowledge of culture help people in business?

International Culture

If people want to be successful in global business, they must understand the cultures of other countries and learn how to adapt to them, or change their practices in different cultures. It's important for them to avoid business decisions that are based on misconceptions—mistaken ideas.

5   One cause of misconceptions is ethnocentrism, the belief that one's own culture's way of doing things is better than the way of other cultures. Ethnocentrism can exist in an individual person or in an organization. In the case of an individual person, ethnocentrism takes the form of "we're better than anyone else." For a global company, there are several examples of ethnocentrism:

10   1. The company uses the same methods abroad that it uses in the home country.

2. It doesn't adapt (change) a product to fit the needs of another country.

3. It sends managers with no international experience to work abroad.

To avoid ethnocentrism, it's necessary to study the different elements of culture. These include language, religion, values, customs, and material elements.

Language

15   A knowledge of the local language can help international businesspeople in four ways. First, people can communicate directly, without relying on someone else to translate or explain what is happening. Second, people are usually more open in their communication with someone who speaks their language. Third, an understanding of the language allows people to infer the implied meanings and other
20   information that is not said directly. Finally, knowing the language helps people to understand the culture better.

Religion

Religion influences everything about people, including their work habits. In the United States, people talk about the *Protestant work ethic*, which simply means a belief that people should work hard and save their money. In many Asian countries, the same
25   idea is called the *Confucian work ethic*. In Japan, it is the *Shinto work ethic*. Such a work ethic may influence even members of the culture who do not practice the religion.

Values and Attitudes

Values are people's basic beliefs about the difference between right and wrong, good and
30   bad, important and unimportant. An attitude is a way of thinking or acting. Values and attitudes influence international business. For example, many people in the United States believe that chocolate from Switzerland is

Common Idioms That Express U.S. Business Values
Time is money.
When in Rome, do as the Romans do.
Let's get down to business. = Let's get down to brass tacks. (= Let's begin to talk about the essential topics.)

35 better than chocolate from other countries (a value), and they buy a lot of it
(an attitude).

Customs and Manners

Customs are common social practices. Manners are ways of acting that the
society believes are polite. For example, in the United States, it is the *custom* to
have salad before the main course at dinner, not after. American table *manners*
40 include not talking with food in your mouth and keeping your napkin in your lap,
not on the table. In some countries, it is polite to arrive at a party very late; in others
it is important to be on time. International businesses need to understand the
customs and manners of other countries, or they will probably have difficulty selling
their products. For example, an American orange juice company in France will have
45 a problem if it sells orange juice as a breakfast drink because the French don't
usually drink juice with breakfast.

Material Culture

Material culture means the things that people make or own. When we study
material culture, we need to think about how people make things (technology) and
who makes them and why (economics). International businesses need to consider the
50 country's *economic infrastructure* such as transportation, communication, and
energy systems; the *social infrastructure*—for example, the health and education
systems; and the *financial infrastructure,* such as banking services.

These—and other—elements of culture help to explain the differences among
people of different cultures. Without an understanding of cultures, global businesses
55 will not be successful. Knowledge of a country's language, beliefs, customs, and
infrastructure can help businesses to avoid costly mistakes.

Source: *International Business: A Strategic Management Approach* (Rugman and Hodgetts)

AFTER READING

Reading Strategy

Finding the Main Idea

A reading, like an essay, has an **introduction**—usually the first paragraph—and a **conclusion**—the last
paragraph. Often, one sentence in the introduction gives the main idea of the reading. The main idea is the
most important idea. It includes all of the smaller, more specific ideas of the reading. Frequently, the main
idea appears again in the conclusion, in different words.

 A. FINDING THE MAIN IDEA Look back at the reading "International Culture." Find one sentence in
the first paragraph and another sentence in the last paragraph that give the main idea. Underline each
sentence.

 Now compare your answers with a partner's answers.

B. VOCABULARY CHECK Match the words to the definitions. Write the correct letters on the lines.

_____e_____ **1.** adapt

a. common social practices

_____ **2.** customs

b. the idea that people should work hard

_____ **3.** economic infrastructure

c. the things that people make or own

_____ **4.** ethnocentrism

d. the belief that one's own culture's customs are best

_____ **5.** financial infrastructure

e. to change in order to fit a new situation

_____ **6.** material culture

f. a country's banks

_____ **7.** social infrastructure

g. a country's health and education system

_____ **8.** work ethic

h. a country's system of transportation, communication, and energy

Reading Strategy

Finding Details

Sometimes you can find important **details** (specific points) quickly if you look for numbers or words such as *first, second, next, finally,* etc.

Example: **First,** people can communicate directly, without relying on someone else to translate or explain what is happening.

C. FINDING DETAILS Look back at the reading on pages 11–12 to find the answers to these questions. When you find the answers, mark them with a highlighter pen.

1. What are three examples of ethnocentrism in a multinational enterprise?

2. In what four ways can knowledge of language help an international businessperson?

3. What two things do we need to think about when we study material culture?

D. MAKING CONNECTIONS In Part 2, you read about five elements of culture: language, religion, values and attitudes, customs and manners, and material culture. In small groups, discuss this question: Which element(s) did each company from Part 1 pages 5–6 **ignore** (not pay attention to)?

Example: KFC ignored the language of the culture.

- KFC   • Traficante   • Samarin   • Nike   • Gerber

E. EXTENSION This is a test of customs in various countries. Take it just for fun. Don't worry about "right" or "wrong" answers. If you know the answer, circle the correct letter. If you don't know an answer, guess. You'll find out the correct answers later. Don't use a dictionary. Try to guess new words.

How Is Your Cross-Cultural Business IQ?

1. In Arab countries, when a man greets another man who has higher status (social position) he should . . .

   A. immediately shake hands.

   B. wait until the other man offers to shake hands.

   C. not shake hands because it's impolite to touch a person he doesn't know.

2. In Turkey, you shouldn't . . .

   A. shake hands.

   B. stand up when an older person enters the room.

   C. sit with crossed legs.

3. In the United States, when a man greets an American businesswoman, he should . . .

   A. shake hands gently because she is a woman.

   B. shake hands firmly and have eye contact.

   C. not shake hands.

4. Two Latin American businessmen are discussing a mutual acquaintance (a person whom they both know). One of the men hits his arm at the elbow. This body language means that . . .

   A. their acquaintance is a skinflint—a miser who won't spend money.

   B. the man's elbow hurts.

   C. their acquaintance is a tennis player, a golfer, or a baseball player.

5. In Japan, when a person gives you his or her business card, you should . . .

   A. put it in your pocket immediately.

   B. accept it with your right hand only and put it in your briefcase.

   C. accept it with both hands, look at it, say something about it, and keep it on the table in front of you during the conversation.

6. In Greece, it's important for a manager to . . .

    A. dress very well in expensive clothes to show the employees that this person is the boss.

    B. give each employee many compliments such as "You're doing a very good job" or "That's a nice shirt."

    C. spend time with employees and learn about their families, their problems, and their lives in general.

7. If a person wants to be successful in business in Russia, it's probably not a good idea to . . .

    A. take a business acquaintance to dinner.

    B. make some helpful suggestions about people's fashion or style of clothing.

    C. accept offers to drink vodka.

8. When you go to someone's home for dinner in Italy, France, or Russia, never bring . . .

    A. an odd number (1, 3, 5, 7) of flowers.

    B. an even number (2, 4, 6, 8) of flowers.

    C. pink flowers.

9. When you discuss business with someone in China, be sure to . . .

    A. use Mr., Mrs., or Ms., and the person's last name.

    B. use the person's first name.

    C. use the person's title such as Chairman, President, or Manager.

10. Two weeks ago, an American acquaintance said: "Let's have lunch or something sometime soon. I'll call you." But he hasn't called. Why not?

    A. He is impolite.

    B. He was closing the conversation.

    C. He had a serious problem.

In small groups, compare your answers.
(Are you curious about the answers? You can find them on page 34.)

PART ③ ACADEMIC READING
Improving CQ: Understanding Cultural Values

BEFORE READING

A. THINKING AHEAD The reading in this section is about cultural values. Think about the importance of these four areas in your culture:

• being a member of a group
• being an individual
• relationships with people
• success in business

Read the two questions below. How would you answer each one about your culture?

1. On a scale of 1–100, how important is being a member of a group or being an individual?

Being a member of a group   Being an individual

1 ←————————————————————————————→ 100

For example, if being a member of a group is very important, give a number of 10–20. If being an individual is very important, give a number of 80–90. Your answer can be any number between 1 and 100.

Answer 1: _____

2. On a scale of 1–100, how important are relationships with others or success in business?

Relationships with others   Success in business

1 ←————————————————————————————→ 100

For example, if relationships with others are very important, give a number of 10–20. If success in business is very important, give a number of 80–90. Your answer can be any number between 1 and 100.

Answer 2: _____

B. TAKING A SURVEY Move around the room and survey 5–10 classmates. Ask them the same two questions you answered in Activity A. Write their information in the chart.

Question 1. On a scale of 1–100, how important is being a member of a group or being an individual?

Question 2. On a scale of 1–100, how important are relationships with others or success in business?

Name	Country	Answer 1	Answer 2

In small groups, compare the numbers on your charts. What are the lowest numbers? What are the highest numbers? Does anything surprise you? Do classmates who are from the same country have similar answers?

Reading Strategy

Guessing the Meaning from Context: Using Logic

Sometimes **logic**—common sense—will help you to guess a new word without using a dictionary. Try this strategy. Imagine a blank in place of the new word. Then think of which words might logically fit in the blank.

Example: **You read:** Kevin pays attention to small social <u>cues</u> in a new culture so that he knows the correct behavior.

You imagine: Kevin pays attention to small social _____ in a new culture so that he knows the correct behavior.

You think of logical words for the blank: *signals, signs, indications*

B. VOCABULARY PREPARATION Read the sentences below. Words and phrases from the next reading are in green. Match the definitions in the box to the words in green. Write the correct letters on the lines.

> a. correct
> b. employer
> c. get
> d. position in society
> e. situation that requires difficult action or thought
> f. stay away from
> g. system for counting an amount
> h. things that happen

_____g_____ **1.** The IQ test is a **measure** of intelligence. The test's score indicates the level of a person's intelligence.

_____ **2.** In today's world, **events** 10,000 miles away can seem as close as something happening next door.

_____ **3.** Globalization creates a new **challenge** for everyone who does business internationally.

_____ **4.** How can people **acquire** the ability to feel at home in other cultures?

_____ **5.** It's important to know the **appropriate** social behavior for different situations.

_____ **6.** In that company, the **boss** listens to the opinions of the workers, but he makes the decisions himself.

_____ **7.** People with high **status** usually have more money or power than people with low status.

_____ **8.** I hope to **avoid** trouble or dangerous situations.

READING

Read about cultural intelligence. As you read, look for the answers to the following questions. When you find the information, highlight it.
• What are the three **components** (parts) of cultural intelligence?
• Which component does most of this reading deal with?

Improving CQ: Understanding Cultural Values

Most people have heard the term *IQ*, a measure of intelligence. In the book *Cultural Intelligence: People Skills for Global Business*, David C. Thomas and Kerr Inkson introduce the term *CQ*—cultural intelligence. They wrote their book for businesspeople. However, this book can be useful to anyone who wants to become
5   culturally intelligent—not only someone in business.

Globalization of People

Why is there a need for a book about cultural intelligence? Thomas and Inkson remind us that "there are seven billion people in the world" from thousands of cultures, "but we live in a village . . . a 'global village' . . . where events 10,000 miles away seem as close as events happening in the next street. We find ourselves
10   in this global village whenever we read a newspaper or watch television."

They explain that the "globalization of people creates a new and major challenge for everyone who works in business." Although we easily cross boundaries when we travel from country to country, it isn't so easy to cross *cultural* boundaries. According to Thomas and Inkson, "the potential problems are enormous. Even
15   when people come from the same culture, interpersonal skills are often poor, and this weakness is costly to business."

The Three Components of Cultural Intelligence

The authors ask the central question: "How can ordinary people in business acquire the ability to feel at home when dealing with those from other cultures, to know what to say and do?" Their answer is for businesspeople to become culturally
20   intelligent. Cultural intelligence has three parts: *knowledge* ("knowing . . . how culture affects behavior"); *mindfulness*, "the ability to pay attention to cues in cross-cultural situations"; and *behavioral skills*—choosing the appropriate behavior for different situations. They include a graphic representation of cultural intelligence (CQ):

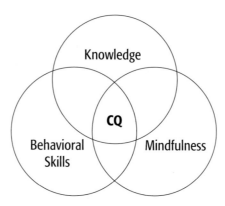

Components of cultural intelligence

Cultural Values

25   A knowledge of cultural values is essential for cultural intelligence. Thomas and Inkson give two ways to look at cultural values. The first is from Geert Hofstede, a Dutch social scientist. In a study first published in 1980, Hofstede analyzed answers on paper-and-pencil questions about the values of more than 100,000 employees of one large multinational company in 40 and later 53 countries and regions. Statistical
30   analysis of the country differences showed these to fall into four separate areas ("dimensions"):

Individualism. In *individualistic* cultures, people think of themselves as individuals and prefer to work alone or to do activities in small "private interactions with

friends." They base their decisions on their own ideas of what is appropriate. In
collectivistic cultures, people think of themselves as "members of groups" and
prefer group activities. They base decisions on the needs of the group.

Power distance. In a culture with *high power distance*, people expect a big
difference between people with high status and people with low status. For
example, at work, they expect the boss to make all the decisions. In a culture
with *low power distance*, people are more equal. There isn't as much difference
between people of high and low status. At work, the boss listens to people at all
levels in the company.

Uncertainty avoidance. In some cultures, there is *strong uncertainty avoidance.*
This means that people try to avoid the unknown: unfamiliar ideas, different-
looking people, new experiences. These cultures are more emotional and
stressed, and tend to like having many rules. In other cultures (with weak
uncertainty avoidance), people accept the unknown more easily, they are
supposed to control their emotions, and they dislike rules.

Masculinity. Hofstede saw some cultures as more "masculine" (male) and some
as more "feminine" (female). In masculine cultures, success in business is very
important. In feminine cultures, it is important to have harmony—good, peaceful
relationships with other people.

Hofstede gave countries a score in each area. For example, cultures with high
individualism, such as Australia, Canada, Great Britain, and the United States, scored
over 75. The countries with low individualism (collectivistic cultures) scored under 20.
Some of these countries were Colombia, Costa Rica, El Salvador, Guatemala,
Indonesia, and Pakistan.

Examples of Hofstede's Scores

Country	Power Distance	Individualism	Uncertainty Avoidance	Masculinity
Argentina	49	46	86	56
Australia	36	90	51	61
Brazil	69	38	76	49
Canada	39	80	48	52
Costa Rica	35	15	86	21
Greece	60	35	112	57
Indonesia	78	14	48	46
Japan	54	46	92	95
Korea	60	18	85	39
Mexico	81	30	82	69
Taiwan	58	17	69	45
Thailand	64	20	64	34
United States	40	91	46	62

In a second study, from 2000, researchers S.H. Schwartz and Lilach Sagiv studied the values of 57 cultures. They looked at seven areas:

60
1. how people see each other as equals
2. harmony with the environment
3. being a member of a group
4. hierarchy (a system in which people with high status have power)
5. use of the natural or social environment

65
6. the ability to pursue (try to have) positive experiences
7. the ability of individual people to pursue their own independent ideas

Thomas and Inkson suggest that people should think about their own culture in these seven areas (or Hofstede's four). They explain that "the first step" to cultural intelligence "is to *understand your own culture*" and how your culture influences

70
how you see others.

Sources: *Culture's Consequences: International Differences in Work-Related Values* (Hofstede), *Cultural Intelligence: People Skills for Global Business* (Thomas and Inkson)

AFTER READING

A. CHECK YOUR UNDERSTANDING With a partner, discuss the two questions asked before the reading.

1. What are the three components (parts) of cultural intelligence?

2. Which component does most of this reading deal with?

B. VOCABULARY CHECK Review vocabulary words from the reading. Write the correct words on the lines.

behavior	costly	~~hierarchy~~
boundaries	harmony	pursue

1. Right now Bill is low in the _____ hierarchy _____ of the company because he is young and new at the company.

2. Some mistakes can be very _____ to a business and cause them to lose a lot of money.

3. When we travel, we cross cultural _____ as well as national borders.

4. Jessica plans to _____ a career in business. She wants to work for a global company.

5. In some cultures, it's especially important to have _____ in the workplace, so people try to find agreement with each other.

6. In international business, you need to learn the _____ that is appropriate in other cultures and then do things in this same way.

Using Graphic Organizers: Venn Diagrams and Charts

A graphic organizer can help you **visualize** (see) the ideas in a reading. It can also help you visualize relationships among ideas. There are many types of graphic organizers. You saw one in the reading on page 19. It **depicted** (showed) the three components of cultural intelligence. This type—with two or more overlapping circles—is called a **Venn diagram.**

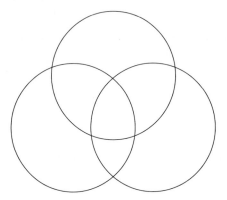

Another type of graphic organizer is a **chart.** You saw a chart on page 7. In this book, you will frequently read and create graphic organizers.

C. USING GRAPHIC ORGANIZERS: VENN DIAGRAMS AND CHARTS The graphic organizer below shows the cultural values in the two studies you read about on pages 18–21. In the chart, the left column shows the values from the Hofstede study; and the right column shows the values from the Schwartz and Sagiv study. With a partner, discuss these questions:

• Which values do both studies discuss? Are the values worded in the same way?
• Which values are discussed only in the Hofstede study?
• Which values are discussed only in the Schwartz and Sagiv study?

Hofstede	Schwartz and Sagiv
• individualism/collectivism	• ability to pursue independent ideas • being a member of a group
• power distance (high/low)	• hierarchy • how people see each other as equals
• uncertainty avoidance (high/low)	
• masculinity/femininity	
	• harmony with the environment
	• use of natural or social environment
	• ability to pursue positive experiences

Look at the Venn diagram below. Finish filling in the diagram with information from the chart above.

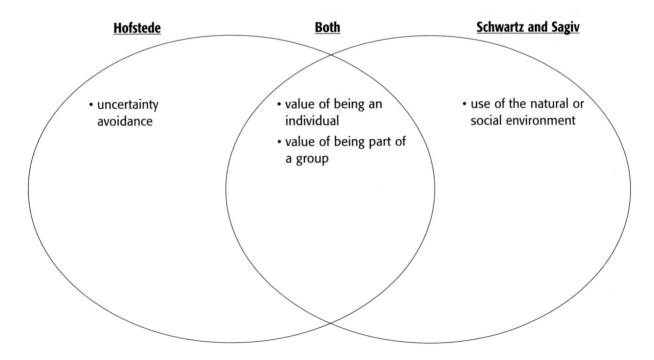

Hofstede — Both — Schwartz and Sagiv

• uncertainty avoidance

• value of being an individual
• value of being part of a group

• use of the natural or social environment

D. MAKING CONNECTIONS You read that not having knowledge of intercultural skills can be costly to people who are doing international business. With a partner, look back at Part 1, pages 5–6. In what way were these mistakes probably costly to these two companies: Traficante and Samarin? What did they lose?

E. ANALYSIS: CULTURAL VALUES In small groups, discuss these questions.

1. Was your country listed in the chart on page 20? If so, do you think the scores are accurate? If not, what scores would you give your country for each area ("dimension"): power distance, individualism, uncertainty avoidance, and masculinity?

2. How well do you "fit" into your culture? In other words, are you happy with the values of your culture? Would you prefer to see some different scores on the chart? (For example, someone from the United States might say, "I would prefer to see a lower score for individualism in my country. I think it's important to be part of a group.")

F. APPLICATION: THE ELEMENTS OF CULTURE On a separate piece of paper, write the five elements of culture listed below. For each one, write notes—not complete sentences—about your culture. Write your own opinion. Give examples for each element. If you aren't sure, put a question mark and spend more time on the other elements. Later in Part 5, you may use some of these ideas for your writing topic.

Elements of Culture:
- Language
- Religion
- Values
- Material Culture
- Customs

G. DISCUSSION In small groups, discuss the elements of your culture.

H. RESPONSE WRITING Choose one of these topics:
- a popular product in your country that comes from another country
- one custom that is important in your culture
- one value that is important in your culture

Write about your topic for 10 minutes. Don't worry about grammar and don't stop writing to use a dictionary. You don't need to worry about being correct. You won't give this paper to your teacher. Just put as many ideas as possible on paper.

PART ④ THE MECHANICS OF WRITING

In Part 4, you will practice using the present and past verbs, modals of advice, adjective clauses, and joining two sentences with coordinating conjunctions. You will need this grammar in Part 5 to write a paragraph about your culture.

Simple Present and Simple Past

The simple present expresses an action that happens repeatedly (sometimes, often, frequently, every day, etc.). In the negative, use *don't* (*doesn't*) and the simple form of the verb.

Examples: The British usually **drink** tea in the afternoon.
Americans **don't drink** as much tea as the British do.

The simple past expresses a finished action. It is used for both short and long actions. Regular verbs end in *-ed*. In the negative, use *didn't* and the simple form of the verb.

Examples: He **picked** up his knife and fork.
She **didn't understand** the gesture.

A. SIMPLE PRESENT AND SIMPLE PAST Fill in the blanks with the simple present or simple past of the verbs in parentheses.

Equality in the Workplace

A person from another country who _____ *does* _____ (do) business in North
                                            1

America _____ (need) to remember that in the United States, women
                  2

_____ (have) equality in the workplace. This _____
        3   4

(mean) that women usually _____ (receive) the same pay, opportunities, and
                                    5

respect as men do. Sometimes this _____ (be) a problem for businesspeople
                                            6

from countries where women _____ (not have) positions of authority
                                        7

in a company.

Several years ago, a multinational company _____ (open) a factory in
                                                      8

the United States. The managers _____ (be not) American. They
                                          9

_____ (be) very polite to all the workers, but unfortunately, they
          10

_____ (follow) the customs of their own country. For example,
          11

they _____ (treat) the women employees as "helpers" with lower status
            12

than the men. These female employees _____ (not appreciate) this and
13

_____ (complain) to the upper management. The upper management
14

_____ (not understand) the problem and _____ (not
15 16

do) anything about it. Finally, the women _____ (feel) so frustrated that they
17

_____ (take) the company to court and _____
18 19

(win) a lawsuit. Then the managers _____ (have) to treat the women the
20

same as they treated the men.

Modals of Advice

When you give advice, you suggest a solution to a problem. To give advice for the present or future, use this structure:

should
ought to } + the simple form of the verb

For the negative, use *shouldn't* + the simple form of the verb. *Ought to* is not usually used in negative sentences in American English.

Examples: Before you travel to another country, you **should learn** something about the culture.

A company that does business internationally **ought to have** a deep understanding of other cultures.

In Japan, you **shouldn't put** a business card in your wallet without studying it first.

To give advice for the past, use this structure:

should
shouldn't } + *have* + past participle*
ought to

Example: The company **should have known** to ask about the customs.

* Past participles of regular verbs end in *-ed*.

B. MODALS OF ADVICE George is leaving for a trip around the world. With a partner, give George some advice. Use *should, shouldn't,* or *ought to* + the simple form of the verb and the phrases below.

Example: In Taiwan, you should flatter your host.

It's a good idea to:

1. flatter (give compliments to) your host (Taiwan)

2. shake hands when you say "hello" or "good-bye" (Italy)

3. learn to bow correctly (Japan)

4. touch your left fingers to your right arm when giving or receiving something (Korea)

5. use the spoon above the plate for dessert (Greece)

It's not a good idea to:

6. refuse a drink (Russia)

7. give an even number of flowers (France)

8. eat with your fingers (Turkey)

9. use the American hand signal for *okay* (Brazil)

George

10. have three people in a photograph (Vietnam)

C. MODALS George has returned from his trip. Poor George! The trip was a failure because he did everything wrong. Give George advice in the past. Use *should(n't) have* or *ought to have* + past participle and use the phrases in Activity B.

Example: In Taiwan, you should have flattered your host.

The Subject *You*

The word *you* is the second person singular and plural pronoun. For example, "You speak English very well." But *you* has another meaning, too. It can also mean *everyone, people in general.*

Example: **You** should remove **your** shoes before entering a Thai home.

In very formal English, the word *one* has this same meaning of "everyone."

Example: **One** should remove **one's** shoes before entering a Thai home.

D. APPLICATION Think of important customs in your culture. On a piece of paper, write five sentences with advice for people who travel to your country. Use *should(n't)* or *ought to*. Begin each sentence with *you*.

Adjective Clauses

An adjective is a word that **modifies** (describes) a noun. It usually comes before the noun. An adjective clause also modifies a noun, but it is a group of words and comes after the noun.

If the information in the adjective clause is essential, there is no comma before it.

An adjective clause might begin with *who* or *that* (for people), *which* or *that* (for things and places), *where* (for places), or *whose* (for possessives). An adjective clause comes immediately after the noun that it modifies.

Examples: A **company** that does business internationally ought to have a deep understanding of other cultures.

The ad listed **places** where you can buy the product.

Note: An adjective clause is also called a relative clause.

E. ADJECTIVE CLAUSES Find the adjective clause in each sentence. Underline it and draw an arrow to the noun that it modifies.

1. The first question that an American usually asks a new acquaintance is "What do you do?"

2. A woman who is traveling in the Middle East should not wear short skirts or low-cut blouses.

3. He spent time in three countries where his company did business.

4. In Arab countries, when a man greets another man who has higher status, he should wait until the other man offers to shake hands.

5. Customs that are very different in various cultures involve the use of gestures—hand movements for communication.

F. SENTENCE COMBINING: ADJECTIVE CLAUSES Combine the sentences. Make the second sentence into an adjective clause and add it to the first.

1. A business will probably not be successful. A business is culturally insensitive.

A business that is culturally insensitive will probably not be successful.

2. The woman was the new manager. The woman called the meeting.

3. One custom is going to public baths. One custom seems a little unusual to some people.

4. We visited an acquaintance. The acquaintance's home was just outside of the city.

_____

_____

5. An American is saying "Good luck." An American crosses his fingers.

_____

_____

6. Kevin went to work for a company. The company did a lot of international business.

_____

_____

Transitional Expressions: Coordinating Conjunctions

An independent clause is a group of words that can stand alone. In other words, with a capital letter at the beginning and a period at the end, an independent clause is a sentence. You can join two independent clauses with a comma and a **coordinating conjunction**. There are seven coordinating conjunctions. One of them, *nor*, will not be covered in this chapter. These are the other six:

And introduces more information; it adds one idea to another.
But introduces information that might be surprising, unexpected, or opposite the information in the first clause.
Yet means "but"; it is very formal.
So means "that's why."
For means "because"; it is very formal.
Or introduces another possibility; it can also join two negative ideas.

Examples: U.S. customers believe that Swiss chocolate is especially good, **and** they buy a lot of it.

International businesses need to understand the culture of other countries, **or** they will probably have difficulty selling their product.

If there isn't an independent clause after the coordinating conjunction, don't use a comma. Usually, this situation happens when the subject in both clauses is the same, and you don't repeat it in the second clause. This is most common with *and*.

Examples: They saw the product, **and** they liked it.
They saw the product **and** liked it.

In a series of three or more nouns, adjectives, verbs, or phrases, use commas between each item. This structure occurs with *and* or *or*.

Examples: You should bring flowers, candy, **or** dessert to a dinner party.

The ad showed dirty clothes on the left, a box of soap in the middle, **and** clean clothes on the right.

G. SENTENCE COMBINING: COORDINATING CONJUNCTIONS Combine these sentences. Use *and, but, yet, or, for,* or *so.*

1. She had lived in Finland for 15 years. She spoke the language fluently.

   She had lived in Finland for 15 years, so she spoke the language fluently.

   _____

2. It's a good idea to bring a gift to the hostess. You shouldn't bring a really expensive gift the first time you visit.

   _____

   _____

3. The company produces cars. The company produces trucks. The company produces vans.

   _____

   _____

4. You need to ask for the bill in a restaurant in Italy. The waiter won't bring it.

   _____

   _____

5. In Spain, an older person may use your first name. You should use an older person's last name.

   _____

   _____

6. You may have tea. You may have juice. You may have water.

   _____

   _____

7. The company wasn't successful. It didn't understand the business customs of the country.

   _____

   _____

8. Most people in that country speak two languages. Some speak three or four.

   _____

   _____

Test-Taking Strategy

Finding Errors

On many standardized tests, there is a section that tests grammar, punctuation, and word choice. In each sentence, you need to find one error out of four possibilities. In such a section, try these suggestions:

- First, read the entire sentence.
- Read it again and pay close attention to the underlined words.
- Check for punctuation, verb tenses, subject-verb agreement, word order, part of speech, and so on.
- Remember that there is just *one* error.

H. FINDING ERRORS Circle the letter under the incorrect word or phrase in the sentences below. There are errors with tenses, modals, adjective clauses, and coordinating conjunctions.

1. Multinational companies, that do business in the United States shouldn't ignore the
                  A   B   C

   importance of diversity, or they will not succeed.
                     D

2. The United States has people from almost any race, religion, language, culture
                  A   B   C

   that you can imagine.
      D

3. The company apparently didn't know about an important value in American culture, for there
                                                                    A

   was no women, blacks, Asians, or Native Americans in the advertisement that I saw.
    B   C   D

4. Diversity is an important value in U.S. culture, so the company should have include minorities
    A   B   C

   and women in its advertisements that appeared in magazines in this country.
                                  D

5. The company ignored the majority of the U.S. population so the people ignored the company and
               A   B   C

   didn't buy the product.
    D

PART ⑤ ACADEMIC WRITING

WRITING ASSIGNMENT

In Part 5, you will write one paragraph to answer this question:
• What is one thing that multinational companies should understand about your culture?

Answer the question in the first sentence. This will be your **topic sentence**. The rest of your paragraph will **support** (give details and evidence for) this first sentence. Include one or more examples in your evidence.

STEP A. CHOOSING A TOPIC It's important to choose a topic that you understand and have ideas about. Choose one element of culture:

• language
• religion
• values
• material culture
• customs

STEP B. NARROWING YOUR TOPIC Look back at the notes you made about elements of your own culture in Activity F (page 24). Choose one of those examples for your topic.

Writing Strategy

Writing an Expository Paragraph

A common type of academic writing is **exposition**. An expository paragraph includes these elements.
• It has *one* **point of view**. There is one way of looking at the topic, one opinion.
• It gives **reasons** to support this point of view.
• It has **specific** evidence. One type of specific evidence is an **example**.

Example:

Multinational companies that do business in the U.S. shouldn't ignore the importance of diversity in U.S. culture. The U.S. is a multiethnic society with people from almost every race, religion, language, and culture. A business that ignores this is probably making a cultural mistake. For example, a car company recently put an advertisement in a national U.S. magazine. In the ad, there were photographs of all the managers of the car dealerships in the country—44 of them. They were all smiling and looked friendly, yet there was one problem. They were all white, middle-aged men. There were no women or people of color. The implied meaning of this advertisement was clear: only white middle-aged men were welcome customers. The company ignored the majority of the U.S. population, so the majority of the U.S. population ignored the company and didn't buy the car.

Note in the example:
- The first line is indented.
- Every sentence begins with a capital letter and ends with a period (.).
- After a period, the next sentence begins on the same line.
- The example supports the main idea.
- The beginning of the paragraph is in the simple present tense because it is about something that is generally true. The example is in the simple past tense because it happened in the past.
- There is a one-sentence conclusion.

 Analysis: In the sample paragraph, look for coordinating conjunctions and adjective clauses. Highlight them.

STEP C. PLANNING YOUR PARAGRAPH Before you begin to write, make notes about your topic. Follow these suggestions:

1. Write your topic at the top of a piece of paper. Under this, write anything about the topic that you can think of. (This will be your evidence or support.) Make sure that you include at least one example. You don't need to write complete sentences. Just write notes.

2. After you write all of your ideas, cross out anything that doesn't belong. A paragraph must be about just one topic.

3. Decide on the organization. The first sentence should answer the question. Your evidence should support your answer. Your conclusion should come after the evidence and examples.

STEP D. WRITING THE PARAGRAPH Use your notes from Step C. Write complete sentences in paragraph form. You might make some mistakes, but don't worry about them at this point.

Test-Taking Strategy

Editing a Test Essay

Sometimes writing a paragraph or short essay is part of a test. Many standardized tests have a writing section. It is important to leave a few minutes at the end to check your writing for errors.

STEP E. EDITING Read your paragraph and answer these questions.

1. Is the paragraph form correct (first line indented)?

2. Does the first sentence answer the question?

3. Does the evidence support the topic sentence?

4. Is there a good example?

5. Is there correct use of coordinating conjunctions (punctuation and choice of conjunction)?

6. If there are adjective clauses, are they used correctly?

7. Are the verb tenses correct?

STEP F. REWRITING Write your paragraph again. This time, try to write it with no mistakes.

Answers to the Cross-Cultural Business IQ Test, pages 14–15:

1. b	**6.** c
2. c	**7.** b
3. b	**8.** b
4. a	**9.** c
5. c	**10.** b

CHAPTER 2

The Global Economy

Discuss these questions:

• Look at the picture. Where is the woman?

• Are group discussions a good way to make decisions? Why? Why not?

• What is the best way for businesses and governments to make decisions about money?

BEFORE READING

Native Americans at a modern powwow (tribal gathering)

A. THINKING AHEAD Look at the picture. Discuss these questions with a partner.

1. In your country, are there **tribal** people—original or native people? If so, do they live in a traditional way or a modern way (or both)? Give examples.

2. Can you name a toy or other item that was suddenly very popular, something that many people wanted to buy? Why was it popular? How long was it popular?

Previewing for Topics

It's a good idea to quickly look over a chapter or reading before you read in order to preview the topics. This will help you know what to expect and to have ideas in mind as you read.

A **topic** is the subject of a reading—what it is about. It is a noun or noun phrase. Most readings have one **main topic** and several more specific but important **sub-topics**. Previewing will help you to know what to expect. Before reading, look over:

• the pictures and their **captions** (words under the pictures)

• the **headings** (the bold titles on the left)

• important new **vocabulary in bold** (darker) print

B. PREVIEWING FOR TOPICS Quickly look over the pictures, captions, headings, and words in bold print in the reading on pages 37–39. What will the sub-topics be? Write your answers on the lines.

1. _____

2. _____

3. _____

READING

Read about economics. As you read, think about the answer to this question. When you find the answer, mark it with a highlighter.

• What goods do people exchange in these three situations?

The Exchange of Material Goods

A term that we often use when we talk about business is "supply and demand." **Supply** is the amount of a product or service that is available for people to buy or
5 use. **Demand** is people's desire or need for a product or service. The term **supply and demand** means the balance between the amount available and the amount that people want or need. The following are
10 three very different examples of the exchange of **goods** and how supply and demand functions in different parts of the world.

A North Pacific Coast Ceremony

A famous cultural and economic event
15 among native people of the North Pacific Coast (southwestern Canada and the northwestern United States) used to be the **potlatch.** (A few tribes still practice this.) In a potlatch ceremony, the hosts *gave away*
20 huge amounts of valuable items such as blankets, food, boats, and large pieces of copper, a metal. It was very expensive for the hosts. They did not receive any items in return. Instead, they received high status.
25 To people coming from Europe, this

A modern potlatch

ceremony seemed like a strange way to pursue status. It didn't seem practical.

Today there is better understanding of the logic of this event. Several villages
30 participated in a potlatch. If one village had a very good year, they hosted the event and gave away their material items to a village that was not doing well. They received status, and the poor village was no longer
35 as poor. A few years later, the tables might be turned—the situation might be reversed. The poor village (now rich) would host a potlatch, give away their wealth, and acquire high status. The result was
40 harmony and balance.

Reindeer Herding

For thousands of years, Samis, the last tribal people of Europe, hunted reindeer. Reindeer were central to their economy and their culture. The animals provided
45 meat, bone for jewelry, and skin for boots, hats, and other clothing. It was a traditional way of life. The Samis had everything they needed and didn't have to exchange goods with the outside world. In the 16th century,
50 they **domesticated** the reindeer—trained them to live with humans. Today, they **herd** the reindeer from one area to another in northern Scandinavia—Finland, Sweden, and Norway. They sell reindeer
55 meat and buy items such as snowmobiles. However, today the government is trying to **regulate**—control—the reindeer industry, and the Samis aren't happy about this because the price they receive for the meat
60 is now lower than before regulation.

Prairie Dogs in the International Economy

In the 1990s, farmers in the American Midwest had a challenge: **prairie dogs.** These animals dig deep holes—burrows— where they live and hide. Prairie dogs have
65 always been a problem for farmers because they destroy the farmers' **crops.** For many years, farmers have tried to kill these

A reindeer

Prairie dogs in the American Midwest

animals in different ways, but nothing has worked. In addition, farmers have a
70 problem with animal rights groups, who don't want animals to suffer.

One man had a strange but successful solution to this problem. He invented a very large vacuum cleaner. It was the size
75 of a truck. He traveled around with this huge machine and *vacuumed* prairie dogs out of their burrows. The prairie dogs were surprised by this experience, but they weren't hurt. The farmers were happy. And
80 the man with the vacuum truck had a successful business. Farmers paid him for his service, and he made more money when he sold pairs of prairie dogs to people in Tokyo who thought they were
85 cuter pets than dogs or cats.

AFTER READING

A. CHECK YOUR UNDERSTANDING Discuss the questions with a partner.

1. What happened in a traditional potlatch?

2. What did reindeer provide the Sami people?

3. In the past, why didn't the Samis need to exchange goods with the outside world?

4. What has always been a problem for farmers in the American Midwest?

5. What did one man invent to solve the problem?

6. In what two ways does this man now make money?

B. APPLICATION On pages 37–39, you read about three examples of the exchange of goods. In each example, what did people sell or give away? What did they receive in return? Write your answers in the chart below.

People	Sold or Gave Away	Received
People of the North Pacific Coast		
The Samis		
Farmers		
People in Tokyo		

PART ② GENERAL INTEREST READING
Business in Literature: Durrell's *Bitter Lemons*

BEFORE READING

THINKING AHEAD In small groups, discuss these questions.

1. In your country, what do people do when they want to buy a house? Do they go directly to the owner of the house, or do they ask a real estate agent for help?

2. In what situations can people negotiate about the price of something? (In a supermarket? A farmers' market? A furniture store?)

3. Do you know someone who is very good at negotiating and buying things cheaply?

4. The next reading takes place on the island of Cyprus. Where is Cyprus? What are the nationalities of the people who live there?

Reading Strategy

Guessing the Meaning from Context: Accepting Incomplete Knowledge

When you're reading a passage that seems difficult, you need to guess the meaning of new words whenever you can. Remember that you don't always have to understand a word exactly. However, if you cannot guess anything about it, you need to learn when to look up the word in a dictionary and when not to worry about it.

Examples: He was perhaps 40 years of age, **sturdily** built, and with a fine head on his shoulders. His actions and words **flowed** from him like honey from a spoon.

"They are all here," he **hissed**. He pointed to the café across the road where the **cobbler** had gathered his family.

• Which new words from the examples above can you guess? Probably only *flowed*. You probably know how honey moves from a spoon, so you can guess that *flowed* might mean "moved slowly, like a thick liquid."

• From the context, you might not know the meaning of *sturdily*, but you probably don't need this word in order to understand the sentence. Don't look it up.

• You can guess that *hissed* means "said" in some specific way, but you don't know the exact meaning. Is it important to know the exact meaning? No, so don't look it up.

• From the context, you can't guess much about the word *cobbler*. You assume that a cobbler is a person, but you don't know anything else. You probably need a dictionary for this word.

READING

As you read, try to guess the meanings of new words. Decide which new words are important and which ones aren't. You'll learn more about the new words after the reading.

Excerpt from Lawrence Durrell's *Bitter Lemons*

A Word to Set the Scene: In the 1950s,
the English writer Lawrence Durrell decided to
live on the Mediterranean island of Cyprus—off
the coast of Greece and Turkey—for a year or
5 two. He planned to teach and write. He wanted
to buy a house in a village there and went to a
Turkish real estate agent for help. Together, they
found a wonderful old house with great wooden
doors and a wonderful view of hills, villages, and a
10 distant castle. Durrell wanted the house very
much but didn't have much money. He needed
an especially smart businessperson to negotiate
the purchase for him from the Greek woman
who owned the house. Luckily, Durrell's real
15 estate agent, Sabri Tahir, was famous on the
island for his cleverness.

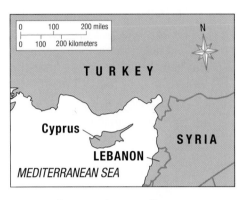

Cyprus and surrounding areas

The following is an excerpt from Lawrence Durrell's book *Bitter Lemons*, about his time
on Cyprus. In this scene, Durrell and Sabri Tahir are in Tahir's office. The owner of the
house, a shoemaker's wife, is across the street in a café with many relatives who are giving
20 her advice. The huge key to the house is on the desk in front of Tahir.

How to Buy a House

[Sabri Tahir] was perhaps 40 years of age, sturdily built, and with a fine head on
his shoulders. He had the sleepy good looks—a rare smile with perfect teeth,
thoughtful brown eyes—which one sees sometimes in Turkish travel posters.

"They are all here," he hissed. He pointed to the café across the road where the
25 cobbler had gathered his family. They sat on a semicircle of chairs, sipping coffee
and arguing in low voices. "Now, whatever happens," said Sabri in a low voice, "do
not surprise. You must never surprise. And you don't want the house at all, see?"

I repeated the words, "I don't want the house. I absolutely don't want the house."
Yet in my mind's eye I could see those great doors. ("God," Sabri had said, "this is
30 fine wood. From Anatolia. In the old days they floated the great timbers over the
water behind boats. This is Anatolian timber, it will last forever.") "I don't want the
house," I repeated under my breath.

[The woman] walked boldly across the road, entering with a loud "Good
morning." She wore the white headdress and dark skirt of the village woman.

35 Sabri cleared his throat, and picking up the great key very delicately between
finger and thumb, put it down again on the edge of the desk nearest her. "We are

speaking about your house," he said softly. "Do you know that all the wood is . . ." he suddenly shouted the last word with such force that I nearly fell off my chair, "rotten!" And picking up the key he banged it down to emphasize the point.

40 The woman threw up her head and taking up the key also banged it down exclaiming: "It is not."

"It *is*." Sabri banged the key.

"It is *not*." She banged it back.

45 "It *is*." A bang.

"It is *not*." A counter bang.

All this was not on a very high intellectual level. I also feared that the key itself would be banged out of shape so that finally none of us 50 would be able to get into the house.

The woman now took the key and held it up as if she were swearing by it. "The house is a good house," she cried. Then she put it back on the desk. Sabri took it up thoughtfully. 55 "And suppose we wanted the house," he said, "which we don't, what would you ask for it?"

"Eight hundred pounds."

Sabri gave a long laugh, wiping away imaginary tears and repeating "eight hundred 60 pounds" as if it were the best joke in the world. He laughed at me and I laughed at him, a dreadful false laugh. We laughed until we were exhausted. Then we grew serious again. Sabri was still fresh as a daisy, I could see that. He had put himself into the patient state of mind of a chess player. Then he suddenly turned to her. "Two hundred 65 pounds and not a *piastre* more."

A village on Cyprus

She turned back to Sabri and banging the key down once more shouted "Six hundred."

"I offer you two hundred pounds."

She let out a yell. "No. Never in this life."

70 My friend leaned back in his chair. "Think of it," he said, his voice full of the poetry of commerce. "This gentleman will [write you a check]. You will go to the bank. They will open the safe. They will take from it notes, thick notes, as thick as a honeycomb, as thick as salami." (Here they both licked their lips and I myself began to feel hungry at the thought of so much edible money.) "All you have to do is agree."

Source: *Bitter Lemons* (Durrell)

AFTER READING

 A. MAKING INFERENCES In the reading on pages 41–42, the people in the scene are talking about business—the sale of a house—but Durrell describes them as if they were actors in a theatrical play. In small groups, discuss these questions.

1. Who is the "star" of this play?

2. What two lies does Sabri tell?

3. From which sentences and paragraphs can you infer that Sabri is acting?

4. What do you think will happen next?

Reading Strategy

Understanding Parts of Speech

When you need to use a dictionary, it's a good idea to know the part of speech of the word that you're looking up *before you open the dictionary*. Why? Many words can be more than one part of speech. You'll save time if you go directly to the correct part of speech and ignore the others. How can you know the part of speech? Look in the sentence.

Examples: She wore a dark **skirt**. (noun)
He **skirted** the topic for several minutes. (verb)

If you're looking up the verb *skirt*, you don't want to waste time reading the definition of the noun *skirt*.

A dictionary will tell you the part of speech with these abbreviations:

n = noun	v = verb
prep = preposition	adj = adjective
adv = adverb	conj = conjunction

> **skirt**[1] /skət/ *n.* [C] a piece of women's clothing that fits around the waist and hangs down like the bottom part of a dress: *She was wearing a white blouse and a plain black skirt.|a short/long skirt*
>
> **skirt**[2] also **skirt around** *v.* [T] **1** to go around the outside edge of a place: *The soldiers skirted around the town and crossed the river.* **2** to avoid talking about an important problem, subject, etc.: *The company spokesman skirted the question.* **3** if you skirt the rules or the law, you do something that is not illegal, but that does not exactly follow the rules

Source: *Longman Dictionary of American English* (2004)

B. PARTS OF SPEECH Decide the part of speech of each green word. Then look it up in a monolingual (English-English) dictionary and write the definition on the line.

1. He **banged** the key on the table to emphasize his point.

Part of Speech: _____

Definition: _____

2. She closed the door with a **bang.**

Part of Speech: _____

Definition: _____

3. The house is strong and well built. It will **last** forever.

Part of Speech: _____

Definition: _____

4. This is my **last** offer.

Part of Speech: _____

Definition: _____

5. They will open the **safe** and take out the money.

Part of Speech: _____

Definition: _____

6. She felt **safe** in the circle of her family.

Part of Speech: _____

Definition: _____

7. The bank teller handed her a thick stack of **notes.**

Part of Speech: _____

Definition: _____

Test-Taking Strategy

Guessing the Meaning from Context

On standardized tests, you often need to be able to guess the meaning of new words from the context. For some test items, you will need to look at the word in the reading passage and then choose a word that is close in meaning or choose a definition for the word. If you take the test on a computer, you will have to **click on** the word or definition to select it.

C. VOCABULARY CHECK Look back at the reading on pages 41–42. Find words or phrases for the definitions below, and highlight them in the reading. Then write them on the correct lines. The numbers in parentheses refer to lines in the reading.

1. drinking in small amounts (20–25)   _____

2. carried in the water (25–30)   _____

3. wood or large wooden beams (25–30)   _____

4. carefully, gently (35–40)   _____

5. gone bad (35–40)   _____

6. promising that one is telling the truth (50–55) _____

7. not real (55–60)   _____

8. something that one can eat (adjective) (70–74) _____

Reading Strategy

Keeping a Word Journal

Keeping a **word journal** is a good way to study, review, and remember new words. In a section of your three-ring binder or in a thin spiral notebook, record words that are important to remember. All of the students in your class will be working with the same readings, but each student might find different words from these readings to put in his or her word journal.

Spend ten to twenty minutes each day adding and reviewing words in your journal.

Include the following information:

• the word (or phrase)

• the part of speech

• a synonym or definition (either your guess or from a dictionary)

• a sentence from the reading with the word in it, but leave a blank in place of the word

You can put this information in a four-section grid.

Example:

emphasize (word)	to put emphasis on; to stress or give special force to something to show that it is important	(definition)
Verb (part of speech)	He banged down the key to _____ his point.	(sentence from the reading with a blank)

D. WORD JOURNAL Go back to "How to Buy a House," pages 41–42. Which new words are important for you to remember? Put them in your Word Journal.

E. VOCABULARY EXPANSION There are traditional expressions of comparison in every language. Durrell uses three in the reading. One is *as fresh as a daisy.* (The structure is *as* + adjective + *as* + noun.) Find and highlight two other expressions with this structure from the last paragraph of the reading on page 42.

In the chart below, read the beginnings of some traditional expressions in English. How do you think they end? Fill in the missing noun for each one. Write your guess or write the way that people in your culture might say this. Then ask two other classmates for their answers.

	My Noun	Classmate 1	Classmate 2
1. as busy as . . .	a bee		
2. as tough as . . .			
3. as free as . . .			
4. as happy as . . .			
5. as soft as . . .			
6. as easy as . . .			
7. as deep as . . .			
8. as pretty as . . .			

Note: You can find out how to say these in English on page 64.

PART ③ ACADEMIC READING Economic Systems

BEFORE READING

 A. THINKING AHEAD In small groups, discuss these questions:
• Do you know the names of any economic systems?
• Can you explain how these economic systems work?

Reading Strategy

Guessing the Meaning from Context: Using the Next Sentence

Sometimes you can find the meaning of a new word in the sentence that follows the word.

Example: Business doesn't **take place** on Fridays in that company. For religious reasons, no business can **occur** on a Friday.

(Here we see that **take place** means "occur.")

Sometimes you will not be able to guess the exact meaning of the word from the next sentence. But since it is not always necessary to know the exact meaning, you do not need to look up the word in the dictionary.

B. VOCABULARY PREPARATION Read the sentences below. Words and phrases from the next reading are in green. Write the part of speech on the line. Then use a highlighter pen to mark the meaning of the word in the next sentence.

1. Each society's values and goals **determine** its economic system. These values and goals decide the type of economy for the country.

   Part of Speech: _verb_

2. That country is rich in **resources.** It has oil, minerals, and timber.

   Part of Speech: _____

3. The government **distributed** food and clothing to people of the neighborhood after the hurricane destroyed their homes. The government gave out these necessities to anyone who needed them.

   Part of Speech: _____

4. That American company wanted to do business in North Korea, but the government **intervened.** The U.S. government stepped in and prevented this.

   Part of Speech: _____

5. These people are **nomadic hunters and gatherers.** They are travelers who move from one area to another to hunt animals and gather fruits and vegetables.

   Part of Speech: _____

C. PREVIEWING Before you read, quickly look over the reading, "Economic Systems," starting on page 49. What are four topics in this passage? Write them on the lines below.

1. _____

2. _____

3. _____

4. _____

Reading Strategy

Marking a Textbook

Students often need to do a huge amount of reading, and there usually isn't enough time to read a chapter several times. You need to learn to highlight the important information in a reading so that you can find it quickly later. One way to do this is to use highlighter pens–bright yellow, green, or orange pens that allow you to find important information later.

• Use one color for main ideas.

• Use a different color for important details.

• Be sure not to highlight too much information. Sometimes you can just highlight key words instead of highlighting an entire sentence.

D. MARKING A TEXTBOOK In small groups, discuss how students in your culture mark up textbooks. Do students highlight main ideas and details? Do students not mark up their books at all?

Reading Strategy

Finding the Topic Sentence

When you read a section of a textbook, you can often find the main idea for the reading in the introductory paragraph and in the concluding paragraph.

In the other paragraphs of a reading, the main idea of each paragraph is usually found in the first sentence. This is the topic sentence. It's a good idea to highlight the topic sentences as you read.

READING

Read about different economic systems. As you read, highlight the following:

• The topic sentence of each paragraph
• The characteristics of each of the four economic systems

Economic Systems

Various countries have different economic systems, but each system must answer the same four basic questions: (1) What goods and services (and how much of each) should be produced? (2) Who should produce them? (3) How should they be produced? (4) Who should be able to use them? Each society answers these questions according
5   to its values and goals, which determine its economic system. Economists have identified four types of economic systems: traditional, command (or controlled), market (or capitalist), and mixed.

Traditional System

A pure traditional economic system answers the four basic questions according to tradition. In such a system, things are done "the way they have always been done."
10   Economic decisions are based on customs, beliefs, and religion—that is, the traditional way of doing things. The San people of southern Africa, for example, are nomadic hunters and gatherers. In other words, the
15   San travel from one area to another to hunt animals and gather fruits and vegetables, and they move on when there is no more food. Traditional economic systems exist today in very few areas of Asia, the Middle
20   East, Africa, and Latin America.

A traditional San hunter

Command (or Controlled) System

In a pure command economic system, an individual person has little—or possibly no—influence over how the basic economic questions are answered. The government controls production and makes all decisions about the use of goods and services. "The government" may be one person, a small group of leaders, or a
25   group of central planners in a government agency. These people choose how resources will be used and decide the distribution of goods and services. They also regulate the amount of education that people receive, so they guide people into certain jobs. These days, the world's only pure command economies are North Korea and Syria. China, once a command economy, has since the late 20th century
30   incorporated more and more elements of market economics into its state-run system.

Market (or Capitalist) System

The opposite of a pure command economic system is a pure market economic system—or capitalism, in which the government does not intervene. In other words, individual people own the factors of production, and they decide for themselves the answers to the four basic economic questions. Economic decisions are made in the
35   market—the freely chosen activity between buyers and sellers of goods and services. Bargaining over the price of items is characteristic of a market exchange. This exchange of goods and services may take place in a neighborhood market for someone's services such as delivering newspapers, or it may happen in a worldwide

market for a good such as oil. People may take, refuse, or change jobs whenever they want to—if there is a demand for their labor. The spread of capitalism is referred to today as globalization.

A capitalist system is based on the law of supply and demand. It assumes that money is necessary to purchase everything. However, other kinds of exchanges, such as gift exchange, continue to coexist along with the market system. There are cultural rules about reciprocal gift exchange. The rules do not require the recipient to return like for like. For example, people often bring gifts when invited for dinner. It is appropriate to bring wine or flowers, but it is not considered appropriate to bring a pound of meat or to give the hostess a $10 bill. This kind of gift exchange is between equals. It is different from the case of government leaders who receive "gifts" for influence. What one person may call a gift, another will call a bribe.

The New York Stock Exchange

Mixed System

Except for the traditional economic system, a *pure* economic system has probably never existed; most economies are mixed. A mixed economy has some characteristics of a command economy and some of a market economy. Two examples are the United States and the People's Republic of China. The U.S. economy tends toward the market system, but there are laws that regulate some areas of business, and many industries, particularly agriculture, are supported by generous state subsidies. The People's Republic of China tends toward the command system but has been gradually moving toward a mixed economy since the late 20th century. In the 1980s, China introduced "special economic zones," where foreign trade could take place without interference by the government, and in the 1990s, the government began transferring ownership of its large state-run industries into private hands. The world system of money and markets has penetrated even places such as Papua New Guinea, where it coexists with a traditional system (of reciprocal exchange) in which people exchange material goods of equal value. The Western economic part of this is called *bisnis*, and continuing traditional systems are referred to as *kastom*.

Sources: *Economics: Today and Tomorrow* (Miller) and *The Tapestry of Culture: An Introduction to Cultural Anthropology* (Rosman and Rubel)

AFTER READING

 A. CHECK YOUR UNDERSTANDING Look back at the first paragraph of the reading on pages 49–50. Which sentence is a "map" that introduces the sub-topics of the reading? Did you highlight it?

Now look at the rest of the paragraphs. If you could choose just one sentence to remember from each paragraph, which one would it be? Did you highlight it?

In small groups, compare and discuss your answers.

Reading Strategy

Using Graphic Organizers: Charts

In Chapter 1, you learned about graphic organizers (page 22). **Graphic organizers** are useful study tools that can allow you to record information such as main ideas, important details, and examples from a reading. They can allow you to see relationships among ideas.

There are many types of graphic organizers. You will use several of them in this book. One type that is good for note-taking is a chart.

B. USING GRAPHIC ORGANIZERS: CHARTS In the box, write the four economic systems mentioned in the reading. Then give a definition (or characteristics) of each system and add an example from the reading. Some of your highlighted information might help you to do this.

System	Definitions/Characteristics	Example
Traditional	Economic decisions are based on customs, beliefs, and religion.	the San people

C. VOCABULARY CHECK: WORDS IN ECONOMICS Look back at the reading on pages 49–50. Find words or phrases for the definitions below, and highlight them in the reading. Then write them on the correct lines. The line numbers in parentheses will help you find the words.

1. people who study economics (5–10)

2. command economy (20–25)

3. market economy (30–35)

4. the freely chosen activity between buyers and sellers of goods and services (35–40)

5. work (noun) (35–40)

6. given or received in return for something else (an adjective) (45–50)

7. money that someone pays in exchange for the influence of a government official (65–70)

8. "leans" in one direction instead of another (70–75)

D. DISCUSSION In small groups, discuss these questions.

1. What is the economic system in the country you live in? If it is a mixed economy, does it tend to be more command or more market? What does the government regulate?

2. What is the effect of religious beliefs and values on the economy where you live? What effect does religion have on the economy of other countries?

3. What are some rules for gift exchange in your culture? For example, what is a typical gift to bring to a dinner party? Do government officials sometimes accept gifts in exchange for their influence? Do people discuss the difference between "gifts" and "bribes"?

Critical Thinking Strategy

Synthesizing and Applying Information

Students often need to **synthesize** information—that is, to put together information from different readings or from readings and their in-class lecture notes. They also need to **apply** information in a reading to a new situation. In doing this, students are making connections between different sources.

E. MAKING CONNECTIONS Look back at the readings in Parts 1 (pages 37–39) and 2 (pages 41–42). What economic system are these people working in? How do you know? Write your answers in the chart below.

People	Economic System
People of the North Pacific Coast	
Sami Reindeer Herders	
The Man Who Vacuumed Prairie Dogs	
Sabri and the Greek Woman (Part 2)	

F. APPLICATION: GATHERING INFORMATION Answer the questions below about the country you were born in or the country you live in now. Check the correct box for each question. Then ask a partner the questions. You will use this information when you write a paragraph in Part 5.

Questionnaire

1. Who decides what a farmer will grow?

   ☐ the farmer   ☐ a group of farmers

   ☐ the government   ☐ other: _____

2. Who decides what a factory will produce?

   ☐ the factory owner(s)   ☐ the workers

   ☐ the government   ☐ other: _____

3. Who is able to receive and use goods and services?

   ☐ anyone who has enough money   ☐ anyone who needs them

   ☐ anyone who works   ☐ other: _____

4. Do some people have more goods and services than others?

   ☐ yes   ☐ no

5. If people are not able to take care of themselves, who takes care of them?

   ☐ nobody   ☐ family members

   ☐ the town or a religious group   ☐ the government

   ☐ a combination (specify: _____)

6. Does the government have laws to regulate conditions in factories?

   ☐ yes   ☐ no

7. Does the government regulate the quality of food, medicine, clothing, or building materials?

   ☐ yes   ☐ no

8. Is there anything that is illegal to grow, produce, buy, or sell?

   ☐ yes (If so, what?) _____   ☐ no

9. Who owns the airlines, railroads (trains), and buses?

   ☐ private companies   ☐ the government

   ☐ a combination (both private companies and the government)

10. How is the price determined for things such as food and clothing?

    ☐ The market determines the price.   ☐ The government sets the price.

    ☐ other: _____

11. Look at your answers for 1–10. The answers should lead you to the answer to this question: What economic system does your country have?

    ☐ traditional   ☐ command

    ☐ market   ☐ mixed

 G. WORD JOURNAL Go back to the readings in this chapter. What words are important for you to remember? Put them in your Word Journal.

H. RESPONSE WRITING Choose one of these topics:

• someone you know who is very good at bargaining or negotiating prices
• the economic system in your country
• how the economic system in your country is changing
• appropriate gifts to bring to the host at a party

Write about your topic for 10 minutes. Don't worry about grammar and don't stop writing to use a dictionary. Just put as many ideas as possible on paper.

PART ④ THE MECHANICS OF WRITING

In Part 4, you will practice using the passive voice and adverbial conjunctions. You will need this grammar in Part 5 to write a paragraph about the economic system of a country.

The Passive Voice

We often use the passive voice instead of the active voice if the subject (in the active voice) is obvious, unnecessary, or unknown.

Example: People **sold** the prairie dogs in Tokyo. (active voice)
The prairie dogs **were sold** in Tokyo. (passive voice)

(It's obvious that *people* sold them, so this is a good place to use the passive voice.)

In the passive voice, the object (from the active voice) is moved into the subject position.

Example: People have always done this in the same way. (active voice)
(object)

This has always been done in the same way. (passive voice)
(subject)

The passive voice uses the verb *be* and the past participle of another verb.

A. THE PASSIVE VOICE Change these active voice sentences to the passive voice. Use the same tense as in the active voice. (The objects are green.)

1. People base **economic decisions** on tradition.

Economic decisions are based on tradition.

2. People exchanged **oil** for wheat.

3. Everyone will need **a lot of natural resources.**

4. Someone may offer **Jim** a job.

5. People make **economic decisions** in the market.

6. People do **things** in the same way people have always done **them.** (Change both parts of the sentence.)

Transitional Expressions: Adverbial Conjunctions

Transitional expressions carry an idea from one sentence to another and show relationships between sentences. They pull a paragraph together and help the ideas to flow smoothly and logically.

One type of transitional expression is an adverbial conjunction. An adverbial conjunction joins two independent clauses. There is a period or semicolon before the adverbial conjunction. There is a comma after it (except for *then*).

Examples: The government is regulating the price of reindeer. **Therefore,** the Sami people are not happy with the government.

The farmer didn't want prairie dogs on his land**; however,** he didn't want to kill or hurt them.

Here are some of the many adverbial conjunctions. They have been separated into groups according to meaning.

in addition
moreover
also
furthermore
} added information (= *and*)

however
nevertheless
even so
} contradiction (= *but*)

therefore
consequently
as a result
for this (that) reason
} cause and effect (= *so* or *that's why*)

for example
for instance
} example

in other words
that is
} explanation, definition (the same information in different words)

next
finally
then (no comma)
} time relationships

mostly
for the most part
to some extent (= *partly*)
to a large extent (= *mostly*)
} degree (how much)

in short
in summary
} conclusion, summary

Note: An independent clause is a group of words that can stand alone. In other words, with a capital letter at the beginning and a period at the end, an independent clause is a sentence.

B. SENTENCE COMBINING: ADVERBIAL CONJUNCTIONS Combine the following pairs of sentences. Choose an adverbial conjunction from the group in parentheses.

1. They discussed the sale of the house for hours and hours. They agreed on a price. (time relationship)

   _____

   _____

2. Sabri Tahir was famous for his cleverness in business. Durrell asked him for help in buying a house. (cause and effect)

   _____

   _____

3. Durrell describes Sabri Tahir as having "an air of reptilian concentration and silence." Sabri was able to sit for a long time without moving or speaking but instead just watched. (explanation)

   _____

   _____

4. There were people of different nationalities living in the village. They got along well without many problems. (degree)

   _____

   _____

C. SENTENCE COMBINING: MORE ADVERBIAL CONJUNCTIONS Combine the following pairs of sentences. Choose a logical adverbial conjunction for each.

1. For many years the country had a socialist economy. Now it has a capitalist economy.

   _____

   _____

2. The taxes on their farm were very high, and they weren't getting good prices for their crops. They sold the farm and moved to the city.

   _____

   _____

3. She studied the language of the country that she was going to live in. She learned as much as possible about the culture.

_____

_____

4. The demand for that book is greater than the supply. There are more people who want to buy the book than there are copies of it.

_____

_____

Recognizing and Repairing Run-Ons and Comma Splices

A common mistake in written (but not spoken) English is the incorrect combination of two sentences.

INCORRECT: My uncle is losing money on his business he refuses to sell it.

This is incorrect because two independent clauses are combined with no punctuation. The problem is between the words _business_ and _he_. This mistake is called a **run-on sentence** because it runs on and on when it should stop.

Sometimes a student tries to "fix" a run-on sentence with a comma.

INCORRECT: My uncle is losing money on his business, he refuses to sell it.

This does not improve the sentence. It simply replaces one mistake with another. A comma alone cannot hold two independent clauses together. This mistake is called a **comma splice.**

There are several ways to repair a run-on sentence or comma splice. Here are some.

1. Simply separate the two clauses with either a semicolon or a period followed by a capital letter.

   Examples: My uncle is losing money on his business; he refuses to sell it.
   My uncle is losing money on his business. **He** refuses to sell it.

2. Use a comma and a coordinating conjunction. (For a list of coordinating conjunctions, see page 29.)

   Example: My uncle is losing money on his business, **but** he refuses to sell it.

3. Use a period or semicolon and an adverbial conjunction with a comma after it.

   Example: My uncle is losing money on his business; **however,** he refuses to sell it.

D. RECOGNIZING AND REPAIRING RUN-ON SENTENCES AND COMMA SPLICES Identify each sentence below as a run-on (R), comma splice (CS), or good sentence (OK). (Hint: look for the place where the two sentences meet.) Then correct the run-ons and comma splices. Do not change the good sentences.

    ; in other words,

_____R_____ **1.** These people are hunter-gatherers^ they hunt animals for meat and gather fruits and vegetables.

_____ **2.** The tribe hunts and gathers in one area they move on when there is no more food.

_____ **3.** Each person in the tribe has a job to do, the young girls find water and firewood.

_____ **4.** Men do most of the hunting women do most of the gathering.

_____ **5.** Old people in the tribe give advice and look after small children.

_____ **6.** There is usually a lot of diversity in the diet the people are generally healthy.

_____ **7.** Hunter-gatherers tend to live in small groups of families that are closely related.

E. REVIEW: FINDING ERRORS Circle the letter of the incorrect word or phrase in each sentence below. There are errors with the passive voice, adverbial conjunctions, and sentence structure (run-ons and comma splices).

1. The Inuit people <u>are</u> hunter-gatherers, <u>so</u> economic decisions <u>are base</u> on traditional <u>beliefs and</u>
            A   B   C   D

    <u>customs.</u>

2. Tradition <u>determines</u> how people hunt and fish <u>and</u> who should do certain jobs<u>, for example,</u> in
               A   B   C

    late summer, families <u>go fishing for salmon</u> in the Yukon River.
                          D

3. <u>However, the native people</u> of modern Alaska <u>are also part</u> of the market <u>economy they have</u>
     A   B   C

    modern houses, engines for their boats<u>, and snowmobiles.</u>
                                    D

4. <u>In addition,</u> the native Alaskan system <u>has</u> one characteristic of a command economy<u>, state laws</u>
      A   B   C

    and U.S. <u>laws regulate the use</u> of the land and wildlife.
                     D

5. <u>On short,</u> the economy of native Alaskans is traditional <u>but</u> <u>has</u> elements of <u>both capitalism and</u>
     A   B   C

    <u>government control.</u>
           D

PART ⑤ ACADEMIC WRITING

WRITING ASSIGNMENT

In Part 5, you will write one paragraph to answer this question:
• What is the economic system in one country you know?

Use your answers on the questionnaire (pages 53–54) as a guide, but you probably won't use all of your answers. Also, you might include information that is not on the questionnaire. You will need to have:
• a topic sentence and a concluding sentence.
• supporting information about the topic sentence.
• details about the supporting information.

STEP A. CHOOSING A TOPIC It's important to choose a topic that you understand and have ideas about. Choose one:

• the country you were born in
• the country you live in
• any other country whose economy you know something about

Writing Strategy ⬤⬤⬤

Writing a Topic Sentence

The topic sentence is usually the first sentence in a paragraph. The topic sentence must be limited and specific enough to develop in one paragraph, but it shouldn't be too specific. The topic sentence has two functions: it gives the topic of the paragraph, and it says something about this topic. What it says about the topic is the **controlling idea.** The topic sentence provides a sort of "promise" to the reader that the rest of your paragraph will give details to support it.

Example: Many farmers in England have been worried about the future of farming in their country.

> Topic: farmers in England
> Controlling Idea: have been worried about the future of farming

Example: In a pure command economic system, an individual person has little–or possibly no–influence over how the basic economic questions are answered.

> Topic: a pure command economic system
> Controlling Idea: an individual person has little or no influence

A topic sentence should not be vague–that is, unclear. Stay away from adjectives that are very general, such as *good, bad, interesting, nice, fun,* and *exciting.*

WRITING A TOPIC SENTENCE In small groups, choose the best topic sentence in each group below. After you choose, circle the topic and underline the controlling idea. Then decide what is wrong with the other sentences. (For example, are they too vague? Are they too general? Is there no controlling idea?)

1. A. It's fun to learn another language.

   B. Knowledge of another language is important.

   C. Knowledge of the local language can help an international businessperson in four ways.

2. A. Religion can have a powerful effect on people's work habits.

   B. There are five major religions in the world: Hinduism, Buddhism, Judaism, Christianity, and Islam.

   C. Religion is important in our lives.

3. A. Albania has an interesting culture.

   B. It's expensive to travel to Albania.

   C. For many years, Albania had a strict command economy, but this has changed enormously since the end of the Cold War.

4. A. Politeness is important in Japan.

   B. International businesspeople who work in Japan need to understand that "yes" doesn't always mean "yes."

   C. It's difficult for international businesspeople to understand Japanese culture.

5. A. Life was hard in Russia.

   B. After living in a mostly command economy for decades, Russians are now adapting to a mixed economy that tends toward capitalism.

   C. My Russian grandmother once stood in line for three hours to buy a pair of shoes.

👥 **IMPROVING TOPIC SENTENCES** The following sentences are poor topic sentences. They are too general or don't have a controlling idea. Rewrite each one and make it into a better topic sentence. When you finish, compare your sentences in small groups. (**Note:** There are many possible answers.)

1. International businesspeople have many problems.

_____

2. There is a lot of unemployment in my country.

_____

3. Farming is hard work for many reasons.

_____

STEP B. WRITING YOUR TOPIC SENTENCE Now write one topic sentence about the topic that you chose in Step A.

_____

_____

Writing Strategy 〰️

Writing a Paragraph of Analysis

A paragraph of analysis looks at the elements (the basic parts) of something. The supporting sentences focus on each part. They give specific information about the topic sentence. The supporting sentences are more specific than the topic sentence, but there are different levels of specificity. (In other words, some supporting sentences are more specific than others.) An outline for a paragraph of analysis might look like this:

Topic Sentence

    Supporting Information
    (about the topic sentence)

        Specific Detail
        (about the supporting information)

    Supporting Information
    (about the topic sentence)

        Specific Detail
        (about the supporting information)

Concluding Sentence

In a real paragraph, there would probably be more information and more details than in this outline. Notice the organization in the example paragraph on the next page.

Example:

In Alaska, the native people have a mixed economic system. For the most part, it is a traditional economy. The people are hunter-gatherers, so economic decisions are based on traditional beliefs and customs. Tradition determines how people hunt and fish and who should do certain jobs. For example, in late summer, families go fishing for salmon in the Yukon River. The men and boys catch the fish. The women and girls work together to cut, dry, and smoke the fish. The older people give advice. The fish is distributed to all members of the group. However, the native people of modern Alaska are also part of the market economy. They have modern houses, engines for their boats, and snowmobiles. To buy these goods, they need to do business in the worldwide market, so they sell fish to Japan and furs to Europe. In addition, the native Alaskan system has one characteristic of a command economy; state laws and U.S. laws regulate the use of the land and wildlife. In short, the economy of native Alaskans is traditional but has elements of both capitalism and government control.

Note in the example:

- One of the details is an example.
- The concluding sentence is similar to the topic sentence but in other words.

Analysis: In the example paragraph, find and highlight five adverbial conjunctions and the punctuation with them.

STEP C. PLANNING YOUR PARAGRAPH Before you begin to write, make notes—not complete sentences—about your topic. Follow these suggestions:

1. Write your topic sentence at the top of a piece of paper. Under this, write information from your questionnaire on pages 53–54. (This will be your evidence or support.) Add details and at least one example for some of this information.

2. After you write all of your ideas, cross out anything that doesn't belong. A paragraph must be about one topic.

3. Decide on the order for your evidence.

STEP D. WRITING THE PARAGRAPH Use your notes from Step C. Write complete sentences in paragraph form. You might make some mistakes, but don't worry about them at this point.

STEP E. EDITING Read your paragraph and answer these questions.

1. Is the paragraph form correct (indentation, margins)?

2. Does the first sentence (the topic sentence) answer the question?

3. Is the topic sentence clear and specific?

4. Is there supporting information?

5. Are there details about the supporting information?

6. Is there correct use of adverbial conjunctions (punctuation and choice of conjunction)?

7. If there is use of the passive voice, is it used correctly?

8. Is there a concluding sentence that is similar to (but not the same as) the topic sentence?

STEP F. REWRITING Write your paragraph again. This time, try to write it with no mistakes.

Answers for Activity E, page 46
In English, these expressions are:
1. as busy as a bee
2. as tough as leather (*or* nails)
3. as free as a bird
4. as happy as a clam (*or* lark)
5. as soft as silk
6. as easy as pie (*or* 1, 2, 3 *or* A, B, C)
7. as deep as the ocean
8. as pretty as a picture

UNIT 1 VOCABULARY WORKSHOP

Review vocabulary that you learned in Chapters 1 and 2.

A. MATCHING Match the words to the definitions. Write the correct letters on the lines.

Words	Definitions
_f_ **1.** acquaintance	**a.** way of acting
_____ **2.** acquire	**b.** expensive
_____ **3.** behavior	**c.** decide
_____ **4.** costly	**d.** business
_____ **5.** determine	**e.** put together information from different sources
_____ **6.** edible	~~**f.**~~ someone whom you know—but not a close friend
_____ **7.** enterprise	**g.** get
_____ **8.** hierarchy	**h.** pay no attention to (something or someone)
_____ **9.** ignore	**i.** something you can eat
_____ **10.** synthesize	**j.** organization into a system of ranks from lowest to highest

B. WORDS IN PHRASES: PREPOSITIONS It will help your vocabulary and grammar to begin to notice words in phrases. In this activity, fill in each blank with the correct preposition that belongs in the phrase. To check your answers, turn back to pages 19–20.

A **knowledge** _____ of _____ **cultural values** is essential for cultural intelligence.
                              1

Thomas and Inkson give two ways to **look** _____ **cultural values.** The first
                                                    2

is from Geert Hofstede, a Dutch social scientist . . . Statistical analysis of the country differences showed

these to fall into four separate areas ("dimensions"):

Individualism. In individualistic cultures, people **think** _____ **themselves**
                                                                            3

as individuals and **prefer** _____ work alone or to do activities in small
                                      4

"private interactions with friends." They **base their decisions** _____ **their**

own ideas of what is appropriate. In collectivistic cultures, people think of themselves as "members of

groups" and prefer group activities. They base decisions on **the needs** _____

the group.

Power distance. In a culture with high power distance, people expect a **big difference**

_____ **people** with high status and people with low status. For example, at

work, they expect the boss to make all decisions. In a culture with low power distance, people

are more equal. There isn't as much difference between people of high and low status. At work,

the boss **listens** _____ **people** at all levels in the company.

C. VOCABULARY EXPANSION Write the different parts of speech for the words in the chart. Use a dictionary to fill in these blanks.

	Verb	**Noun**	**Adjective**
1.	determine	determination	
2.			nomadic
3.		distribution	
4.	regulate		
5.	tend		

Stems and Affixes

Parts of words, usually from Greek or Latin, will help you to guess the meaning of many new words. These word parts are prefixes (at the beginning of a word), stems (the main part of a word), and suffixes (the ending of a word). Prefixes and suffixes are called affixes. Here are some examples from this passage.

Prefixes	**Meaning**	**Stems**	**Meaning**	**Suffix**	**Meaning**
infra-	under or within	centr	center, middle	-ism	belief in
inter-	between	ethic	moral system		
mis-	wrong	ethno	race, culture, people		
multi-	many				

Example: **multiethnic**

multi- = many   **ethnic** = race, culture, people

A multiethnic society has many different cultures.

D. STEMS AND AFFIXES What do you know about these words? Use stems and affixes in the box to analyze the word parts with a partner.

1. misconception

2. international

3. ethnocentrism

4. Buddhism

5. multinational

E. THE ACADEMIC WORD LIST In the box below are some of the most common academic words in English. Fill in the blanks with these words. When you finish, check your answers in the reading on pages 49–50. For more words, see the Academic Word List on pages 259–262.

appropriate	~~economic~~	individual	jobs	purchase
assumes	factors	intervene	labor	require
cultural	globalization	items	over	

The opposite of a pure command economic system is a pure market ___economic___
1

system—or capitalism, in which the government does not _____. In other
2

words, _____ people own the _____ of production,
3   4

and they decide for themselves the answers to the four basic economic questions. Economic decisions

are made in the market—the freely chosen activity between buyers and sellers of goods and

services. Bargaining _____ the price of _____ is
5   6

characteristic of a market exchange. This exchange of goods and services may take place in a

neighborhood market for someone's services such as delivering newspapers, or it may happen in a

worldwide market for a good such as oil. People may take, refuse, or change _____
7

whenever they want to—if there is a demand for their _____. The spread of
8

capitalism is referred to today as _____.
9

A capitalist system is based on the law of supply and demand. It _____
10

that money is necessary to _____ everything. However, other kinds of
11

exchanges, such as gift exchange, continue to coexist along with the market system. There are

_____ rules about reciprocal gift exchange. The rules do not
                  12

_____ the recipient to return like for like. For example, people often bring
                  13

gifts when invited for dinner. It is _____ to bring wine or flowers, but it is not
                                              14

considered appropriate to bring a pound of meat or to give the hostess a $10 bill.

UNIT 2

ART

Chapter 3
Themes and Purposes

Chapter 4
The Ancient World: Egypt

Themes and Purposes

Discuss these questions:
- Look at the picture. What images do you see in the painting? Are they realistic?
- What do you like or dislike about this painting? Why?
- What is your favorite work of art? Why do you like it?

PART ① INTRODUCTION Looking at Art: What's the Story?

BEFORE READING

A. THINKING AHEAD Look at the mysterious figure above. Discuss these questions with a partner.

1. Is this a man or a woman?

2. What is the figure doing?

3. What might the figure be made of?

4. How do you think it was made?

5. What condition is it in?

6. In your opinion, what is this figure? Circle your answer.
   a. a medicine container
   b. a flower vase
   c. an **anthropomorphic** (human-form) perfume jar
   d. an anthropomorphic figure to hold an offering to a god or to burn incense
   e. a waiter carrying a bowl of soup

B. DISCUSSION In small groups, look over the pictures on pages 74–75. Which one do you like the most? Why? Do you know something about any of these pieces of art?

READING

Read about how to look at art. As you read, think about this question:
• What are two ways to look at art?

Looking at Art: What's the Story?

People without much experience in art often do not know what to look for in a work of art. They might glance quickly at a painting or sculpture and decide immediately if they like it or not. In a museum, they hurry past much of the art and, unfortunately, in the process miss out on a lot. However, students of art learn to
5   look at art using two special approaches: they use *art criticism* and *art history*.

In art criticism, students learn first to describe the work of art: What people and things are in the work? What are the details, colors, lines, shapes, and space relationships? Then they analyze the work: How are the various parts organized?

Art history allows students to learn the story behind the work of art. To do this,
10 they try to answer four questions. When, where, and by whom was it made? What is the style? How was the artist influenced by the world around him or her? How important is the work?

Let's look back at the figure on page 72 from an art-criticism approach. What might an art critic say? This is an anthropomorphic figure that is carrying a bowl in
15 its right hand. The top of the head also seems to be a bowl. The figure is made of clay. Although it has a human form, it does not look natural. There are two tiny arms and no legs. Instead, the body of the figure is round, shaped almost like a cylinder. We know that it was broken at one time because there are crack marks. From this example, you can see that art criticism allows us to *see* a piece of art.

20 An art historian can add the story behind this mysterious figure: it was found in Israel, with many other broken figures, and is about 2,600 years old. It either burned incense or held a religious offering to a god of the Edomite people. Possibly, it was broken in the seventh century B.C.E.* when King Josiah ordered his soldiers to destroy the culture of "pagan" or non-Jewish religions. It is art history that allows us
25 to appreciate the story behind the work. For most of us, it is the history that makes the art come alive.

*B.C.E. = Before the Common Era (also known as B.C. or before Christ)
Sources: *Art in Focus* (Mittler) and *Biblical Archaeology Review*

AFTER READING

Determining Point of View

Determining a writer's **point of view** (opinion, way of looking at a subject) involves making inferences (see page 6). One way to determine point of view is to pay attention to adjectives and adverbs that express opinion. Another way is to keep in mind that a writer often saves the best for last—in other words, puts the most important reason, point, or argument at the end of a passage. Recognizing a writer's point of view helps a reader to understand a passage on a deeper level.

A. DETERMINING POINT OF VIEW According to the reading on page 73, there are two ways to look at art. Which one does the writer seem to prefer? Explain your answer to a partner.

B. APPLICATION In small groups, discuss the three pieces of art by using the art-criticism approach; that is, discuss what you see. Then fill in the chart on page 75. Use a dictionary if necessary. If someone in your group knows about the history of the piece (the story behind it), that person should use the art-history approach to explain it to the others.

A

B

C

Piece of art	List the components: people, things, and shapes.	What is your opinion of it?	What do you already know about this piece?
A			
B			
C			

When you finish, turn to page 104 to find the story behind each piece of art.

PART ② GENERAL INTEREST READING The Sacred Realm of Art

BEFORE READING

A. THINKING AHEAD In small groups, think of as many religions as you can. Then discuss the art that is important to each religion.

B. VOCABULARY PREPARATION Read the sentences below. Words from the next reading are in green. What can you guess about each word in green? First, write the part of speech: *noun, verb,* or *adjective.* Then guess the meaning from the context.

1. Today, most ancient Greek buildings are white stone, but two thousand years ago, they were brightly painted. If you look very closely at some of them, however, you'll notice that a small amount of paint is still **visible.**

   Part of Speech: _____

   Guess: _____

2. When he's alone, high up in the mountains, he sometimes gets a very **spiritual** feeling. There is no church or temple, but he feels that God is all around him.

   Part of Speech: _____

   Guess: _____

3. The culture **flourished** for over a thousand years, but then it began a decline. It became less "healthy," less successful, and finally disappeared.

   Part of Speech: _____

   Guess: _____

4. The painting **portrays** an important event in the country's history. It shows the time when the country gained independence.

   Part of Speech: _____

   Guess: _____

5. The figure of Mary holds the **infant** Jesus. She gestures toward the baby, and they both look toward the viewer.

   Part of Speech: _____

   Guess: _____

6. The ancient Olmec people often **depicted** this figure—half man, half jaguar—in their art. They represented this man-cat in thousands of statues.

Part of Speech: _____

Guess: _____

Now compare your answers with a partner's answers.

Reading Strategy

Guessing the Meaning from Context: Pictures and Captions

Pictures and the captions under them can often help you to understand new words. Photos or art can provide a sort of "picture dictionary" for new vocabulary in the caption or text. Sometimes the caption itself explains a word.

C. PICTURES AND CAPTIONS Look over the pictures and captions on pages 78–79. Find **bolded** words for the definitions below. Write the words on the lines.

1. a green stone: _____

2. golden circles of light around the head of a very spiritual being: _____

3. terrible and angry: _____

4. are around: _____

5. deep thought, usually about something religious: _____

Reading Strategy

Finding Main Ideas: Major Sub-Topics

You learned in Chapter 1 that the introduction to a reading usually includes the main idea of the whole reading. Frequently, there is also a sentence that provides a "map" of two or more of the most important sub-topics, so you know what to expect as you read. In the introduction, the sub-topics are given in the same order in which you will find them in the reading.

READING

Read about religious art. As you read, highlight the answers to these questions when you find them:
• What is the role of art in religion?
• What are the sub-topics?

The Sacred Realm of Art

Since earliest times, art has served religion. Art attempts to take something invisible, something spiritual, and make it visible. Through the centuries, art has
5 given people visual images of the people, stories, and events described in the religion. We will look at art from four religions—the ancient Olmecs, the Bwa, Buddhism, and Christianity.

10 Art is often the only evidence we have of the beliefs of cultures that have come and gone without leaving written records. An example is this jade figure from the Olmec culture, which flourished
15 from about 1500 to 300 B.C.E. in what is today southern Mexico. The statue seems to portray a shaman, a person who communicates with both the human and spirit worlds and acts as an
20 intermediary between the two. The shaman holds up a small creature whose fierce expression contrasts with his own calm look. The creature's headband, catlike eyes, and large down-turned
25 mouth identify him as the infant man-jaguar, a magical creature that combines animal and human characteristics. The man-jaguar was clearly an important figure in Olmec culture and is often
30 depicted in the art, but we do not know its purpose.

Among the most important art forms ever developed to give visual presence to the spirit realm are the masks of
35 Africa. Among the Bwa people of West Africa, these masks manifest (make physically present) nature spirits, and with the costumes completely hide the human identities. Masks do not appear casually in the community. Rather, people call on them during times when
40 the help of the spirits and the natural forces that they control are especially needed. For example, masks may appear at funerals to make sure that the spirit of the dead person leaves the community and takes its place in the spirit world of ancestors.

An Olmec figure in **jade** (a green stone) holding a baby with a **fierce** expression on its face

Our next two examples, one Buddhist and one Christian, are very different from each other in subject. It may be surprising, however, that they are very similar in form. The works were created at about the same time but four thousand miles apart.

An image from Tibet shows the Buddha sitting in meditation. He is the largest figure and faces front. His hands are in a classic *mudra*—a hand position that symbolizes the giving of gifts. Around him are *bodhisattvas*—people who have postponed their goal of *Nirvana* (freedom from the cycle of birth, death, and rebirth) because they want to help other people to reach that goal. All of the figures wear halos—golden circles of light around their heads.

A Tathagata Buddha from Central Tibet; the Buddha is sitting in **meditation**–deep thought, usually about something religious. The figures of *bodhisattvas* **surround** him.

The final example is by the 13th-century Italian master Cimabue. In this painting, the Virgin Mary is the central figure. She is holding her son Jesus. Mary is sitting on her throne, with her hand in a gesture toward Jesus, who is the hope of the world. On both sides of her are angels. These angels are spirit beings who help humans reach heaven. Again, all of the figures in the painting wear halos. Again, the Virgin is the largest figure because she is the most important.

From these pieces of art of four very different religions, we have examples of how artists can make religion more concrete—more real—to believers.

Sources: *Living With Art* (Gilbert, 4th ed., and Getlein, 6th ed.)

Madonna Enthroned by Cimabue, Uffizi, Florence; the mother of Jesus is surrounded by angels with **halos** around their heads.

AFTER READING

A. CHECK YOUR UNDERSTANDING Look back at the sentences that you highlighted in the reading to answer these questions.

- What is the role of art in religion?
- What four religions does the reading include? Write them on the chart. Then go back to the reading and find the paragraphs that discuss art from these religions. Fill in the chart with examples.

Religion	One Example of a Piece of Art from This Religion
ancient Olmec	

B. VOCABULARY CHECK Fill in blanks with words from the box.

ancestors	concrete	faith	funerals	intermediary	shaman

1. Buddhism is the major _____ of several Asian countries.

2. Most religions use art to make spiritual ideas more _____ because belief is invisible.

3. In some religions, people go to a(n) _____ for spiritual advice. This person seems to be able to communicate not only with humans but also with spirits. In other words, he acts as a(n) _____ between living and dead people.

4. Two of my friends died recently, so I had to go to two _____. Both were beautiful ceremonies.

5. In some religions, people believe that they can communicate with their _____. The belief is that these family members who lived before them can help and guide them.

C. VOCABULARY EXPANSION Use a dictionary to help you complete this chart.

Noun (Religion)	Adjective	Noun (Person Who Believes)
Buddhism	Buddhist	Buddhist
Hinduism		
Judaism		
Christianity		
Islam		

Understanding Pronouns

On reading tests and when reading in general, it's important to understand the meaning of subject pronouns (such as *he, she, it, they*) and object pronouns (such as *him, her, it, them*). Each pronoun refers to a noun or **noun phrase** (small group of words) that comes before it. Writers use pronouns because they want to avoid repeating a noun.

Examples: <u>People without much experience in art</u> often do not know what to look for in a work of art. **They** might glance quickly at <u>a painting or sculpture</u> and decide immediately if they like **it** or not.

D. UNDERSTANDING PRONOUNS What do the pronouns in green mean in the sentences below? Highlight the noun or noun phrase that the pronoun refers to.

1. Art attempts to take something spiritual and make **it** visible.

2. The creature's catlike eyes identify **him** as the infant man-jaguar.

3. Masks do not appear casually in the community. Rather, people call on **them** during difficult times.

4. An image from Tibet shows the Buddha sitting in meditation. **He** is the largest figure and faces front.

5. The *bodhisattvas* have postponed their goal of Nirvana because **they** want to help other people to reach that goal.

Comparing and Contrasting Two Works of Art

When reading, students often need to compare and contrast two things—in other words, look for similarities and differences between two or more things. This frequently happens in an art history class because it is often necessary to compare and contrast works of art.

One way to compare two things is to make a **simple list.**

Example: In both the Olmec and Bwa cultures:
- art is evidence of the religion.
- communication with the spirit realm is important.
- the art involves animals.

The best way to contrast two things is with a specific graphic organizer called a **T-chart.** It's called a T-chart because of its shape, like the letter T.

Example:

Olmec	Bwa
ancient	present-day
figures	masks
purpose unclear	purpose is to manifest nature spirits

👥 **E. COMPARING AND CONTRASTING TWO WORKS OF ART** In small groups, find the similarities and 🔄 differences between the painting of Buddha from Tibet and the painting of the Virgin Mary from Italy. Look back at the illustrations and reread the paragraphs on page 79. Write a list of similarities. Then put the differences on a T-chart.

Similarities: _____

_____

_____

_____

_____

Differences:

A Tathagata Buddha	Madonna Enthroned

👥 **F. DISCUSSION** In small groups, discuss these questions:

• What kind of religious art can you find in your culture? (Sculpture? Paintings? Architecture?)

• What are some topics of this art?

• Does this art make the religion more visible? Explain your answer.

PART ③ ACADEMIC READING
Art as the Mirror of Everyday Life

BEFORE READING

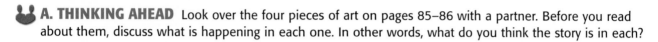

A. THINKING AHEAD Look over the four pieces of art on pages 85–86 with a partner. Before you read about them, discuss what is happening in each one. In other words, what do you think the story is in each?

B. VOCABULARY PREPARATION Read the sentences below. Words from the next reading are in green. What can you guess about each word? Match the definitions in the box below with the words in green. Write the correct letters on the lines. Then compare your answers with a partner's answers.

> a. full of life and with movement
>
> b. great piece of art
>
> c. handwritten book, before the printing press was invented
>
> d. having very strong emotions about something
>
> e. places (usually large and with decoration) for dead people
>
> f. supervisors
>
> g. system in which some people can own other people, who work without pay and without freedom

_____ **1.** This painting is a **masterpiece** of Chinese art.

_____ **2.** This is one page from an early French **manuscript.**

_____ **3.** Jim and Alex were excited, and their gestures were **animated.**

_____ **4.** **Overseers** watched as the workers prepared the tomb for the king.

_____ **5.** To make sure that people who died had a good afterlife, ancient Egyptians painted pleasant scenes on the walls of their **tombs.**

_____ **6.** Until 1864, **slavery** was legal in the United States. There was a terrible civil war between the North and the South which finally ended this system.

_____ **7.** Many people had a **fervent** belief that it was completely wrong to own another human being.

C. VOCABULARY IN PICTURES AND CAPTIONS Look at the figures in the following reading to help you guess the meaning of the green words. Write your guess on each line. Then compare your ideas with a partner's ideas.

Figure 2

1. There are three people inside a **hut.**

   Guess: _____

2. Outside the small house, the rest of this picture is a snow-covered **landscape.**

   Guess: _____

3. On the far right, one man is rushing toward the hut with his **cloak** over his face to keep in the warm breath.

   Guess: _____

Figure 3

4. People are using sticks to move **cattle** along and to count them.

   Guess: _____

Figure 4

5. The figure of John Brown is sitting on a **wagon** that is pulled by two white horses.

   Guess: _____

6. Over his head is a **bare tree limb.**

   Guess: _____

7. In the lower right corner, a woman **stares** out at us.

   Guess: _____

READING

Read about art in everyday life. As you read, think about this question:
• What's the story behind each of these pieces of art?

Art as the Mirror of Everyday Life

When children start to draw and paint, they deal with the images that they know best: mother and father, sisters and brothers, the teacher, the house, the dog. Many artists never lose their interest in everyday things, so much of our finest art depicts subjects that are close to the artist's personal world.

5   Art that depicts the moments of everyday life and its surroundings is known as *genre*. Often, its purpose is a simple one—to record, to please the eye, to make us smile. Images like this

10   occur in all periods of the history of art, in all cultures and parts of the world. A charming example from China is *Court Ladies Preparing Newly Woven Silk*. No grand political or

15   social issues are presented here. Instead, the artist has depicted a delightful scene of daily activity: Three women and a girl stretch and

Figure 1: *Court Ladies Preparing Newly Woven Silk,* from China, 12th century

iron a piece of silk, while a little girl peeks underneath to see what is going on. The women's pastel kimonos, their quiet gestures, and the atmosphere of pleasant shared work give us a gentle masterpiece of Chinese genre.

Equally charming genre pieces occur in an early French manuscript, one page of which we shall study here. During the Middle Ages (about 1100–1500 A.D.), wealthy people paid artists to illuminate (hand-paint) books, especially prayer books. In the early 15th century, the Limbourg Brothers illuminated one of the most famous books in the history of art, *Les Très Riches Heures* ("the very rich book of hours"). It contains a calendar, with each month's painting showing a seasonal activity.

The *February* page, shown here, depicts a small hut with three people around a fire. They have pulled their clothes back to get maximum

Figure 2: *February* page from *Les Tres Riches Heures du Duc de Berry.* Illumination. Musee Conde, Chantilly

warmth from the fire. Outside
this small house, we see a
snow-covered landscape.
There are sheep and birds and
three men. One man is
rushing toward the hut with
his cloak over his face to keep
in the warm breath. Another
man is chopping wood. The
third is walking up a hill with
a donkey. In the background
there is a church.

Figure 3: A model depicting the counting of **livestock**, from the tomb of Meketre, Deir el-Bahri. Dynasty 11, 2134–1991 B.C.E. Painted wood. Egyptian Museum, Cairo

Among the earliest images
of daily life to have come
down to us are those in the
tombs of ancient Egypt.
Egyptians imagined the
afterlife to be the same as
earthly life in every detail. To
make sure that the person
had a *good* afterlife, scenes of the pleasures of life in Egypt were painted on the tomb walls.
Sometimes models were used instead.

This model was one of many found in the tomb of an Egyptian official named Meketre,
who died around 1900 B.C.E. Meketre himself is depicted at the center, seated on a chair in
the shade. Seated on the floor to his right is his son; to his left are several scribes (professional
writers) with their writing materials ready. Overseers of Meketre's estate stand by as men herd
his cattle in front of Meketre so that the scribes can count them. The herders' gestures are
animated as they move the cattle along with their sticks, and the cattle themselves have
beautiful markings.

Figure 4: *John Brown Going to His Hanging,* 1942, by Horace Pippin. The Pennsylvania Academy of Fine Arts, Philadelphia

Artists have often turned to
stories for subject matter. History
has furnished artists with many
stories, for history itself is nothing
more than a story we tell ourselves
about the past, a story we write
and rewrite. In his 1942 painting
called *John Brown Going to His
Hanging*, Horace Pippin took for
his subject an event from history
to which he had a personal
connection. During the 1850s, the
United States was politically and
emotionally divided by the
conflict between people who were
in favor of slavery and those who
hated it, called abolitionists.
Among the most fervent of the
abolitionists was a white man
named John Brown, whose

(sometimes violent) activities to try to free the slaves caused him to be arrested and put on trial in the state of Virginia. He was found guilty and put to death by hanging on December 2, 95 1859. The artist Horace Pippin, a descendant of black slaves, was not yet born, but his grandmother was present at the hanging of John Brown, and she pictured the scene, many times, in words. Her grandson later transformed the word-picture into this painting.

We see John Brown at center, against the white jailhouse in the background. His arms are bound to his sides. All the people on the wagon are dressed in black, but the wagon is drawn 100 by two white horses—surely symbolic of the black-white drama. Directly over Brown's head is a bare tree limb—again, surely symbolic of the tree from which he will soon be hanged. Most of the people watching this are white. A lone black woman, at far right, turns her back on the scene and stares out fiercely, her arms crossed in anger. This figure is the artist's grandmother.

Sources: *Living With Art* (Gilbert, 4th ed., and Getlein, 6th ed.)

AFTER READING

A. MAKING CONNECTIONS In Part 1, you learned about two approaches to use when looking at art: art criticism and art history. Choose one of the four pieces of art on pages 85–86. Look at the piece using both approaches. On the chart below, summarize what you know about it. Answer as much as you can.

Title of the Piece: _____

Art Criticism	Art History
• Describe it. What people and things are there? • What are the details and space relationships?	• When, where, and by whom was it made? • How was the artist influenced by the world around him or her? • How important is the work?

 In small groups, discuss your chart.

B. VOCABULARY CHECK Look back at the reading on pages 85–87. Find words or phrases for the definitions below, and highlight them in the reading. Then write them on the correct lines. The numbers in parentheses refer to lines in the passage.

1. art that depicts the moments of everyday life (5–10)   _____

2. hand-paint (30–35)   _____

3. life after death (60–65)   _____

4. professional writers (65–70)   _____

5. people who hated slavery (85–90)   _____

6. a person who is related to a specific ancestor (95–100)   _____

7. changed (95–100)   _____

8. pulled (95–100)   _____

Reading Strategy

Understanding Italics

Writers use *italics* (slanted letters) for different reasons. Some of the reasons are:

• The words in italics are the title of a book, movie, newspaper, magazine, or painting.
• A word in italics might be a foreign word used in an English sentence.
• The writer is using italics to emphasize a word.

Examples: *Art in Focus* was written by Gene A. Mittler.
                     The museum had a large collection of *artesanias,* handicrafts from Mexico.
                     Art criticism allows us to *see* a piece of art.

Note: The Tathagata Buddha in the reading on page 79 is not in italics because it is a description of the piece, not the title given by the artist.

C. UNDERSTANDING ITALICS Look over the readings in Parts 2 (pages 78–79) and 3 (pages 85–87) with a partner. Find the words in italics. What is the reason for the italics?

D. VOCABULARY EXPANSION: A GAME Work in small groups. Go back to the reading on pages 85–87 and quickly find as many adjectives (words that describe nouns) as you can. Put them into the categories below, if possible. If you're not sure about the category for some adjectives, put them in the box below the chart and discuss them later with the whole class. The group that finds the most adjectives wins the game.

Opinion

_____

_____

_____

_____

_____

Size

_____

_____

_____

_____

_____

Condition or Quality

_____

_____

_____

_____

_____

Age

_____

_____

_____

_____

_____

Color

_____

_____

_____

_____

_____

Nationality

_____

_____

_____

_____

_____

Not Sure about the Category

_____   _____   _____

_____   _____   _____

_____   _____   _____

E. WORD JOURNAL Go back to the readings in this chapter. What words are important for you to remember? Put them in your Word Journal.

F. APPLICATION In small groups, discuss each pair of paintings using the art-criticism approach. What are the similarities between each pair? What are the differences?

1a. *Lamentation,* from Avignon, France. 1320–1350

1b. *The Death of General Wolfe,* by Benjamin West (American). 1770

2a. *Cooling Off by the Riverbank,* by Kitagawa Utamaro (Japanese). Late 18th century

2b. *In the Omnibus,* by Mary Cassatt (American). 1891

G. RESPONSE WRITING Choose one of these topics.

• one of the pieces of art in this chapter
• anything that interested you in this chapter
• something that you learned from these reading passages
• your favorite piece of art from any culture

Write about your topic for 10 minutes. Don't worry about grammar and don't stop writing to use a dictionary. Just put as many ideas as possible on paper.

PART ④ THE MECHANICS OF WRITING

In Part 4, you will practice using appositives, adjective clauses, participial clauses, prepositional phrases, and transitional expressions of comparison and contrast. You will need this grammar in Part 5 to write a comparison-contrast paragraph about two paintings.

Appositives

An **appositive** is a noun or noun phrase that comes after another noun or noun phrase. The appositive either means the same as the noun or gives more information about it. An appositive comes between commas, or it comes after a comma.

Examples: Dr. Chen, **our art history professor,** has written several textbooks.

The king of Israel, **King Josiah,** ordered the destruction of all pagan cultures.

She picked up the strange little figure, **an ancient perfume bottle.**

A. SENTENCE COMBINING: APPOSITIVES Combine the pairs of sentences below. Make the second sentence in each pair into an appositive and add it to the first.

1. This is from the tomb of Meketre. Meketre was an Egyptian official.

_____

_____

2. A 13th-century Italian master painted *Madonna Enthroned.* A 13th-century Italian master was Cimabue.

_____

_____

3. The Buddha's hand position symbolizes the giving of gifts. The Buddha's hand position is a *mudra.*

_____

_____

4. Mary Cassatt lived in France. Mary Cassatt was a famous American painter.

_____

_____

5. Cartier-Bresson took this photo at what he called the "decisive moment." Cartier-Bresson was a well-known French photographer.

_____

_____

Adjective Clauses

In Chapter 1 (page 28), you learned that adjective clauses modify nouns. If the adjective clause adds extra information to a sentence, use a comma before it and a comma or period after it.

Examples: **Cassatt, who was an Impressionist painter,** is very popular today.

The painting depicts a **Mayan ball game,** which was very different from ball games these days.

B. SENTENCE COMBINING: ADJECTIVE CLAUSES Combine the pairs of sentences below. Make the second sentence in each pair into an adjective clause and add it to the first. Use *who, which,* or *whose* and include a comma (or commas).

1. He took a class in art history. Art history is a required course.

_____

_____

2. This figure is actually a perfume bottle. This figure looks like a doll.

_____

_____

3. The painting is a memorial to John Brown. John Brown was a famous abolitionist.

_____

_____

4. Impressionist artists are now favorites among museum goers. Impressionist artists' work was not appreciated at the time it was created.

_____

_____

5. The Buddha is surrounded by *bodhisattvas*. *Bodhisattvas* help other people reach Nirvana.

_____

_____

Participial Phrases

A participial phrase, like an appositive (or adjective clause), gives information about a noun. One type of participial phrase is a reduced adjective clause.

Examples: The painting has a large central figure <u>that is facing front</u>. =
(adjective clause)

The painting has a large central figure <u>facing front.</u>
(present participial phrase)

The painting <u>that is shown on this page</u> is by West. =
(adjective clause)

The painting <u>shown on this page</u> is by West.
(past participial phrase)

Present participial phrases begin with a present participle (*-ing*). They are in the active voice. Past participial phrases begin with a past participle (*-ed* for regular verbs). They are in the passive voice.

C. PARTICIPIAL PHRASES For each sentence that follows, highlight the adjective clause and draw an arrow to the noun or noun phrase that it modifies. Then change the adjective clause to a participial phrase by crossing out the unnecessary words.

1. The central figure is surrounded by smaller figures ~~who are~~ wearing halos.

2. Two artists who were unknown to each other created similar works of art.

3. The anthropomorphic figure that is holding a small bowl is an incense burner.

4. The central figure, who is surrounded by angels, is the Virgin Mary.

5. The women who are folding the silk are court ladies.

6. The people who are working in the fields are peasants from the nearby village.

7. *Cooling Off by the River Bank,* which was painted many years before *In the Omnibus,* probably influenced Mary Cassatt.

8. Impressionist artists, who were unappreciated in their lifetime, are favorites among museum goers today.

Prepositional Phrases

These prepositional phrases may be useful when you describe a picture.

in the upper left-hand corner

in the upper right-hand corner

at the top

in the background

in the middle (of the picture)

in the foreground

in the lower left-hand corner

at the bottom

in the lower right-hand corner

In addition, you may need other phrases to explain *which figure* you're discussing in a painting.

Examples: A girl **with a bow in her hair** is in the middle of the picture.
(= a girl who is wearing a bow in her hair)

A woman **in a hat** is next to her.
(= a woman who has a hat)

A basket **with food in it** is in the foreground.
(= a basket that has food in it)

D. PREPOSITIONAL PHRASES Use prepositional phrases to answer these questions about the painting *February,* from *Les Très Riches Heures du Duc de Berry* (page 85).

1. Where is the calendar?

_____

2. Where is a single tree?

_____

3. Where are three women?

_____

4. Where are some birds?

_____

5. Where is the man with a donkey?

_____

6. Where is the forest?

_____

Adjectives

Adjectives are important when you describe art. An adjective usually comes before a noun.

Examples: It's a **flat** painting.
These are **realistic** figures.
It's a **dramatic** scene.

An adjective can also come after a verb such as *be, seem,* or *look* (= seem).

Examples: The people look **wealthy**.
The painting is **mysterious**.

Participles are often used as adjectives. A present participle (-ing) expresses a *quality*. A past participle (-ed) expresses a *result* or *effect*.

Examples: This is a **charming** little figure.
Everyone is **charmed** by it.
People in 1905 thought it was a **shocking** painting, but nobody is **shocked** anymore.

Note: Adjectives in English are never plural.

E. BRAINSTORMING ADJECTIVES Look at the pictures on pages 72–75 and 78–79. Think of as many adjectives as possible to describe these pictures. Put them into the categories below. If you aren't sure about a category, put the word in the box below the chart and discuss the words later with the whole class.

Opinion	Size	Condition or Quality
_____	_____	_____
_____	_____	_____
_____	_____	_____
_____	_____	_____
_____	_____	_____

Age	Color	Nationality
_____	_____	_____
_____	_____	_____
_____	_____	_____
_____	_____	_____
_____	_____	_____

Not Sure about the Category

_____	_____	_____
_____	_____	_____
_____	_____	_____

Order of Adjectives

Sometimes you will use two adjectives to modify a noun. When you do, the usual order of those adjectives follows the same order that you see in Activity E (above): opinion, size, condition or quality, age, color, nationality.

Examples: **INCORRECT:** This is a little charming figure.
                CORRECT: This is a <u>charming</u> <u>little</u> figure.
                                        (opinion) (size)

                INCORRECT: It's an Edomite ancient figure.
                CORRECT: It's an <u>ancient</u> <u>Edomite</u> figure.
                                        (age)   (nationality)

Sometimes, you will need to use three adjectives. When you do, follow this same order.

Example: This is a <u>charming</u> <u>little</u> <u>Edomite</u> figure.
                        (opinion) (size)(nationality)

👥 **F. ORDER OF ADJECTIVES** Add the adjectives in parentheses to the sentences below. Put them in the correct order.

1. It's a statue. (Italian/huge)

It's a huge Italian statue.

2. There is a house in the foreground. (large/unpainted)

_____

3. This is a painting. (modern/strange/American)

_____

4. These are rooms. (dark/small/uncomfortable)

_____

5. It's a scene. (Chinese/little/pleasant)

_____

6. In the foreground, there is a dog. (black/tired/old)

_____

Transitional Expressions: Comparison-Contrast

In Chapter 2 (page 56), you learned many transitional expressions. Here are some more.

similarly
in a similar way   } Use these to express how two items are similar.
both . . . and

in contrast   } Use these to express how two items are different.
while

Follow the rules for adverbial conjunctions (page 56) for *similarly, in a similar way,* and *in contrast.*

Examples: In the Tibetan painting, the Buddha is surrounded by smaller figures wearing halos. **Similarly,** in the Italian painting, Mary is surrounded by angels with halos.

Pablo Picasso's early paintings were realistic; **in contrast,** his later work is completely abstract.

For **similarities** you can also use this structure with a plural verb:

both + noun (or noun phrase) + *and* + noun (or noun phrase)

Example: **Both** the Buddha **and** Mary are surrounded by smaller figures.

For **differences** you can also use the subordinating conjunction *while* (= *although* or *but*) between two independent clauses.

Example: Pablo Picasso's early work is realistic, **while** his later work is abstract.

G. SENTENCE COMBINING: EXPRESSIONS OF COMPARISON-CONTRAST Combine the pairs of sentences below. Choose a logical transitional expression for each.

1. The central figure of the Buddha isn't holding anything. The Virgin Mary is holding the baby Jesus.

   _____

   _____

2. The Tathagata Buddha is a religious painting. *Madonna Enthroned* is a religious painting.

   _____

   _____

3. The Tathagata Buddha was created for Buddhists in Tibet. *Madonna Enthroned* was created for Christian Italians.

   _____

   _____

4. The Buddha has a serene expression. The Virgin Mary has a serene expression.

   _____

   _____

H. REVIEW: FINDING ERRORS Circle the letter under the incorrect word or phrase in each sentence below. There are errors with appositives, adjectives, participial phrases, prepositional phrases, adjective clauses, and transitional expressions of comparison-contrast.

1. In the Tathagata Buddha a Buddhist painting the figure of the Buddha is in the middle of the
                              A   B
   picture; similarly, the Virgin Mary is in the central position of *Madonna Enthroned*.
              C   D

2. The Buddha isn't holding anything in contrast, the Virgin Mary,
                  A   B
   the central figure in *Madonna Entroned,* is holding the baby Jesus.
                    C   D

3. The painting of the Buddha, that has nine figures, made the religion more concrete to
                                A   B   C
   believers in 13th-century Tibet.
                        D

4. Both the Buddha and the Virgin Mary are surrounded by smaller figures wear halos.
       A   B   C
   In the Tathagata Buddha, these smaller figures, *bodhisattvas,* help people to reach Nirvana.
                                                          D

5. Similarly, the angels surrounded the Virgin Mary, the Madonna, help people to reach heaven.
       A   B   C   D

PART 5 ACADEMIC WRITING

WRITING ASSIGNMENT

In Part 5, you will write a paragraph comparing and contrasting one of the pairs of paintings on page 90 or 91. You will need to have:
• a topic sentence and a concluding sentence
• both similarities and differences between your two paintings
• logical organization for your supporting details

STEP A. CHOOSING A TOPIC It's important to choose a pair of paintings that you feel comfortable with. You need to have enough—but not too much—to write about these paintings. Choose one pair from page 90 or 91. (You can change your mind later.)

1. A. *Lamentation*
    B. *The Death of General Wolfe*

2. A. *Cooling Off by the Riverbank*
    B. *In the Omnibus*

STEP B. CHOOSING A GOOD TOPIC SENTENCE Read each pair of sentences and circle the letter of the better topic sentence. When you finish, decide if you want to keep your topic or change it.

1.
   A. The theme of both *Lamentation* and *The Death of General Wolfe* is the death of a leader, but the two paintings differ greatly in the details and in style.
   B. *Lamentation* and *The Death of General Wolfe* are both about death.

2.
   A. Mary Cassatt's *In the Omnibus* clearly shows the influence of Japanese woodblock prints in general and perhaps Kitagawa Utamaro's *Cooling Off by the Riverbank* in particular.
   B. Kitagawa Utamaro's *Cooling Off by the Riverbank* and Mary Cassatt's *In the Omnibus* both depict two women and a child.

Writing Strategy

Gathering Supporting Material

After you choose a topic and topic sentence, you need to **gather** (collect) information to support your topic sentence. At this point in the process, you shouldn't write complete sentences or worry about grammar. You just need to write down all of your ideas. You can brainstorm ideas and then list them in a graphic organizer. You probably won't use all of these ideas in your paragraph.

STEP C. GATHERING SUPPORTING MATERIAL Fill in the chart below with information about the pair of paintings that you have chosen. Use words and phrases about the painting. Don't use complete sentences. (You might want to work with another student.)

Elements	Painting 1 Title: _____	Painting 2 Title: _____
Subject (theme)		
Artist (if known)		
Period (time)		
Culture/Country		
Emotional Qualities (dark? dramatic?)		
Style (realistic? stylized?)		
Space (deep or flat)		
Details		

STEP D. GROUPING YOUR SUPPORTING MATERIAL Use the information from the chart on page 101 to help you find similarities and differences between the two paintings. (You don't have to include every element.) Write your ideas in the Venn diagram below.

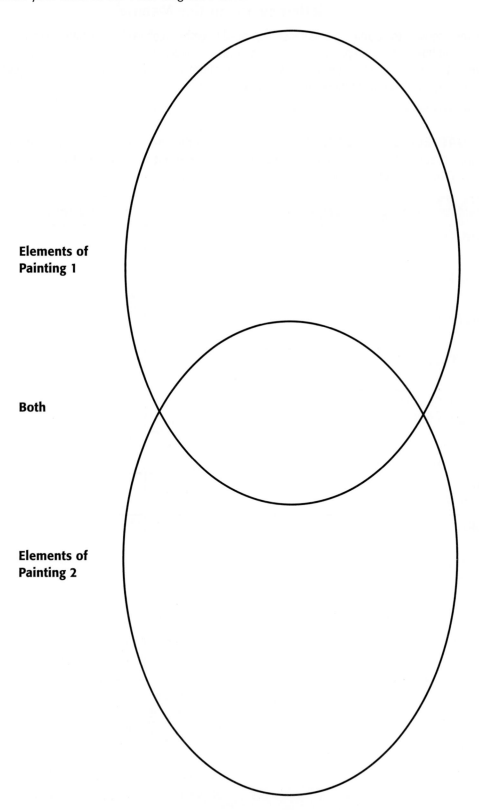

Elements of Painting 1

Both

Elements of Painting 2

Writing a Paragraph of Comparison-Contrast

In a paragraph of comparison-contrast, you *compare* two items and *contrast* them. Both items must be in the same **class** (group); in other words, they have to be related to each other in some way. You can compare and contrast two houses, two animals, two economic systems, or two paintings, for example. However, you cannot compare or contrast a house and an animal because they don't belong to the same class. After you choose two items to compare and contrast, you must have *at least* one similarity and one difference. In your paragraph, you need to give equal weight to each point; that is, don't spend most of the paragraph telling about just one point.

One way to organize information in a comparison-contrast paragraph is with an **alternating pattern**. In this pattern, after the topic sentence, present each point (for example, *subject, period, artist*) and discuss the similarities or differences. One way to visualize this is AA, BB, CC, DD, etc. In other words, write about one element for *both* things that you are comparing. Then write about the next element for both things, and so on. Group the similarities together and the differences together.

Example: Comparing and contrasting the Tathagata Buddha and *Madonna Enthroned*

The Tathagata Buddha	*Madonna Enthroned*	
• Buddhist	• Christian	
• holding nothing	• holding the baby Jesus	} Differences
• wearing very little	• wearing long robes	

- period: 13th century
- large central figure facing front
- emotional qualities: calm, serene
- details: symbolic hand gesture
  - central figure surrounded by figures with halos
  - small figures with halos help people

} Similarities

After you have organized the similarities and differences, you can expand your phrases into sentences and write your paragraph. You can present the similarities first or the differences first. *Whichever is more important* (in the case of your topic) should come second. Save the most important points for last.

Example:

   Two religious paintings, the Tathagata Buddha from Tibet and Cimabue's *Madonna Enthroned* from Italy, were created four thousand miles apart and for different religions, so they are quite different in content; nevertheless, they are surprisingly similar in form. The Tathagata Buddha is, of course, a Buddhist painting, and *Madonna Enthroned* is Christian. The Buddha, the central figure in the Tathagata Buddha, isn't holding anything; in contrast, the Virgin Mary, the central figure in *Madonna Enthroned*, is holding the baby Jesus. The Buddha is wearing very little clothing except for elaborate jewelry, while the Virgin is wearing long robes. However, these paintings have more similarities than differences. Both were created in the 13th century and have a large central figure facing front. The central figure in each painting has a calm, serene expression and a symbolic hand gesture; the Buddha's hand position symbolizes the giving of gifts, while Mary gestures toward her son, symbolic of the hope of the world. Finally, both the Buddha and the Virgin Mary are surrounded by smaller figures wearing halos. In the Tathagata Buddha, these smaller figures, *bodhisattvas*, help people to reach

Nirvana. Similarly, the angels surrounding the Virgin Mary help people to reach heaven. Clearly, two artists unknown to each other created quite similar paintings for their different religions.

Note in the example:

• the use of expressions for comparison and contrast: *both . . . and, similarly, in contrast, while*
• the use of appositives
• the alternating pattern

Analysis: In the sample paragraph, find the topic sentence, conclusion, and transition expressions of comparison and contrast. Highlight these. Then find the similarities and differences. Which come first? Which come second? Why?

STEP E. WRITING THE PARAGRAPH Use your notes from Step D. Decide which information to include. Also, decide which are more important in your paragraph—the similarities or differences—and which should come first. Write complete sentences in paragraph form. You might make some mistakes, but don't worry about them at this point.

STEP F. EDITING Read your paragraph and answer these questions.

1. Is the paragraph form correct (indentation, margins)?

2. Is there a topic sentence that includes the main topic and a controlling idea?

3. Are the painting titles in italics or underlined?

4. Is there at least one similarity between the two paintings?

5. Is there at least one difference between the two paintings?

6. Is there a clear alternating pattern?

7. Are the more important points last?

8. Is there correct use of transition words?

9. Is there a concluding sentence?

STEP G. REWRITING Write your paragraph again. This time, try to write it with no mistakes.

Information about the three pieces of art on pages 74–75:
a. This is a painting of a street scene by 20th century Haitian folk artist Laetitia.
b. This illustration by American artist Norman Rockwell is called *The Art Critic.* Rockwell was famous for charming, often funny but sometimes sad paintings that told a story. Many of his paintings appeared on the cover of a magazine called the *Saturday Evening Post.*
c. This famous photograph by the French photographer Henri Cartier-Bresson is called *Aquila* (Abruzzi, Italy, 1951). The geometric lines in this photo are immediately noticeable, of course, but the photo is especially successful because Bresson took it at the "decisive moment" when the woman with a pan of bread was walking upstairs. The round loaves of bread seem to match the paving stones beneath her feet.

CHAPTER 4

The Ancient World: Egypt

Discuss these questions:
- Look at the photo. What country was it taken in?
- What is the name of the statue? How old is it?
- What is the oldest piece of art that you have seen? Describe it.

PART ① INTRODUCTION The Rules of Egyptian Art

BEFORE READING

Nakht and His Wife. Copy of a wall painting from the tomb of Nakht, c. 1425 B.C.E.* Thebes, Egypt.
The Metropolitan Museum of Art, New York

👥 **THINKING AHEAD** Look at the wall painting above. Examine the details of the painting and discuss these questions in small groups.

1. Which people are Nakht and his wife? Explain your answer.

2. Who might the other people be?

3. What are the people doing? Describe as many activities as possible.

4. Do these figures look realistic? Why or why not? What seems strange about them?

*c. 1425 B.C.E. = circa (about) 1425 Before the Common Era

READING
Read about Egyptian art. As you read, think about this question:
• Why did the style of Egyptian art stay almost the same for 3,000 years?

The Rules of Egyptian Art

Just for a few moments, imagine some famous paintings of one or two hundred years ago. Can you picture these in your mind? Now imagine the most modern abstract art of today. In only one to two hundred years, there have been huge changes in the form and content of art. In contrast, the characteristics of ancient Egyptian art remained nearly the
5   same for almost three *thousand* years.

The principal message of Egyptian art is continuity—an unbroken span of time reaching back into history and forward into the future. The Greek philosopher Plato wrote that Egyptian art did not change for ten thousand years; while this is an exaggeration, there were many features in Egyptian art that
10   remained the same over long periods of time.

The so-called *Palette of King Narmer* (as art historians call it), a famous piece of Egyptian art, was created during the Old Kingdom (2686–2181 B.C.E.). It illustrates many
15   characteristics of Egyptian art. The piece is called a palette because it looks like a stone the Egyptians used to mix their cosmetics. The palette portrays a victory by the armies of Upper (southern) Egypt, led by King Narmer,
20   over the armies of Lower (northern) Egypt. Narmer is the largest figure and is near the center of the palette to indicate his high status. He holds an enemy by the hair and is about to kill him. To the left, a servant holds Narmer's
25   sandals, which indicates that Narmer is probably standing in a temple or on holy ground. In the lowest section of the tablet are two more defeated enemies. In the upper right is a falcon representing Horus, the god of
30   Upper Egypt.

Palette of Narmer, from Hierakonpolis, about 3100 B.C.E., Egyptian Museum, Cairo

Narmer's pose is typical of Egyptian art. When depicting an important person, the Egyptian artist attempted to show each part of the body to the best advantage, so it could be
35   "read" clearly by the viewer. Thus, Narmer's lower body is seen in profile, his torso full front, his head in profile, but his eye front again. This same pose recurs throughout most two-dimensional art in Egypt. It is believed that the priests (religious leaders), who had much control over the art, established this figure type and decreed that it be maintained for the sake of continuity. It is not a pose that suggests motion, but action was not important to
40   Egyptian art. Order and stability were its main characteristics, as they were the goals of Egyptian society.

Why did this flat style remain constant for thousands of years? It wasn't due to a lack of ability. Egyptian artists were certainly *able* to create full, natural images. We know this from the lovely realistic animals in many of their wall paintings. And, of course, there is the famous portrait of Queen Nefertiti, which seems real enough to come alive and speak to us. Nevertheless, the flat artistic style remained the same in most Egyptian art because the artists were following a strict set of rules written by powerful priests. If these rules had been written down, they might have looked like the list below.

Queen Nefertiti, about 1345–2181 B.C.E.
Staatliche Museen zu Berlin

Rules for Artists

1. The pharaoh (king) or most important person must be the largest. Servants, children, and unimportant wives must be smaller.

2. Men have dark or red skin. Women have light or yellow skin. (It doesn't matter what their real skin color is.)

3. People of high status—especially the pharaoh—must look stiff and serious. They should appear frozen and unmoving.

4. People of low status may be shown in more natural positions as they hunt, fish, plant or harvest crops, and do other work.

5. Depict animals as naturally as possible in correct biological details.

6. Don't leave empty areas. Fill the space with human figures, animals, plants, or hieroglyphs (writing).

7. When you create a human image (especially an important person), be sure to show all parts of the body from the most familiar point of view:
   - The head, arms, and feet must be seen from the side.
   - The shoulders and eyes must be seen from the front.
   A complete, clear image is necessary. If an arm, for example, is hidden behind the body, the person's *ka* (spirit) will live forever without an arm.

8. In the tomb of a dead pharaoh or important person, paint his wife, servants, and slaves. They will be with him and take care of him for all eternity—forever.

Sources: *Living with Art* (Getlein) and *Art in Focus* (Mittler)

AFTER READING

A. CHECK YOUR UNDERSTANDING Go back to the reading. When you find the answers to the questions below, highlight them.

• If Egyptian art didn't change much for 3,000 years, was there a problem with the ability of the artists?
• Why didn't Egyptian art change much?

B. VOCABULARY CHECK Look back at the reading to find the words that match the definitions. Don't use a dictionary. Line numbers are in parentheses. Write the correct letters on the lines.

_____ **1.** continuity   **a.** a situation without interruption or change (5–10)

_____ **2.** decreed   **b.** a bird of prey (a hunting bird) (25–30)

_____ **3.** falcon   **c.** a position of the body (30–35)

_____ **4.** frozen   **d.** the face or body seen from the side (35–40)

_____ **5.** pharaoh   **e.** the human body from the stomach to the shoulders (35–40)

_____ **6.** pose   **f.** occurs again and again (35–40)

_____ **7.** profile   **g.** said; officially commanded (35–40)

_____ **8.** recurs   **h.** a situation in which things are not easily changed or upset (40–45)

_____ **9.** stability   **i.** king of Egypt (55–60)

_____ **10.** torso   **j.** unnatural and without moving (60–65)

C. APPLICATION With a partner, look back at the painting of *Nakht and His Wife* (page 106). Fill in the chart below with examples and add the number of the rule (page 108).

Elements	Examples in the Wall Painting from the Tomb of Nakht	Rule
Space	The painting is full of figures, things, and writing. There is no empty space.	6
Animals		
People		
color		
size		
actions		
style		

PART ② GENERAL INTEREST READING
Finds Reveal Much of Life at Pyramids

BEFORE READING

Egyptian pyramids at Giza–tombs of several
Old Kingdom pharaohs, built c. 2550 B.C.E.

A. THINKING AHEAD Most people know that the pyramids of ancient Egypt were tombs for the dead pharaohs. However, until recently, we didn't know much about the people who built the pyramids. With a partner, discuss these questions.

1. In your opinion, who built the pyramids? What was the status of these builders?

2. What might their lives have been like? How were their lives different from the pharaohs' lives?

B. VOCABULARY PREPARATION Read the sentences below. Words from the next reading are in green. What can you guess about the words in green? Write your guesses on the lines.

1. The builders of the pyramids lived in a village not far from their worksite. When they died, their families buried them in tombs in a nearby **cemetery**.

Guess: _____

2. The town is on a mountainside. Houses up at the top of the **cliff** are the most expensive because they have a beautiful view. Houses at the bottom of the **slope** are cheap because there is no view.

Guess: _____

Guess: _____

3. Art historians and archaeologists are excited about the new discoveries. Every day, diggers at the **excavations** find another ancient perfume jar or cooking pot. Sometimes they find a tomb.

Guess: _____

Compare your answers with a partner's answers.

Reading Strategy

Guessing the Meaning from Context: Using Opposites

Sometimes you can guess the meaning of a new word if its opposite is in the context.

Example: Houses down at the bottom of the cliff were <u>undesirable</u> and <u>unwanted</u> because of the bad location, but houses up at the top of the cliff were **sought after**.

Here we see that *sought after* means the opposite of *undesirable* or *unwanted*. Therefore, you can guess that *sought after* means "desirable" or "wanted."

C. VOCABULARY PREPARATION: USING OPPOSITES Read the sentences below. Words and phrases from the next reading are in green. What is the opposite meaning of the word or phrase in green? Work with a partner. Write your guesses on the lines.

1. The pharaohs often had more than one wife, but most ordinary Egyptians were **monogamous**.

    Guess: _____

2. His moustache wasn't large or messy. It was **neatly trimmed** and as thin as a pencil.

    Guess: _____

3. Most of the people who built the houses were workers with no special ability; however, a few were **artisans**.

    Guess: _____

D. VOCABULARY PREPARATION: PARTS OF SPEECH Circle the part of speech of each green word below. Then write your guess about the meaning on the line.

1. I don't know why people just **dump** their garbage here!   **Verb   Noun**

    Guess: _____

2. These days, there are huge garbage **dumps** outside most big cities. In ancient   **Verb   Noun**
    times, of course, there were garbage dumps, too. Archaeologists can learn
    a lot about people from the things that they threw away.

    Guess: _____

3. Zahi Hawass is an Egyptologist who studies ancient life in the area of the   **Verb   Noun**
    pyramids in Giza. Every year, he **finds** more information about the people
    who built the pyramids.

    Guess: _____

4. There are some exciting new **finds** in Egypt.   Verb   Noun

Guess: _____

5. A mystery **remains**: How did the pyramid builders move the huge stones?   Verb   Noun

Guess: _____

6. We had a wonderful dinner party, but after the guests left, we had to clean   Verb   Noun
up the **remains**.

Guess: _____

 Compare your answers with a partner's answers.

Reading Strategy

Recognizing Style: Newspaper Feature Stories

Textbooks, essays, magazines, and newspapers all have different styles. As a student, you may sometimes use newspapers as **source material** (information) when you write a research paper, but you cannot use the newspaper style. For example, you will notice that in newspaper articles, a paragraph frequently consists of only one sentence. This does not occur in essays.

There are two distinct newspaper styles. **Hard news articles** are usually found on the first page and the rest of Section A. They contain facts but no opinion. They should have the main idea of the article in the first paragraph. Also, this first paragraph usually answers these questions: *Who?, What?, Where?,* and *When?* The rest of the article contains more detailed information such as *How?* and *Why?* **Feature stories** may contain the writer's opinion and use more conversational language, such as idioms. The main idea is not always in the first paragraph.

E. RECOGNIZING STYLE The next reading is a feature story from a newspaper. As you read, notice:
• how many paragraphs consist of just one sentence.
• how many idioms you can find.

READING

The following newspaper feature story has not been simplified, so it may contain many words and expressions that you don't know. Try to focus on what you *do* understand instead of what you don't.

As you read, highlight the sentence that gives the main idea. In another color, highlight anything that surprises you or is interesting about life in ancient Egypt.

Finds Reveal Much of Life at Pyramids

Old clues: Cemetery dig gives new look at ancient Egypt workers.

GIZA PLATEAU, Egypt (AP)

Life wasn't all work and no play for the workers who built the pyramids, tombs and temples of Giza Plateau.

"History is life," said Egyptologist Zahi
5 Hawass, in charge of an ancient cemetery yielding volumes of information about the life and times of the pyramid work force.

Archaeologists poking through garbage dumps, examining skeletons, probing texts,
10 and studying remains of beer jars, wine vats and bakeries have discovered all kinds of information about the pyramid builders:

■ Beer was dished out three times daily. There were five kinds of beer and four
15 kinds of wine available.

■ They could build strong bodies in 12 ways—with 12 varieties of bread.

■ Neatly trimmed pencil moustaches were in vogue, and workers had nicknames still
20 popular today, like Didi and Mimi.

■ Their lives averaged 36 to 38 years, and industrial accidents took a toll. Six skeletons revealed deaths from injuries. Many others had bent spines from the
25 weight of stone blocks they carried.

■ Ordinary Egyptians were monogamous, but some played around. And they kept up with the Joneses.

Much of the new information comes
30 from excavations over the past nine months in cemeteries found near the pyramids about three years ago.

Recently found texts show that the pyramid builders were not slaves, as was
35 long believed, but were free Egyptians working for the gods. The pharaoh provided them with food, clothing, and shelter.

"Everything about this cemetery disputes the idea that these people were
40 slaves," Hawass said last week.

It is not clear how many workers were involved in building them, but the three major pyramids at Giza and the queen's pyramids nearby were built over a 70-year
45 period beginning about 2551 B.C.E., when Cheops ascended to the throne.

Skilled workers, probably sought-after artisans, were buried in 43 tombs lined up at the top of the cliffside cemetery. They were
50 the prime burial sites, affording views of the pyramids a few miles across the dunes.

Foremen were buried in smaller tombs just down the slope. At the bottom were workers, often buried only in deep shafts.

55 Archaeologists have found 600 tombs of foremen and workers. Job descriptions include "decorator of tombs," "the official in charge of one side of the pyramid," or "overseer of the stone movers."

60 The most important tomb found so far belonged to She-dou, a blue-collar worker identified as a servant of the goddess of war and hunting, Neith.

In a secret compartment to the rear,
65 archaeologists found four painted statues of She-dou. The largest, measuring 29 inches, represents She-dou in a short white kilt, his neck ringed by a wide collar adorned with blue, white, and yellow stones.

70 A neighboring tomb gave excavators another surprise. It was already known that, unlike the pharaohs, ordinary Egyptians were monogamous. But the man buried in this tomb lay between his wife
75 and another woman.

"Texts show she had to be a girlfriend," said Hawass. "It's surprising the wife put up with it."

The upper classes avoided such scandal
80 because they were in the public eye.

Source: "Finds Reveal Much of Life at Pyramids" from *The Star Free Press*

AFTER READING

👥 **A. FINDING THE MAIN IDEA** Which one-sentence paragraph gives the main idea of the article? Share with a partner the sentence you highlighted.

Test-Taking Strategy

Understanding Idioms

On the reading section of some standardized tests, you will often find unknown idioms. An idiom is a phrase that has a different meaning from the meaning of each individual word. Idioms are often fun to learn, but they can also be difficult to learn. Because there are thousands of idioms in English, you need to read a lot and listen to a lot of spoken English to absorb as many as possible. Work *actively* at learning idioms by putting them in your Word Journal and reviewing them daily.

Sometimes, you will be tested to see if you can figure out the meaning of an idiom from the context. You will need to choose the best of four possible answers.

Example: I bought only ten apples at the farmers' market, but the seller was really nice and threw in a couple of free apples **for good measure**.
  A. to make a dozen (12)
  B. in case an apple is bad
  C. as something more or extra
  D. to fill the bag

The best answer is *C,* "as something more or extra."

B. UNDERSTANDING IDIOMS Read the sentences below. Circle the correct meaning for the idioms in green.

1. Dylan worked very hard all his life and didn't often relax. He smoked a lot, ate junk food, and worried all the time. Unfortunately, this lifestyle **took a toll on his health**.

   took a toll on his health
   A. made him happy
   B. caused him to make a lot of money
   C. caused him to be healthy
   D. took away his good health

2. Social status and wealth are important to Dylan and his wife. They try hard to **keep up with the Joneses**: they wear stylish clothes, have hairstyles that are **in vogue**, have new cars, and buy fashionable furniture. However, it's hard for them to pay for all of this because they're both **blue-collar workers**.

keep up with the Joneses

- A. compete with their neighbors for higher status
- B. run in a race with a family named "Jones"
- C. wear nice clothes
- D. work hard

in vogue

- A. attractive
- B. easy to take care of
- C. fashionable
- D. in a magazine

blue-collar workers

- A. workers who wear blue shirts
- B. workers who do hard work and don't usually make a high salary
- C. workers who are sad and tired
- D. people without a job

3. I think Dylan has a girlfriend. Of course, his wife doesn't know that he's **playing around**. If she knew, she would never **put up with** this kind of behavior. She would tell him to leave his girlfriend or to get out.

playing around

- A. playing a game
- B. playing a musical instrument in a nightclub, for entertainment
- C. spending time romantically with another person
- D. going around the city with someone

put up with

- A. complain about
- B. discuss openly
- C. postpone
- D. suffer without complaining

Now go back to the reading on page 113 and highlight these idioms.

C. WORD JOURNAL Go back to the reading. Which words or idioms are important for you to remember? Put them in your Word Journal.

Critical Thinking Strategy

Identifying Causes and Effects

It's often possible to identify **causes** (reasons) or **effects** (results) in a reading by paying attention to **cause and effect conjunctions** such as *because, so, for, since, as, therefore, thus, as a result,* or *consequently.* However, there is frequently no cause and effect conjunction used. Then you have to use your own logic and **infer**—use logic to guess—the cause or effect.

D. IDENTIFYING CAUSES AND EFFECTS Read the causes. Then match the causes to the correct effects. Draw a line to connect the cause and effect.

<u>Effects</u>

1. Workers had bent spines because they

2. Some workers were buried in tombs at the top of the cliffside because they

3. Some workers were buried at the bottom of the cliffside cemetery because they

4. Workers died quite young; their lives averaged only 36 to 38 years because they

5. The upper classes avoided "playing around" because they

<u>Causes</u>

a. had higher status than others

b. suffered accidents and injuries

c. were in the public eye

d. carried heavy stone blocks

e. had lower status than others

E. MAKING INFERENCES The inferences below can be made from the newspaper article (page 113). Find specific information in the article to support each inference.

1. **Inference:** Life for the builders of the pyramids wasn't all bad.

    Support: _____

2. **Inference:** Life was physically hard on the workers.

    Support: _____

3. **Inference:** There were three classes of pyramid workers.

    Support: _____

In small groups, discuss the support that you found in the newspaper article.

PART ③ ACADEMIC READING
Egyptian Civilization: A Brief History

👥 BEFORE READING

A. THINKING AHEAD Before you read, briefly review the "Rules for Artists" on page 108 and look over the pictures in the reading on pages 118–119. Then answer these questions in small groups:
• Which pictures appear to follow the rules? In what ways? Which seem to break the rules? In what ways?

B. VOCABULARY PREPARATION Read the sentences below. Match the definitions in the box with the words or phrases in green. Write the correct letters on the lines.

> a. bring it back to its original condition
>
> b. great, grand, wonderful
>
> c. king
>
> d. a set of actions, one following after another
>
> e. trip
>
> f. were prepared to do anything, no matter how difficult
>
> g. without any goal or reason

_____ **1.** There was a succession of wars—one after another after another.

_____ **2.** The ruler who sat on the throne of Egypt was not always a great leader, but in the eyes of his people, he was both pharaoh and a god.

_____ **3.** King Tutankhamen's tomb was filled with magnificent art—gold and silver, paintings, statues, and beautiful furniture.

_____ **4.** After 4,000 years, the wall painting was in poor condition, but art experts at the museum were able to restore it. Now it looks almost exactly as it looked when it was new.

_____ **5.** Ramses and his wife made the journey from Memphis to the new capital, Thebes. When they finally arrived, they were hot and tired.

_____ **6.** Ikhnaton walked aimlessly through the old city. He had no purpose, no idea of where to go or what to do.

_____ **7.** Ancient Egyptians went to great lengths to protect the body of the pharaoh. They were prepared to do anything necessary to keep his body safe.

👥 Now compare your answers with a partner's answers.

Read about ancient Egypt. As you read, think about this question:
• How was art a mirror for the three periods in ancient Egyptian history?

Egyptian Civilization: A Brief History

It is usual to divide the long history of Egypt into three periods: the Old Kingdom, the Middle Kingdom, and the New Kingdom. These are further divided
5 into dynasties. A dynasty was a period when a single family provided a succession of rulers. When one pharaoh died, a successor was chosen from the same family. It was important to keep the blood of the
10 royal family pure; therefore, the pharaoh was not allowed to marry outside the immediate family.

The Old Kingdom

The earliest dynastic period began around 3100 B.C.E. when Upper and
15 Lower Egypt were united by a powerful pharaoh named Menes [perhaps another

The *ka* statue of Khafre, c. 2600 B.C.E., Egyptian Museum, Cairo, Egypt

name for Narmer]. Menes established his capital at Memphis and founded the first of the thirty-one Egyptian dynasties.

20 It was during the Old Kingdom that the pyramids were built. These massive tombs were an attempt to keep the body of the pharaoh safe. The Egyptians believed that the soul, or *ka*, remained with the body
25 until death. At death, the *ka* left the body for a time, but it later returned and united with the body again for the journey to the next world. If the body was destroyed, the *ka* had to travel aimlessly for all eternity.
30 For this reason, the Egyptians went to great lengths to protect the body—especially the body of the pharaoh, for he was both a king and, in the eyes of the people, a god.

Often, however, thieves broke into the
35 pyramids. They stole the gold and other treasures and destroyed the pharaoh's body. Consequently, sculptors began to create statues of the pharaoh, such as the portrait of Khafre on his throne. They put these
40 statues inside the tomb so that the *ka* could enter this stone statue for the journey to the next world.

The Middle Kingdom

The Middle Kingdom was a time of law and order in Egypt until foreign armies
45 attacked Egypt for the first time, around 1800 B.C.E. The Hyksos from western Asia had horses and chariots. They easily won battles because the Egyptians were fighting on foot. The Hyksos remained in Egypt for
50 two hundred years. When the Egyptians finally learned how to use horses and chariots, they forced the Hyksos to leave their country.

During the Middle Kingdom,
55 Egyptians stopped building pyramids and began to build pharaohs' tombs in rock

cliffs instead. Many of the statues were destroyed by the Hyksos. Perhaps one incomplete portrait of King Sesostris III,
60 which was created during this difficult period, represents the time. This portrait is very different from Old Kingdom portraits of rulers. It is a surprisingly realistic face.

Portrait of Sesostris III, c. 1850 B.C.E. (Middle Kingdom), Metropolitan Museum of Art, New York

The firmly set mouth and lines above the
65 eyes express deep worry and a troubled emotional condition.

The New Kingdom

The third period of Egyptian history, the New Kingdom, began in 1570 B.C.E. With a knowledge of horses and chariots,
70 Egypt became a military power and ruled over neighboring nations. Thebes, the royal capital, became the most magnificent city in the world. It was a golden age of Egypt.

In 1372 B.C.E., one pharaoh broke with
75 Egyptian tradition for a short time. When Amenhotep IV came to power, he moved the capital, changed his name to Ikhnaton, and established a monotheistic religion with Aton (symbolized as the sun) as the
80 one god. This was an attempt to break the enormous power of the priests of other gods. However, after Ikhnaton's death, this

new religion did not remain. The capital was returned to Thebes, and the old
85 polytheistic faith—having many gods—was restored. But Egypt's time of power and glory was ending. When Alexander the Great of Macedonia brought his army to Egypt in 332 B.C.E., the era of the New
90 Kingdom came to a close.

Statue of Ikhnaton (Akhnaten), c. 1360 B.C.E.

Ikhnaton influenced not only the religion but also the art of his time. The strict rules for artists became relaxed, and art became less stiff, more realistic. From
95 this period we have the wonderful lifelike portrait of Nefertiti, Ikhnaton's wife. And a charming wall painting of his daughters shows them with natural, playful gestures. Most surprisingly, portraits of Ikhnaton
100 himself show him as he really looked—and he was not handsome.

With Ikhnaton's death, the old rules for artists returned. Nevertheless, we can still see some of his influence in much of the
105 art, such as the tomb art of Ikhnaton's famous young successor, Tutankhamen.

Source: *Art in Focus* (Mittler)

AFTER READING

A. FINDING DETAILS The events in the list below are not in the correct order. What happened during the Old Kingdom? The Middle Kingdom? The New Kingdom? Write the events in the correct box on the chart. Then write the art that we associate with each period on the chart.

Events
- great military power
- Menes founded the first dynasty
- Ikhnaton changed the religion and capital
- foreign armies took over Egypt for 200 years
- Golden Age of Egypt
- difficult period for Egypt
- Tutankhamen became king

Art
- rules for artists became relaxed
- pyramids
- tombs in rock cliffs
- began to create *ka* statues
- stopped building pyramids
- portraits surprisingly realistic and sad

	Old Kingdom (c. 3100 B.C.E.)	**Middle Kingdom** (c. 2040 B.C.E.)	**New Kingdom** (c. 1570 B.C.E.)
Historical Events			
Art Associated with the Period			

 In small groups, share your chart.

B. VOCABULARY CHECK Look back at the reading on pages 118–119. Find words or phrases for the definitions below, and highlight them in the reading. Then write them on the correct lines. Line numbers are in parentheses.

1. a period when a single family leads a country (5–10) _____

2. began or set up (15–20) _____

3. huge and heavy (20–25) _____

4. very beautiful and valuable things (35–40) _____

5. vehicles from ancient times that horses pulled (45–50) _____

Reading Strategy

Guessing the Meaning from Context: *in other words, that is, i.e.*

In academic reading, there is often a definition or synonym of a new word after one of these expressions: *in other words, that is,* or *i.e.* The abbreviation *i.e.* stands for the Latin *id est,* meaning "that is." These expressions are followed by a comma.

Example: He was the pharaoh; i.e., he was the ruler of the land.

C. GUESSING THE MEANING FROM CONTEXT Read about the possible murder of King Tutankhamen. Then answer these questions with a partner.

1. What did Ankhesenamen mean by the expression "a servant of mine"?

2. What is a vizier?

3. Who is a commoner?

A Murder Mystery?

Most people have seen pictures of the magnificent tomb furnishings of King Tutankhamen, also known as King Tut. The number of valuable items of gold, silver, alabaster, and ebony is truly astonishing. The quality of the art is amazing. However, this pharaoh was only a minor king. He died at age 18 after a very short period on the throne. Many people wonder what the tombs of other pharaohs were like—pharaohs who lived long and ruled for fifty, sixty, seventy years. These tombs were all robbed in ancient times, so today we can only ask ourselves, how much more magnificent would these tombs have been?

There is another question that some Egyptologists are asking: Is it possible that Tutankhamen was a murder victim? According to Bob Brier, a professor at Long Island University and the author of *The Murder of Tutankhamen* (1998), there is some evidence for this. It is known that Tutankhamen was the successor to Ikhnaton; however, it is unclear if he was Ikhnaton's younger brother or son by a minor wife, Kiya (not the "Great Wife," Nefertiti). We know that he married Ankhesenamen, who was probably his half-sister. Brier makes the following points:

• Tutankhamen died suddenly, unexpectedly.

- After his death, his wife, Ankhesenamen, sent a mysterious letter to the King of the Hittites, in the area that is now Turkey. The Hittites were traditional enemies of Egypt. In this letter, she told the foreign king of her fears.

She wrote:

> "My husband has died. I have no sons. They say that you have many sons. Send me one of your sons, and I will marry him and make him king of Egypt. Never will I marry a **servant of mine** [in other words, a commoner]. I am afraid."

- The Hittite king sent one of his sons. This prince was murdered at the border with Egypt, before reaching Ankhesenamen.

- The successor to Tutankhamen was Aye, his **vizier** (that is, a high official, similar to a prime minister). This man was a **commoner**–i.e., a person with no royal blood.

- There is one piece of evidence that Aye married Ankhesenamen: there is a finger ring in a Berlin museum with their names together.

- Ankhesenamen disappears from history after this. We don't know what happened to her.

Reading Strategy

Finding Evidence

Textbook passages that present a **theory**–an opinion–must also present evidence, that is, support for that theory. The evidence is a reason or number of reasons for the reader to believe the theory. In the boxed selection ("A Murder Mystery?"), the evidence is very clearly stated. Often, it is not as clear.

As the reader, you need to examine the evidence before deciding if you agree with a writer's theory.

D. FINDING EVIDENCE Look over "A Murder Mystery" again. In small groups, discuss these questions.

1. What is the theory?

2. What is the evidence?

3. In your opinion, what is the strongest piece of evidence?

4. Is there sufficient (enough) evidence to persuade you?

E. WORD JOURNAL Go back to the readings in this chapter. Which words are important for you to remember? Put them in your Word Journal.

F. PRONOUN REFERENCE Circle the noun or noun phrase that the pronoun in green refers to in each sentence below.

1. At death, the *ka* left the body for a time, but **it** later returned and united with the body again.

2. Thieves often broke into the pyramids. **They** stole gold and other treasures.

3. Sculptors began to create statues of the pharaoh, such as the portrait of Khafre. **They** put these statues inside the tomb.

4. A charming wall painting of his daughters shows **them** with natural, playful gestures.

G. IDENTIFYING CAUSES AND EFFECTS Look back at the reading on pages 118–119 to find answers to these questions. (Hint: Look for conjunctions of cause and effect: *therefore, for this reason, consequently,* and *because.*)

1. Why was the pharaoh not allowed to marry outside of the immediate family?

   _____

   _____

2. Why did the Egyptians go to great lengths to protect the body of the pharaoh?

   _____

   _____

3. Why did sculptors begin to create statues of the pharaohs?

   _____

   _____

4. Why did the Hyksos easily win battles against the Egyptians?

   _____

   _____

H. ANALYSIS Look at the wall painting below. In the chart that follows, fill in as much information as possible. If you don't know a piece of information, put a question mark.

Fragment of a wall painting from the tomb of Nebamun, Thebes, Egypt, c. 1450 B.C.E.

Elements	Wall Painting from the Tomb of Nebamun
Time (year and period– which kingdom?)	
Use of space	
Other figures or animals	
Central figure (pose, size, actions, style)	
Adjectives to describe this work of art	

In small groups, compare your charts and discuss the wall painting.

PART ④ THE MECHANICS OF WRITING

In Part 4, you will practice using infinitives and different kinds of conjunctions to describe causes, effects, and purposes. You will need this grammar in Part 5 to write a paragraph about a piece of Egyptian art. You will explain an artist's reasons for the style of a painting.

Infinitives of Purpose

An infinitive (*to* + the simple form of a verb) can be used to show the **purpose** (the reason why something was done). The purpose answers the question *Why*.

Example: Artists depicted the pharaoh as stiff and unmoving **to show his high status.**

To show his high status is the purpose. It shows why the artists did what they did.

A. INFINITIVES OF PURPOSE Match each phrase below with a purpose from the box. Then write complete sentences on the lines that follow. Use an infinitive of purpose in each sentence. Follow the example.

a. fill empty space	**d. show his importance**
b. make green	**e. take care of the pharaoh for eternity**
c. make orange	

_____b_____ **1.** mix blue and yellow

_____ **2.** mix red and yellow

_____ **3.** use plants, animals, and hieroglyph

_____ **4.** make the pharaoh larger than other figures

_____ **5.** there should be servants in tomb art

1. _Mix blue and yellow to make green._____

2. _____

3. _____

4. _____

5. _____

Transitional Expressions of Cause and Effect: Subordinating Conjunctions

Subordinating conjunctions are a common type of transitional expression. To express a cause and effect relationship between two sentences, you can join the sentences with one of these subordinating conjunctions:

because
since
as

Examples: The artist used hieroglyphs **because** he needed to fill in empty space. (no comma)

Because the artist needed to fill in empty space, he used hieroglyphs. (comma)

There is a comma after the first clause if the sentence begins with the subordinating conjunction. There is no comma if the subordinating conjunction is in the middle.

Because, since, or *as* begins the clause that contains the cause or reason. The other clause (the main clause) expresses the effect or result. *Because* is more frequently used than *since* or *as*, but all three words have the same meaning.

B. SENTENCE COMBINING: SUBORDINATING CONJUNCTIONS Combine the pairs of sentences in two ways each. Use subordinating conjunctions. (**Note:** Before you write, decide which sentence is the cause and which is the effect.)

1. Art historians now know more about the lives of the pyramid builders. Archaeologists have been excavating the workers' tombs.

   A. _____

   _____

   B. _____

   _____

2. Many people had thought that the pyramid builders were all slaves. Many people were surprised by the new discoveries. (**Note:** Use a pronoun.)

   A. _____

   _____

   B. _____

   _____

3. Expert opinion is that pyramid builders did not all have the same status. Pyramid builders had tombs of different quality. (**Note:** Use a pronoun.)

   A. _____

   _____

   B. _____

   _____

Transitional Expressions and Phrases

If the cause is a noun or noun phrase (instead of a clause), use *due to* or *because of.*

Examples: Skilled artisans were buried in tombs of better quality **because of** <u>their higher status</u>.
(noun phrase)

Because of <u>their higher status</u>, skilled artisans were buried in tombs of better quality.
(noun phrase)

C. TRANSITIONAL EXPRESSIONS In the paragraph below, write *because, since, as, because of,* or *due to* on the lines. Don't use the same expression more than once.

_____ 1 ancient Egyptian religious beliefs, much of what we know

today about the people comes from their tombs. Great care was taken to protect and preserve the

body after death _____ 2 people believed that a person's *ka,* or soul, needed a

body in which which to live. It was especially necessary to preserve the body of the pharaoh

_____ 3 he was seen as both a king and a god. People believed that he would

join the other gods when he died. _____ 4 a need to keep his body safe, the

Egyptians built the massive, amazing pyramids that we see today. However, the enormous effort that

went into the pyramids was not just for the sake of the pharaoh himself. The people of ancient Egypt

would do almost anything for their king _____ 5 he was seen as responsible for

order in the universe.

Conjunctions of Cause and Effect: Review

In Chapters 1 and 2, you learned the rules for coordinating and adverbial conjunctions. (To check these rules, see pages 29 and 56.) You now know several ways to combine pairs of sentences. This is good to know because in a paragraph that gives many causes or reasons, you don't want to use *because* over and over. You'll want to use a variety of transitional expressions. So far, you have studied three groups of conjunctions for cause and effect:

Coordinating	so (= that's why) for (= because)	
Subordinating	since as because	
Adverbial	consequently as a result for this reason therefore	} (= so)

D. REVIEW: CONJUNCTIONS OF CAUSE AND EFFECT Rewrite each sentence below in two different ways. Use the conjunction in parentheses. You'll need to change the order of the clauses in some sentences. The subject of the first clause is a noun and the subject of the second clause is a pronoun.

1. Workers had bent spines because they carried heavy stone blocks.

   A. (for) _____

   _____

   B. (therefore) _____

   _____

2. Some workers were buried in tombs at the top of the cliffside cemetery because they had higher status than other workers.

   A. (so) _____

   _____

   B. (for this reason) _____

   _____

3. Some workers were buried at the bottom of the cliffside cemetery because they had lower status than others.

   A. (for) _____

   _____

   B. (consequently) _____

   _____

4. Many workers died quite young because they suffered accidents and injuries.

   A. (so) _____

   _____

   B. (as a result) _____

   _____

5. The upper classes avoided "playing around" because they were in the public eye.

   A. (since) _____

   _____

   B. (therefore) _____

   _____

E. REVIEW: FINDING ERRORS Circle the letter under the incorrect word or phrase. There are errors with infinitives of purpose, subordinating conjunctions, and conjunctions of cause and effect.

1. The figures on Tutankhamen's magnificent throne <u>seem somewhat unnatural</u> to the modern
A

observer <u>, because</u> the artist <u>was following</u> the strict rules <u>for artists</u> in ancient Egypt.
B   C   D

2. These figures <u>are depictions of the pharaoh</u> and his queen, <u>so</u> they appear inactive and unmoving
A   B

<u>show their high status</u>. The queen appears in this piece of tomb art <u>to be with her husband</u> for all
C   D

eternity.

3. <u>Since</u> her figure is <u>the same size as</u> her <u>husband's we can assume</u> that she <u>was considered his equal</u>
A   B   C   D

in status.

4. Egyptian religion <u>required artists to depict</u> all parts of the body from the most familiar point of
A

view<u>, consequently,</u> we see <u>the feet, arms, and head</u> of these figures in profile
B   C

<u>and their shoulders and eye</u> from the front.
D

5. The pharaoh almost casually hooks his right arm <u>over the back of the throne,</u> and in a charming
A

gesture, the queen has bent toward her husband <u>to touch him</u> on the shoulder. <u>As a result</u>
B   C

figures appear less stiff and <u>less frozen than</u> most figures in earlier periods of Egyptian art.
D

PART ⑤ ACADEMIC WRITING

WRITING ASSIGNMENT

In Part 5, you will write a paragraph of cause and effect about one piece of ancient Egyptian art from this chapter. You will need to:
• Explain the use of space in this painting. How did the artist fill the space and for what reasons?
• Briefly describe the animal and human figures in the painting and give reasons for the style.

STEP A. CHOOSING A TOPIC In some class assignments and tests, you will not have a topic choice. In this chapter, you will write about the painting on page 124.

Test-Taking Strategy

Applying Information

On an essay exam, you will need to answer one or more questions in complete paragraphs. The instructor will want to find out if you (1) have done the reading for the class, (2) understand it, and often (3) can apply it to a new situation. Clearly, it is not enough simply to memorize information for an essay exam.

There are three types of essay exams:
• in-class, closed-book exams (the most common)
• in-class, open-book exams
• take-home exams

It's important to read the essay questions and the directions carefully. It's also important to stay on target in writing your paragraph. In other words, keep on the specific topic that the instructor has given.

One common type of question on an essay exam is cause and effect. For this type of question, you analyze something and give reasons for it, based on the readings that you had in class.

STEP B. APPLYING INFORMATION You have already analyzed the elements of the painting on page 124. Now you need to apply what you know about the ancient requirements for art. In other words, what were the reasons for each element?

1. Turn back to the *Rules for Artists* (page 108). How can the rules explain the elements in the wall painting on page 124?

<table>
<tr><td><u>**Elements**</u></td><td><u>**Reasons**</u></td></tr>
<tr><td>_____</td><td>_____</td></tr>
<tr><td>_____</td><td>_____</td></tr>
<tr><td>_____</td><td>_____</td></tr>
<tr><td>_____</td><td>_____</td></tr>
<tr><td>_____</td><td>_____</td></tr>
<tr><td>_____</td><td>_____</td></tr>
</table>

2. Review the history of the period in which the painting on page 124 was created. Is there any information from the reading on pages 118–119 that can help you understand something about your painting? If so, write it here.

_____

_____

_____

_____

_____

_____

Writing a Paragraph of Cause and Effect

There are many possible directions on an essay exam. In this chapter, we are focusing on essay questions that require a cause and effect paragraph. Notice in the examples below that sometimes an essay "question" is not a question at all; instead, it is in the form of a command.

Examples: Explain why . . .
Discuss the causes of . . .
Identify the major reasons for . . .
Give three reasons for . . .

In an art history class, it is common to be required both to **describe** a piece of art and to **explain** what you have described. In other words, give causes and effects.

Example: **Briefly describe the figures on the throne of Tutankhamen and identify reasons for their naturalness or unnaturalness.**

    The figures on Tutankhamen's magnificent throne seem somewhat unnatural to the modern observer because the artist was following the strict rules for artists in ancient Egypt. These figures are depictions of the pharaoh and his queen, so they appear inactive and unmoving to show their high status. Since the queen's figure is the same size as her husband's, we can assume that she was considered his equal in status. Egyptian religion required artists to depict all parts of the body from the most familiar point of view. Consequently, we see the feet, arms, and head of these figures in profile and their shoulders and eye from the front. Also, arms and legs of both people are clearly shown so that their *ka* can live forever in a complete body. This throne was created in the New Kingdom. As a result, it is clear that there is some influence from the naturalness of art at that time. For example, both figures appear less stiff, less frozen than most figures in earlier periods of Egyptian art.

Note in the example:

- The topic sentence very generally describes the figures ("somewhat unnatural") and also gives the general reason for this unnaturalness ("strict rules for artists").
- There is a lot of support for the topic sentence.
- The paragraph stays on target. It deals only with the figures—not with the use of space or details around the figures.

Analysis: In the sample paragraph, look for the transition words of cause and effect and purpose. Highlight them. Notice the punctuation.

STEP C. WRITING THE PARAGRAPH Use the information from the chart on page 124 and reasons for these elements from Step B. Decide which information to include. Write complete sentences in paragraph form. You might make some mistakes, but don't worry about them at this point.

STEP D. EDITING Read your paragraph and answer these questions.

1. Is the paragraph form correct?

2. Is the piece of art mentioned in the topic sentence?

3. Are several elements described?

4. Are clear reasons given for each element?

5. Is there correct use of transition words?

6. Is there variety in the use of transitions?

STEP E. REWRITING Write your paragraph again. This time, try to write it with no mistakes.

UNIT ② VOCABULARY WORKSHOP

Review vocabulary that you learned in Chapters 3 and 4.

A. MATCHING Match the words to the definitions. Write the correct letters on the lines.

Words

_____ **1.** aimlessly

_____ **2.** cliff

_____ **3.** dynasty

_____ **4.** funeral

_____ **5.** genre

_____ **6.** infant

_____ **7.** jade

_____ **8.** monogamous

_____ **9.** profile

_____ **10.** recur

Definitions

a. a ritual for a person who has died

b. baby

c. a period when a single family rules a country

d. happen again and again

e. green stone

f. art that shows the moments of everyday life

g. a steep side of a mountain

h. having one husband or wife

i. the face seen from the side

j. without any plan or goal

B. TRUE OR FALSE? Which statements are true? Which are false? Write T for *True* or F for *False* on the lines.

_____ **1.** A **cloak** is something to eat.

_____ **2.** A **landscape** is a painting of an outdoor scene.

_____ **3.** If you **go to great lengths** to do something, you try hard.

_____ **4.** A **masterpiece** is a great work of art.

_____ **5.** **Blue-collar workers** probably work in an office.

_____ **6.** If something is **sought after**, many people want it.

_____ **7.** People who are trying to **keep up with the Joneses** probably don't care what other people think about them.

_____ **8.** **Feature stories** in the newspaper are about very serious subjects such as politics, economics, and war.

C. ODD ONE OUT Read each row of words below. In each row, cross out the word without a connection to the other two. Then compare your answers with a partner's answers and explain your logic, if necessary.

1. ancestor ~~scribe~~ descendent
2. pharaoh ruler abolitionist
3. falcon livestock cattle
4. concrete visible spiritual
5. tomb hut cemetery
6. wagon chariot journey
7. surround portray depict
8. continuity stability change

D. VOCABULARY EXPANSION Write the different parts of speech for the words in the chart. Use a dictionary to fill in these blanks.

	Verbs	Nouns	Adjectives
1.	describe		
2.		analysis	
3.			excavated
4.	stabilize		
5.			founded
6.		animation	
7.	rule		
8.			established

E. THE ACADEMIC WORD LIST In the box below are some of the most common academic words in English. Fill in the blanks with words from this box. When you finish, check your answers in the reading on page 107. For more words, see the Academic Word List on pages 259–262.

abstract	established	illustrates	philosopher	section	stability
contrast	features	indicate	pose	so-called	status
created	goals	maintained	principal		

Just for a few moments, imagine some famous paintings of one or two hundred years ago. Can

you picture these in your mind? Now imagine the most modern _____ art of
₁

today. In only one to two hundred years, there have been huge changes in the form and content of art.

In _____, the characteristics of ancient Egyptian art remained nearly the same
                   2

for almost three *thousand* years.

     The _____ message of Egyptian art is continuity—an unbroken span of
                       3

time reaching back into history and forward into the future. The Greek _____
                                                                                    4

Plato wrote that Egyptian art did not change for ten thousand years; while this is an exaggeration, there

were many _____ that remained the same over long periods of time.
                    5

     The _____ *Palette of King Narmer* was _____
                       6   7

during the Old Kingdom. It _____ many characteristics of Egyptian art. The
                                      8

palette (so named because it takes the form of a slab for mixing cosmetics) portrays a victory by the

forces of Upper (southern) Egypt, led by Narmer, over those of Lower (northern) Egypt. Narmer is the

largest figure and is near the center of the palette to _____ his high
                                                                      9

_____. He holds an enemy by the hair and is about to kill him. To the
         10

left, a servant holds Narmer's sandals, which indicates that Narmer is probably standing in a temple or

on holy ground. In the lowest _____ of the tablet are two more defeated
                                        11

enemies. In the upper right is a falcon representing Horus, the god of Upper Egypt.

     Narmer's _____ is typical of Egyptian art. When depicting an important
                       12

person, the Egyptian artist attempted to show each part of the body to best advantage, so it could be

"read" clearly by the viewer. Thus, Narmer's lower body is seen in profile, his torso full front, his head

in profile, but his eye front again. This same pose recurs throughout most two-dimensional art in

Egypt. It is believed that the priests (religious leaders), who had much control over the art,

_____ this figure type and decreed that it be _____
         13   14

for the sake of continuity. It is not a pose that suggests motion, but action was not important to

Egyptian art. Order and _____ were its main characteristics, as they were the
                                 15

_____ of Egyptian society.
         16

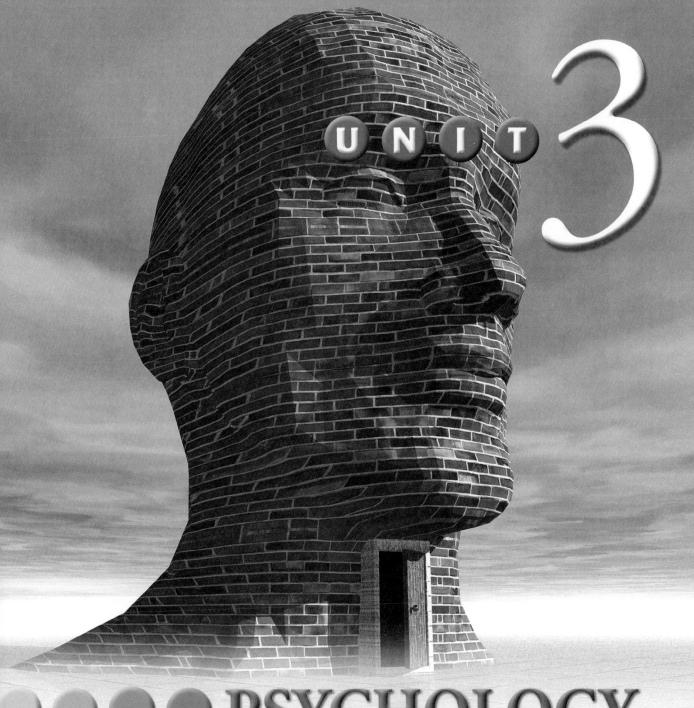

CHAPTER 5

States of Consciousness

Discuss these questions:
- Look at the picture. What do you think is happening?
- How many hours do you sleep each night? How much do you want to sleep?
- Do you remember your dreams? Describe a dream you have had.

PART ① INTRODUCTION Lucid Dreaming

BEFORE READING

Home-Study Guide to Lucid Dreaming

Would you like to remember your dreams, to experience the joy of flying in your nightly dreams? Can you imagine knowing when you are dreaming and becoming a "director" of your dreams? Learn to explore the world of your dreams! Become a lucid dreamer with this 3-month program.

How to Become a Lucid Dreamer
(Order # MHC9697) $59.00

Dream Catcher

Native Americans place "dream catchers" over their beds at night. The net is believed to catch nightmares and protect sleepers from these bad dreams. It also attracts good dreams and helps the dreamer remember them! Made by Native Americans in the Soutwest. Willow bark, natural color beads and feathers. Our mini-dreamcatcher is 2.5 inches (6.4 centimeters) wide. You can take it wherever your journey takes you.

Dream Catcher
(Order # MHC97998) $15.99

THINKING AHEAD With a partner, look at these ads from a catalog and discuss these questions.

1. From the first ad, what can you guess that **lucid dreaming** is?

2. Why would someone buy a **dream catcher**?

READING

Read about lucid dreaming. As you read, think about these questions:
• What can a dreamer do in lucid dreaming?
• How can a person become a lucid dreamer?

Lucid Dreaming

The History of Lucid Dreaming

In a lucid dream, the dreamer becomes consciously aware that he or she is dreaming while participating in the events and emotions of the dream. That is, the dreamer can be a character experiencing the dream, an observer watching the dream, and a director creating the dream. As far back as the fourth century B.C.E.,
5 Aristotle commented: "Often when one is asleep, there is something . . . which declares that what . . . presents itself is . . . a dream." Lucid dreams were given a special status in early Christianity, Tibetan Buddhism, and Islam.

In England, Oliver Fox independently discovered lucid dreaming in 1902. He called lucid dreams "dreams of knowledge." In such dreams, Fox felt "free as air,
10 secure in the . . . knowledge that I could always wake if danger threatened."

Several modern popular books have focused attention on lucid dreaming. Patricia Garfield included a chapter on lucid dreams in *Creative Dreaming* (1974). She wrote that the lucid dreamer would have an "unbelievable freedom from all restrictions of body, time, and space":

15 When you become lucid you can do *anything* in your dream. You can fly anywhere you wish, . . . converse with friends long dead or people unknown to you; you can see any place in the world you choose, experience all levels of positive emotions, receive answers to questions, . . . observe creative products, and, in general, use the full
20 resources of the material stored in your mind. *You can learn to become conscious during your dreams.*

Techniques for Developing Lucidity

Stephen LaBerge, at the Stanford University Sleep Lab, has developed a method called the MILD technique (Mnemonic Induction of Lucid Dreams). This involves waking up from a dream, imagining yourself back in that same dream, seeing
25 yourself becoming lucid, and telling yourself, "Next time I'm dreaming, I want to recognize I'm dreaming." LaBerge claims that with practice using his MILD technique, he was able to have lucid dreams on any night he wished.

To gain access to your dreams, you don't have to use any physical energy. The only mental energy required is that of paying attention to the dreams that are given
30 to you and being willing to consider the possible messages.

You can start your preparation today by finding a notebook or diary to record your dreams tomorrow morning. Place it on your nightstand or under your pillow tonight.

When you wake up during the night or in the morning, don't open your eyes
35 immediately. Lie very still and try gently to recall any imagery. Were you in some
building or unusual location? Was anyone else present? Did you notice something
unusual? If you can recall any specific image (D), try to reconnect it with whatever
event or activity preceded it (C), and what preceded that (B), and what preceded that
(A). Think about these events or images a few times before opening your eyes and
40 recording the dream in its ABCD order. Describe the dream as fully as you can
without crossing out any words.

As you begin to experience the personal rewards of your dream explorations,
your dream journal will achieve a special place in your life. Review your journal from
time to time to note how your life patterns are changing. Good journeying!

Source: *Our Dreaming Mind* (Van de Castle)

AFTER READING

 A. CHECK YOUR UNDERSTANDING Go back and answer the two questions on page 141. Highlight the
sentences in the reading where you found the answers.

Critical Thinking Strategy

Determining Point of View

Some readings (such as newspaper articles or chapters in textbooks) are **objective**. In other words, the
writer does not include his or her opinion but, instead, gives equal weight to all sides of an issue.

Other readings are **subjective**; the writer expresses his or her opinion. Such readings have a point of view–a
way of considering the topic.

When reading subjective passages, you need to be able to determine an writer's point of view. Often, it is
possible to do this by noticing the writer's choice of adjectives. Adjectives of opinion (such as *good, bad,
interesting, boring, beautiful, ugly*) signal the writer's point of view.

 B. DETERMINING POINT OF VIEW Does the writer of the reading believe that it's *good* or *bad* to be a
lucid dreamer? Look through the reading quickly and highlight the adjectives and phrases that support your
answer. Then discuss your answer with a partner.

Reading Strategy

Understanding Ellipses (. . .)

When the writer is quoting a source, the writer must copy the source's words exactly. However, sometimes the writer wants to omit (leave out) one or more words. In this situation, the writer puts in ellipses (. . .) to indicate that something was taken out. Look at these quotes from the Chapter 3 reading on page 78.

Example:
Complete quote: "Art attempts to take something invisible, something spiritual, and make it visible."

Quote with ellipses: "Art attempts to take something invisible . . . and make it visible."

C. UNDERSTANDING ELLIPSES Look back at the reading on pages 141–142 and find the ellipses within the quotations. Circle them. Why are they there?

D. TAKING A SURVEY Read the questions in the chart and think about your answers. Then move around the classroom and ask classmates the questions. Record their answers on the chart, using slashes. For example, 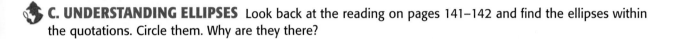 = 5 people answered this way.

Questions	No, never	Very rarely	Sometimes	Often	Yes, every day
Do you remember your dreams?					
Do you talk about dreams with friends or family?					
Do you have flying dreams?					
Do you have lucid dreams?					
Do you write down your dreams?					

E. DISCUSSION In small groups, talk about the results of your survey. How rare are flying dreams and lucid dreams? How often do most students remember dreams, talk about them, or write them down?

F. APPLICATION For the next week (beginning tonight), keep a notebook and pen beside your bed. When you wake from a dream, write it down quickly before you forget it. You might want to use these notes in your writing in Part 5.

BEFORE READING

A. THINKING AHEAD The next reading explains cultural beliefs about dreams. Using the questions below, discuss in small groups what your culture believes about dreams. When your group finishes the discussion, share your answers with the rest of the class.

1. Do people in your culture think that dreams are important? Do they talk about the meaning of dreams? Do some people take dreams more seriously than others do?

2. What do most people in your culture think that dreams mean? What are some **folk beliefs** (traditional ideas) about the meaning of dreams? In other words, what did your grandparents or great-grandparents believe about dreaming?

B. VOCABULARY PREPARATION Read the sentences below. Try to guess the meaning of the words from:
• the context
• stems and affixes
• your own knowledge of the situation

With a partner, write on the lines words that have the same meaning as the green words.

1. The artist took a piece of wood and used several different knives to **carve** a sculpture of an ancestor.

   When people carve something, they _____ it.

2. In ancient times, when people were sick and wanted to be **healed**, they went to special healing centers.

   When people are sick, they want to be _____.

3. In some religions, an animal is **sacrificed** before or during a ceremony.

   What happens to an animal in some religious ceremonies? It is _____.

4. Everyone is hoping that scientists will soon find a **cure** for cancer and other terrible sicknesses.

   We want (a) _____ for cancer.

5. The police are **seeking** information about a lost child; they have no idea, yet, what happened to her.

   When a child is lost, the police _____ information.

6. When we go on our hike in the mountains next weekend, Alan is going to **guide** us because it's easy to get lost in that area.

   What will Alan do to help us? _____

Having Questions in Mind

It's always a good idea to have questions about a reading in mind as you read. If you do, some of the answers will "pop out" at you as you read. Also, it is easier to stay focused on the reading if you are looking for answers while reading.

Example:

You know: The reading is about lucid dreaming.

You think about questions as you read:
• What can a dreamer do during lucid dreaming?
• How can a person become a lucid dreamer?

READING

Before you read about dreaming, look over the questions in Activity A on page 147. As you read, look for the answers.

Dreaming Across Cultures

The famous anthropologist Edward Tylor studied dreaming in many cultures. Tylor believed that "primitive" early humans developed the idea of a soul
5 from their attempts to explain dreaming. According to Tylor's theory, these people thought a part of their body seemed to go someplace else during dreams. If his theory is correct, our early
10 ancestors decided that this part of their body was not physical—in other words, it was the *soul*—and this was the beginning of religion. Whether or not Tylor was correct, it's clear that people
15 in all cultures do dream; however, how they view dreaming and how they use dreams varies from culture to culture.

Artists' Use of Dreams

Anthropologists have pointed out the importance of dreams to artists
20 worldwide. Artists in very different cultures receive inspiration for their art from dreams. In West Africa, for

A *malanggan* sculpture

example, an artist will carve a mask for the Poro Society after a dream gives him guidance. In New Ireland (now part of Papua New Guinea, in the South Pacific), sculptures are carved for the *malanggan* ceremony, in which people remember dead ancestors. Although the basic design is traditional, each sculpture is also unique. The artist receives his inspiration for it through a dream. This form of inspiration is probably not surprising to artists, writers, or composers of music from any culture, for dreams are often seen as a source of inspiration.

The Ancient Egyptians

Ancient Egyptians sometimes dreamed about gods or people who had died. Some events in dreams were seen as lucky and some as unlucky. People would go to a priest at a temple or to a scribe— someone who could read and write— who could find an interpretation of these dreams in a dream book or recite a spell (magic words) to prevent unlucky dreams.

The Ancient Greeks and Medieval Christians

The ancient Greeks looked to their dreams to guide them to good health. When they were sick and wanted to be healed, they went to the temple of Asklepios, the god of healing. They paid for an animal—a chicken, goat, or sheep—to be sacrificed. Then they slept on the temple floor in the belief that the god would come to them in a dream and tell them what to do in order to be cured.

Over a thousand years later, during the Middle Ages, the tradition continued. European Christians used to sleep in churches in the hopes of having a dream to cure their sickness. The Church, however, did not approve of this practice. The Church saw itself as the intermediary between God and people. If people could listen to God directly, in their dreams, then the power of the Church was lessened.

In the Middle Ages, European Christians would sleep in churches to dream.

The Senoi of Malaysia

The Senoi people of Malaysia are famous for their art of dream interpretation, which they practiced until recently. Traditionally, they used their dreams to control their waking life. Each day, adults used to meet with each other to discuss their dreams in order to solve personal and community problems. At breakfast every day, children told their dreams to older family members and learned dream interpretation in the discussion and analysis that followed. Children learned to use their dreams creatively and change feelings of ill will— fear, anger, or hatred—into feelings of good will. For example, if a child had a nightmare about falling, his elders told him that it was a wonderful dream; it was the quickest way to contact the spirit world, and there was nothing to be afraid of. In his next falling dream, he should relax and see where the dream might take him. If a child

90 dreamed that she was attacking
someone, she needed to apologize to
that person and share something good
with him. The goal was for dreamers to
gain control of their dream world and
95 then the waking world. In this way, the
Senoi lived peacefully within themselves
and their society, without psychological
problems, crime, or violence.

Native Americans

Dreams have always been important
100 in Native American culture, too, but in
quite a different way from the Senoi.
Native Americans* in North America
who follow their people's traditions may
seek a vision—a rare and special kind of
105 dream—in two ways: through the use of
peyote or through a *vision quest*. Peyote
is a kind of drug from the cactus plant.
When people eat it as part of a religious
ceremony, sometimes they experience
110 visions of God or Jesus or a spirit. Their
visions are associated with images from
their specific cultures. A Mexican native,
for example, might see beautiful colored

The Senoi were famous for
their creative use of dreams.

birds. A Native American from the
115 flatlands of the United States might
envision buffalo. In a vision quest,
people suffer hunger, physical pain, and
loneliness for several days in an attempt
to have a vision that will guide them or
120 their people.

*In the U.S., the term "Native American" is more widely accepted than "Indian."

AFTER READING

A. CHECK YOUR UNDERSTANDING In small groups, discuss these questions.

1. How were the Christians of the Middle Ages similar in their dream life to the ancient Greeks? How were they different?

2. What do some traditional Native Americans do as part of their dream life that is different from the other cultures in the reading selection?

B. MAKING CONNECTIONS In Part 1, you read about lucid dreaming. Which group of people in the reading seems to practice lucid dreaming? Explain your answer to a partner.

Reading Strategy

Finding the Topic Sentence

As you know, you can find the main idea of a paragraph in the **topic sentence**. Usually, this is the first sentence of the paragraph. However, sometimes the first sentence is either too general or too specific to be the topic sentence. Instead, you will find the main idea in another sentence. When this happens, look for an "umbrella" sentence that covers all of the details in the paragraph.

C. FINDING THE TOPIC SENTENCE In the reading on pages 145–147, the topic sentence was the first sentence in only two of the paragraphs. Which ones? In the other paragraphs, where were the topic sentences? Highlight them.

In small groups, compare your highlighted sentences. Did everyone highlight the same sentences?

D. IDENTIFYING GENERAL AND SPECIFIC IDEAS Look back at the topic sentences you highlighted in the reading on pages 145–147. In the chart below, write how the groups of people use or understand dreams. Then write examples or details from the reading that support your answers.

Group of People	How They Use or Understand Dreams (general ideas)	Examples or Details (specific ideas)
Artists		
Egyptians		
Greeks/Medieval Christians		
Senoi		
Native Americans		

Compare your answers with a partner's answers.

E. VOCABULARY CHECK Look back at the reading on pages 145–147 to find the words for these definitions. Line numbers are in parentheses. Write the correct words on the lines.

1. magic words (40–45) _____

2. experiencing (a dream) (55–60) _____

3. fear, anger, or hatred toward another person (80–85) _____

PART ③ ACADEMIC READING
The Function and Meaning of Dreaming

BEFORE READING

A. THINKING AHEAD In small groups, discuss this question and make a list of the possible answers.
- What might be the function of dreams? In other words, why do we dream?

B. VOCABULARY PREPARATION Read the sentences below. Words and phrases from the next reading are in green. What can you guess about each word in green? Write your guesses on the lines. Then compare your answers with a partner's answers.

1. I woke up late on the day of the final exam and realized that the exam started in 15 minutes. **In a panic,** I threw on some clothes, grabbed my keys, and rushed out the door.

   Guess: _____

2. I hate the sound when a dentist **drills** my teeth to fill a cavity.

   Guess: _____

3. Some psychologists think there is great **significance** in the new evidence, but others disagree.

   Guess: _____

4. We can never **fulfill** all of our wishes, but it is possible to satisfy many of them.

   Guess: _____

5. On Halloween, the children **disguised** themselves as ghosts, Superman, and cartoon heroes.

   Guess: _____

6. There are often both **overt** reasons for some things that we do and hidden or secret reasons.

   Guess: _____

7. I closed my eyes and pointed to a place on the map. In this way, I decided **at random** where to go.

   Guess: _____

8. Without **sufficient** information, we couldn't reach a conclusion.

   Guess: _____

9. Professor Smith and her **colleagues** at the university disagree with that theory.

   Guess: _____

10. That's a **plausible** explanation. You've persuaded me.

    Guess: _____

Reading Strategy

Choosing the Correct Dictionary Definition

Some words have just one meaning. Many words, however, have more than one meaning. When you use a dictionary, you need to find the definition that fits the context in which you found the word. First, determine the part of speech of the word. Then look at each definition of the word in the dictionary. Look back and forth from the sentence to the dictionary to see which definition matches the word in the sentence. Be sure to read the dictionary examples of how to use the word; sometimes these help you more than the definitions.

vi-sion /ˈvɪʒən/ *n.* **1** [U] the ability to see [= sight]: *Will the operation improve my vision? | She has good/poor vision.* **2** [U] the area that you can see: *For a moment, the passing car was outside my **field of vision**.* **3** [C] an idea of what you think something should be like: *He had a clear **vision of** how he hoped the company would develop. | The President outlined his **vision for** the future.* **4** [C] something you seem to see, especially in a dream as part of a religious experience, especially in a dream: *She said that an angel appeared to her **in a vision**.* **5** [U] the knowledge and imagination that are needed in planning for the future with a clear purpose: *We need a leader with vision.*

Example: Native Americans in North America who follow their people's traditions may seek a **vision** of a spirit to guide them.

You see that definitions 1, 2, 3, and 5 don't fit at all. Definition 4 is the correct one for *vision* in this context.

Source: *Longman Dictionary of American English* (2004)

C. VOCABULARY PREPARATION: DICTIONARY USE As you did in Activity B on page 149, guess the meaning of words in green. Then check a dictionary to see if your guess was correct. Focus on choosing the correct definition of each word.

1. Sleep is **critical** to good health.

   Guess: _____

   Dictionary Definition: _____

2. These are some of the **key** concerns in his life these days.

   Guess: _____

   Dictionary Definition: _____

3. She got 45 hours of sleep last week. That **works out to** about 6½ hours per night.

   Guess: _____

   Dictionary Definition: _____

Read about dreaming. As you read, highlight the sentences that answer these questions:

• What are three main theories about the meaning of dreams?
• What are two other ideas about dreams?

The Function and Meaning of Dreaming

I was sitting at my desk when I remembered that this was the day of my chemistry final! I was terrified because I hadn't studied a bit for it. In fact, I had
5 missed every lecture all semester. In a panic, I began running across campus desperately searching for the classroom, to which I'd never been. It was hopeless; I knew I was going to fail and flunk out of college.

Landscape from a Dream by Paul Nash

10   If you have had a similar dream—a surprisingly common dream among people involved in the academic world—you know how completely convincing the panic and fear are in such a dream.
15 Nightmares, unusually frightening dreams, occur fairly often. In one survey, almost half of a group of college students who kept records of their dreams over a two-week period reported having at least
20 one nightmare. This works out to some twenty-four nightmares per person each year, on average (Wood & Bootzin, 1990; Berquier & Ashton, 1992; Tan & Hicks, 1995).

25   On the other hand, most of the 150,000 dreams the average person experiences by the age of 70 are much less dramatic (Snyder, 1970; Webb, 1992). They typically include such
30 everyday events as going to the supermarket, working at the office, or preparing a meal. Students dream about going to class; professors dream about lecturing. Dental patients dream about
35 getting their teeth drilled; dentists dream of drilling the wrong tooth. The English take tea with the queen in their dreams; in the United States, people go to a bar with the president (Solomon, 1993; Potheraju
40 & Soper, 1995; Domhoff, 1996).

But what, if anything, do all these dreams mean? Whether dreams have a specific significance and function is a question that scientists have considered
45 for many years, and they have developed several alternative theories.

Do Dreams Represent Unconscious Wish Fulfillment?

Sigmund Freud viewed dreams as a guide to the unconscious (Freud, 1890). In his **unconscious wish fulfillment**
50 **theory,** he proposed that dreams represented unconscious wishes that dreamers desire to see fulfilled. However, because these wishes would create too much guilt or anxiety in the
55 dreamer's conscious awareness, the actual wishes—called the **latent content of dreams**—are disguised. The true subject and meaning of a dream, then, may have little to do with

60 its overt story line, which Freud called the **manifest content of dreams.**

To Freud, it was important to cut through a dream's manifest content to understand its true meaning. To do this, 65 Freud tried to get people to discuss their dreams, associating symbols in the dreams to events in the past. He also suggested that certain common symbols with universal meanings appear in 70 dreams. For example, to Freud, long objects such as snakes, umbrellas, and sticks represented male sex organs, and round objects or empty spaces such as closets, caves, or tunnels represented 75 female sex organs. Actions such as climbing stairs, crossing a bridge, or riding in an elevator represented the sexual act.

Today, many psychologists do not accept Freud's view that dreams 80 represent unconscious wishes and that particular objects and events in a dream are symbolic. For example, we now know that some dreams reflect events occurring in the dreamer's environment 85 as he or she is sleeping. Sleeping participants in one experiment were sprayed with water while they were sleeping. These unlucky volunteers reported more dreams involving water 90 than a comparison group of participants who were left to sleep undisturbed (Dement & Wolpert, 1958).

Dreams-for-Survival Theory

According to the **dreams-for-survival theory**, dreams permit 95 information that is critical for our daily survival to be reconsidered and reprocessed during sleep. According to this theory, dreams represent concerns about our daily lives, illustrating our 100 uncertainties, indecisions, ideas, and desires. Dreams are seen as consistent with everyday living. Rather than being disguised wishes, as Freud suggested, they represent key concerns growing 105 out of our daily experiences (Pavlides & Winson, 1989; Winson, 1990).

Up and Down, by M.C. Escher

Research supports the dreams-for-survival theory, suggesting that certain dreams permit people to focus on and 110 combine memories, particularly dreams that are connected with "how-to-do-it" memories. For instance, in one experiment, people learned a visual memory task late in the day. They were 115 then sent to bed, but awakened at certain times during the night. When they were awakened at times that did not interrupt dreaming, their performance on the memory task typically improved the next day. But when they were awakened during rapid eye movement (REM) sleep—the stage of sleep when people dream—their performance was worse. The conclusion: Dreaming can play a role in helping us remember material to which we have been previously exposed (Karni et al., 1992, 1994).

Activation-Synthesis Theory

According to psychiatrist J. Allan Hobson, who proposed the **activation-synthesis theory**, the brain produces random electrical energy during REM sleep, possibly due to changes in the production of particular neurotransmitters—chemicals in the brain that transmit messages from one nerve cell to another. This electrical energy randomly stimulates memories found in various areas of the brain. Because we have a need to make sense of our world, even while asleep, the brain takes these chaotic memories and creates a logical story line (Hobson, 1996; Porte & Hobson, 1996). Hence, what starts out as a random process becomes something meaningful.

Dream Theories in Perspective

The difference in theories about dreaming clearly illustrates that dream researchers do not agree on the fundamental meaning of dreams. However, new research is suggesting that the different approaches might be closer together than originally thought.

For instance, according to work by Allen Braun and colleagues, the parts of the brain associated with emotions and visual imagery are strongly activated during REM sleep. At the same time, the areas that control logical analysis and attention are inactive during REM sleep (Braun et al., 1998).

The results support several aspects of Freudian theory. For example, the high activation of emotional and motivational centers of the brain during dreaming makes it plausible that dreams might reflect unconscious wishes and instinctual needs, just as Freud suggested. On the other hand, critics of Freudian explanations for dreams disagree that the new research findings support Freud. There is still no evidence that the meaning of dreams is hidden behind symbols found in the storyline of the dream.

One thing is clear: despite the advances in our understanding of the biological aspects of dreaming, the debate about the meaning of dreams is not yet resolved. But Freud would probably take satisfaction in the fact that a hundred years after he published his first book on the meaning of dreams, scientists are still debating his theory.

Source: *Essentials of Understanding Psychology* (Feldman)

AFTER READING

A. FINDING MAIN IDEAS Go back to the reading on pages 151–153. Look at the sentences you highlighted. Fill in the chart below with a partner.

Theory	Person(s) Associated with This Theory	Main Ideas of This Theory
	Freud	Dreams are unconscious wishes dreamers want to fulfill.
Dreams-for-survival		
	J. Allan Hobson	
New research		

B. VOCABULARY CHECK Look back at the reading to find words for these definitions. Write the correct word on the line. Line numbers are in parentheses.

1. unusually frightening dreams (15–20) _____

2. a person's disguised wishes in dreams (according to Freud) (55–60) _____

3. the overt story line of a dream (according to Freud) (60–65) _____

4. the stage of sleep when people dream (120–125) _____

C. WORD JOURNAL Go back to the readings in this chapter. What words are important for you to remember? Put them in your Word Journal.

Answering Questions about Details

A reading exam almost always asks about details in a passage. A typical multiple-choice question asks which one of four statements is *not* true.

Example:

All of the following statements about Senoi dream interpretation are true except:

    A. Children learned to use their dreams to change feelings of ill will into feelings of good will.

    (B.) Adults met once a week to discuss their dreams.

    C. Dreams helped the Senoi to solve community problems.

    D. People said falling dreams were a quick way to contact the spirit world.

According to the reading on page 146, statement B is incorrect. All of the other statements are true. B is the answer.

Another way to word this type of test question is:
Which of the following statements about Senoi dream interpretation is *not* true?

 D. ANSWERING QUESTIONS ABOUT DETAILS Look back at the reading on pages 151–153. Circle the letter of correct answer.

1. According to Freud's theory, all of the following are true except:

    A. Dreams can often be interpreted in terms of everyday concerns and stress.

    B. Dreams represent unconscious wishes.

    C. The actual wishes in dreams are disguised.

    D. Dreams contain universal symbols often associated with sexuality.

2. The section on the dreams-for-survival theory indicates all of the following except:

    A. These psychologists disagree with Freud.

    B. They believe dreams represent concerns about everyday life.

    C. Dreams can help us remember material.

    D. Dreams are disguised wishes.

3. According to Hobson, which of the following is *not* true?

    A. Random electrical energy is produced during REM sleep.

    B. Electrical energy creates symbols that are associated with wishes.

    C. Electrical energy stimulates memories.

    D. The human brain creates a logical story line from chaotic memories.

E. DISCUSSION In small groups, discuss these questions.

1. Which of the dream theories from the reading seem similar to each other? What do these theories have in common?

2. Which theory is the most plausible to you? Explain your answer.

F. APPLICATION Analyze the three dreams below with a partner. Interpret each dream according to the dreams-for-survival theory.

Dream 1

I was going into a thick forest. There were so many trees that it was hard to see very far. I decided to climb a tree to try to see better. It was difficult to climb, and I was going really slowly. Finally, just as I got close to the top of the tree, I slipped and fell down, down, down. I was more scared than I had ever been. I knew I was going to die. Then I woke up.

—dream of an 18-year-old male student

Dream 2

I was at work. Someone had found a baby fox. I was amazed that this wild animal was here, in a city. It was a perfect creature but in miniature—just one-inch long. (I didn't seem to notice the impossibility of this.) There were three evil scientists who were excited about this animal. They wanted to raise it and then do terrible experiments on it some day. I was so angry, so furious, that I couldn't express myself. I took the baby fox and ran away. I put the animal in my purse to keep it safe. I decided to take it up into the mountains and let it go free where it would be safe. As I was climbing the mountain, my husband joined me. We passed farms and parks and lots of people. We had to find the wilderness. Finally, near the top, we stopped to rest at a university. When I opened my purse to check on the fox, he wasn't there. I absolutely panicked. He couldn't be gone! I was so careful! I looked everywhere, but he was gone. I knew I would never find him.

—dream of a 40-year-old professional woman

Dream 3

I was at a conference in Europe. It had been pleasant. One evening, we were invited to a dinner party at the home of a wealthy woman in Vienna. We walked into the home, which was incredibly beautiful. It was a combination of a castle, museum, and art gallery. There was rich, dark wood and Old Masters' paintings everywhere. I had never seen such art in a private home before. We were in a huge, elegant dining room, where waiters served many courses of fabulous food. There was so much to see. I kept turning around to watch the people and see the art. I realized that I was missing out on some of the food because others at my table took it while I was marveling at the art. But this didn't bother me because this experience was so special. I was completely happy.

—dream of a 66-year-old retired man

G. RESPONSE WRITING Choose one of these topics:
- a dream that you have had recently
- the most memorable dream that you have ever had
- folk beliefs about dreaming
- the psychological theory about dreaming that seems most plausible to you
- anything that interested you in this chapter

Write about your topic for 10 minutes. Don't worry about grammar and don't stop writing to use a dictionary. Just put as many ideas as possible on paper.

PART ④ THE MECHANICS OF WRITING

In Part 4, you will practice using expressions for explaining symbols and transition words of time. You will need this grammar in Part 5 to write two paragraphs about a dream—one a narration of the dream and the other an analysis.

Using Transition Words of Time

Here is a brief review of adverbial conjunctions of time.

Adverbial Conjunctions of Time

first	second	third (etc.)
finally	then	afterwards

Examples: I had an awful nightmare last night. **Afterwards,** I couldn't remember the details, but I remember the feeling.

I was trying to run from a murderer when I felt a hand on my shoulder. **Then** I woke up.

There are several things you can do to become a lucid dreamer; **first,** you need to learn to value your dreams.

Note: Adverbial conjunctions often begin a sentence or independent clause. There is a period or semicolon before the adverbial conjunction. There is a comma after it (except for *then*).

When you tell a story in **chronological order** (order of time), you need to use transition words of time. Here are some of the subordinating conjunctions of time.

Subordinating Conjunctions of Time

when	as (while)	before
while	after	as soon as (immediately after)

Examples: I was relieved **when** I woke up.
When I woke up, I was relieved.
I couldn't remember the dream **after** I woke up.
After I woke up, I couldn't remember the dream.

Notes:
1. If the sentence begins with the subordinating conjunction, there is a comma after the first clause. There is no comma if the subordinating conjunction is after the independent clause.

2. *While* and *as* are often used with continuous tenses.

Examples: While I **was dreaming**, it was raining outside.
As I **was running**, I wondered who was chasing me.

A. SENTENCE COMBINING: TRANSITION WORDS OF TIME Combine the pairs of sentences. Use the adverbial and subordinating conjunctions in parentheses.

1. Lucid dreamers know that they're dreaming. The dream is happening. (while)

_____

_____

2. You need to replay the dream in your mind. You open your eyes. (before)

_____

_____

3. He realized that it was only a dream. A dream enemy was chasing him. (as)

_____

_____

4. Replay the dream in your mind. Open your eyes and write it down. (then)

_____

_____

5. Greeks were sick. They went to the temple of Asklepios. (when)

_____

_____

6. You should focus on thoughts of flying during the day. You need to think about past flying dreams at night. (first/second)

_____

_____

Using Verbs in Narration

A narrative is a story. When we tell a story, we usually use the simple past. Within the narrative, we may also occasionally use the past continuous (for an action occurring when something else happened) or the past perfect (for something that happened *before* a past action). Because a dream is a narrative, these three tenses are usually used to describe it.

Example: In my dream, I **was going** into a thick forest. There **were** so many trees that it **was** hard to see very far.

However, it is also common to use the "narrative present" in describing a dream. This involves mostly the simple present, with some present continuous, present perfect, and future.

Example: I **realize** that I'm **missing** out on some of the food because others at my table **take** it while I'm marveling at the art.

B. USING VERBS IN NARRATION Notice the use of tenses in the narrative of a dream below. Highlight each tense. Then turn back to page 156 and highlight the tenses in the three dreams.

> I go into my uncle's office. It's late at night, after hours. Nobody is there. I haven't come to take anything. I'm just curious. I look around and find it uninteresting. I'm moving from room to room. I notice that it's not a beautiful office at all, just functional. I notice with shock that there are video cameras hanging from the ceiling. There are several of them, and they're following me. I'm going from one room to another. I'm terrified and want to escape. I try to hide under a desk, but I know the cameras have already caught me.

Writing Strategy

Writing about Symbols

Dreams are filled with symbols—objects or actions that represent something else. Sometimes the same symbol might have a different meaning to different people. However, some symbols seem to be universal; in other words, they appear to have the same meaning to people everywhere. To write about symbols (for example, in a psychology, anthropology, or literature class), it is useful to know a variety of expressions to explain them. Here are a few.

Noun or Noun Phrase		**Noun or Noun Phrase**
Light	**is a symbol of**	understanding or knowledge.
The ankh (☥)	**is symbolic of**	life, the universe, and humankind.
A flag	**represents**	a country.
A circle	**is associated with**	the self and wholeness.
Snakes around a staff	**symbolize**	medicine.

C. WRITING ABOUT SYMBOLS Write what each symbol below means to you. (There are no "right" or "wrong" answers.) Use structures from the box above.

Example: I think a road is symbolic of a person's life.

1. a road _____

2. a star _____

3. an owl _____

4. a cross _____

5. breath _____

6. water _____

7. a crescent _____

8. five interconnected rings _____

 In small groups, compare your answers. Were your answers similar or different?

D. TALKING ABOUT SYMBOLS Ask your classmates about each symbol in the chart below. Write the person's name and answer in the chart. Ask questions such as these:
- What does the color red represent to you?
- What does a door symbolize to you?
- What do you think an eagle is symbolic of?

Symbols	Classmates	Meanings	Classmates	Meanings
1. the color red				
2. a door				
3. an eagle				
4. the ocean				
5. a mirror				

When you finish, write five sentences based on your chart. Use the five structures from the box on page 159.
Example: To Anne, the color red is associated with passion.

E. REVIEW: FINDING ERRORS In the paragraphs below, there are at least seven errors. These are errors with tenses, conjunctions of time, and expressions to explain symbols. Find and correct them.

In my dream, I was going into a thick forest. There were so many trees that it was hard to see very far. I decided to climb a tree to try to see better. It was difficult to climb, and I was going really slowly, finally, just as I got close to the top of the tree, I was slipping and fell down, down, down. I was more scared than I had ever been. I knew I was going to die then I woke up.

I think this dream concerns my anxiety about beginning college. Freud would say that the forest is a "female symbol," and the tree is a "male symbol," but this doesn't make sense to me. According to the dream-for-survival theory, we dream about things that concern us in everyday life. I've been worried about this big change in my life, so I think this theory is logical. The forest is probably symbolic of I am starting college. It was hard to see far into the forest represents my difficulty in imagining my future. Climbing the tree associated with my attempt to control my own future. Falling is a symbol of I am afraid of failure in college.

PART ⑤ ACADEMIC WRITING

WRITING ASSIGNMENT

In Part 5, you will write two paragraphs. The first will be a narrative of one dream. (Decide if you want to use past tenses or the narrative present. See page 158.) The second paragraph will be your analysis of this dream.

STEP A. CHOOSING A TOPIC Choose one dream that interests you. This should be a dream that you think you can interpret. It's best to work with one of your own dreams because the symbols may have a personal meaning to you. However, you could choose another person's dream. Also, choose one of these theories of dream interpretation: Freudian or dreams-for-survival.

Here are some dreams you could use:
• the dream from your Response Writing in Part 3 (page 156)
• one of the dreams that you wrote down during the week
• any dream that you can remember well
• Dream 3 on page 156
• a dream of one of your classmates

STEP B. ORGANIZING INFORMATION You will organize the information for your two paragraphs differently. Read the box below about organizing information for your narrative paragraph.

Writing Strategy ⬤⬤⬤⬤

Gathering and Organizing Ideas

Before writing, you need to gather ideas and organize them. For a paragraph in chronological order (such as the narration of a dream), simply list the events or actions in the order in which they happened.

Example: This is how the dreamer of Dream 2 on page 156 might start a list.

1. found baby fox
2. 3 scientists wanted to take it
3. was angry
4. took fox & ran away
5. (etc.)

GATHERING AND ORGANIZING IDEAS On a piece of paper, list the events or actions from the dream you have chosen to write about.

Using Graphic Organizers: Idea Maps

For a paragraph of analysis, create an idea map. Put the theme (subject of the dream) at the center and important details or elements around it. For any element that you think you understand, note the meaning. Don't worry about the other elements.

Example: This is how the dreamer of Dream 2 might map it.

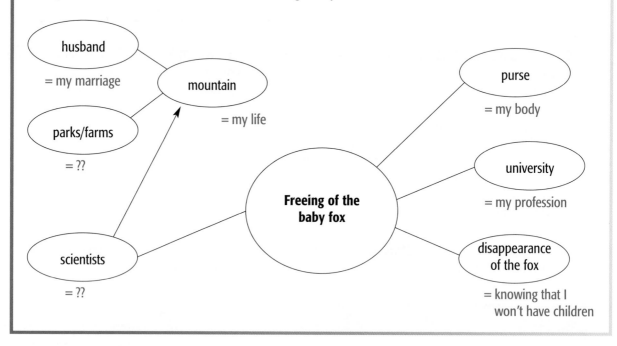

USING GRAPHIC ORGANIZERS: IDEA MAPS On a piece of paper, create an idea map. Use your list from page 161. Put the theme at the center and the elements around it. Add notes on any elements or symbols that you understand. Don't worry about the others.

Writing Strategy

Writing a Paragraph of Analysis

One way to organize a paragraph of analysis is to begin with the topic sentence, which gives the general meaning of the dream. Follow this with support that examines each detail. End with a concluding sentence. To be more persuasive, you can add reasons.

Example:

> My dream about freeing the baby fox is, I think, about my desire to have a child because in the dream I felt protective and maternal toward the fox. The mountain is symbolic of my life, and the fact that my husband joined me symbolizes our marriage. Freud would say that the purse is a "female symbol," and I think this is probably true. It's an "empty space," and I put the fox in it to keep it safe. The university represents education. To me, it is associated with my profession. I've worked for many years to reach this level in my work, and I haven't left much room in my life for a child. For this reason, it seems clear that "losing" the animal means that I know, unconsciously, that I won't have children.

Note in the example:

The details are in chronological order because it is the analysis of a dream, a narrative.

Analysis In the sample paragraph, look for expressions of symbolism. Highlight them when you find them. The writer gives reasons to explain most of her interpretations. What are these reasons?

STEP C. WRITING THE PARAGRAPHS Use the list of events in your dream to write your paragraph of narration. Choose either past tenses or present tenses, and be careful to use transition words of time appropriately. Then use your idea map as the basis for your paragraph of analysis. Write complete sentences. Use correct expressions of symbolism and whenever possible, add reasons for your interpretation.

STEP D. EDITING Read your paragraph and answer these questions.

1. Is the paragraph form correct (indentation, margins)?

2. Are the transition words of time used correctly?

3. Are the tenses used correctly?

4. In the second paragraph, does the topic sentence give the general meaning of the dream?

5. Are both paragraphs in chronological order?

6. Are expressions of symbolism used correctly?

7. Are some reasons given for the symbols that were chosen?

STEP E. REWRITING Write your paragraph again. This time, try to write it with no mistakes.

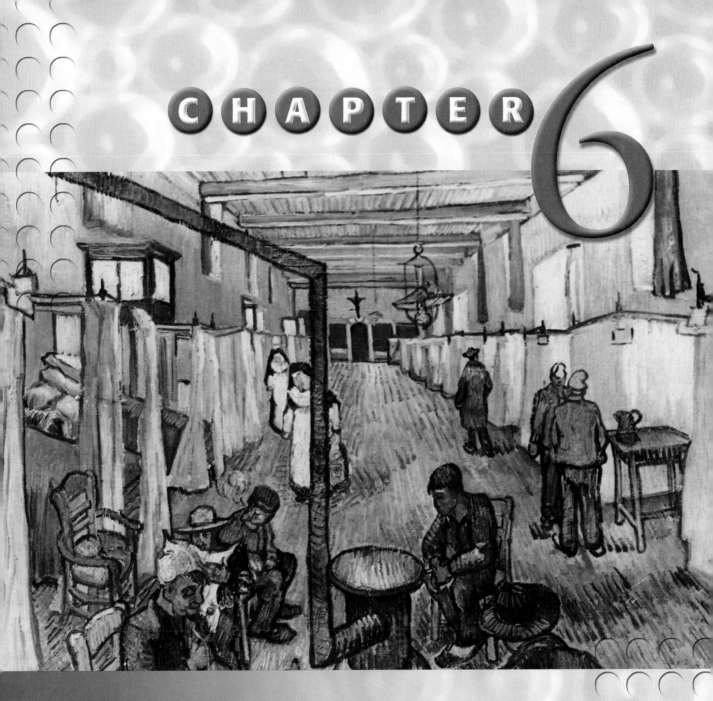

CHAPTER 6

Abnormal Psychology

Discuss these questions:
- Look at the picture. What's happening in the picture?
- Who do you think the people are? What kind of place is this?
- What is the best way to help people with mental problems?

BEFORE READING

Is it possible to tell from someone's appearance if he or she has a mental illness?

THINKING AHEAD The reading in this section deals with **psychological disorders**—mental diseases—in several different cultures. Before you read, discuss in small groups your culture's views about **abnormal** (not normal) behavior.

1. In your culture, when do people seek the help of psychologists? How do people deal with abnormal behavior in a friend or relative?

2. Do you know of any psychological disorders that exist in some cultures but not others? Explain your answer.

3. What's the difference between being *abnormal* and just being *different*? Can the same person be considered abnormal in one culture but not in another? Explain your answer.

READING

Read about culture and mental illness. As you read, highlight each psychological disorder as you find it. Also, highlight important new vocabulary and try to guess the meanings of new words from the context.

Culture and Mental Illness

Society has long placed labels on people who display abnormal behavior—labels such as *crazy, insane, neurotic, psycho, strange, possessed,* and *nuts.*
5 Unfortunately, most of the time, these labels have reflected the intolerance of the people using them and have been used with little thought as to what the label signifies.

10 Finding appropriate and specific names and classifications for abnormal behavior has been a major challenge for psychologists. It is difficult simply to distinguish normal from abnormal
15 behavior. Yet classification systems are necessary. Over the years, many classification systems have been used. Today, the standard system created by the American Psychiatric Association is
20 used by most professionals in the United States to diagnose and classify abnormal behavior. This classification system is the *Diagnostic and Statistical Manual of Mental Disorders, Fourth Edition*—
25 the *DSM-IV*. However, what is regarded as a symptom of mental illness in one society may be just one aspect of a normal, healthy life in another.

In most people's view, a person who
30 hears voices of the recently deceased is probably a victim of some psychological disturbance. Yet members of the Native American Plains Indian tribes routinely hear the voices of the dead calling to
35 them from the afterlife.

This is only one example of the role that culture plays in the labeling of behavior as "abnormal." In fact, of all the major adult disorders listed on the
40 *DSM-IV*, just four of them (schizophrenia, bipolar disorder, major depression, and anxiety disorders) are found across all cultures of the world.

Take, for instance, anorexia nervosa.
45 This is a weight disorder in which people, particularly women, develop inaccurate views of their body appearance, become obsessed with their weight, and refuse to eat, sometimes
50 starving in the process. This disorder occurs only in cultures which believe that slender female bodies are most desirable. In countries where such a standard does not exist, anorexia
55 nervosa does not occur. Interestingly, it is a fairly recent disorder. In the 1600s and 1700s, it did not occur in western society because the ideal female body at that time was a plump—somewhat fat—
60 one.

Similarly, dissociative identity (multiple-personality) disorder is only seen as a problem in societies in which a sense of self is fairly concrete. In
65 places like India, when an individual displays symptoms of what people in western society would call multiple-personality disorder (in which one person has more than one separate,
70 distinct personality), it is assumed that this individual is possessed by demons (which is viewed as a problem) or by gods (which is not a cause for treatment).

75 Other cultures have disorders that do not appear in the west. *Amok* is a mental illness, found in Malaysia and Indonesia, that has a specific set of symptoms. It is characterized by a wild
80 outburst in which a person who is

usually quiet and withdrawn kills or severely injures another person and doesn't remember the murder, experiencing complete amnesia
85 afterward. Some researchers consider *amok* a disease specific to these cultures, while others consider it a form of depression psychosis produced by extreme stress. English gets the
90 expression "to run amok" from this mental illness of Southeast Asia. It has been pointed out that *amok* occurs in societies where individuals also may go into a trance. A suggested explanation
95 for *amok* in Malaysia is that it may be an extreme expression of aggression in a society which strictly prohibits such expression.

In Algeria, a sick person is believed
100 to be possessed by *jinn* (spirits), and this is considered to be a form of "madness." People believe that someone else, motivated by envy, will use the "evil eye"; this causes the victim's behavior
105 and desires to come under the control of supernatural beings. The *marabout* is one type of traditional therapist who treats such patients. In an exorcism, the *marabout* talks with evil spirits through
110 the patient. The use of traditional therapists like the *marabout* are not only legal but on the increase in Algeria. In countries like Iraq, Kuwait, and Tunisia, such therapies are illegal
115 because they are associated with underdevelopment, in contrast to modernization.

Some West African men develop a disorder when they first attend college
120 that they call "brain frag"; it includes feelings of heaviness or heat in the head, as well as depression and anxiety.

Finally, *ataque de nervios* is a disorder found most often among
125 Latinos from the Caribbean,* characterized by trembling, crying, uncontrollable screams, and incidents of verbal or physical aggression.

In sum, we should not assume that
130 the *DSM-IV* provides the final word on psychological disorders. The disorders it includes are very much a creation and function of Western cultures at a particular moment in time, and its
135 categories should not be seen as universal.

* Studies of *ataque de nervios* now show that the disorder is found among most Latino cultures and not specifically Latinos from the Caribbean.

Sources: *Essentials of Understanding Psychology* (Feldman) and *The Tapestry of Culture: An Introduction to Cultural Anthropology* (Rosman and Rubel)

AFTER READING

A. FINDING THE MAIN IDEA Which sentence contains the main idea of the reading? Highlight it. Then compare your answer with a partner's answer.

B. VOCABULARY CHECK Look back at the reading on pages 167–168. Find words or phrases for the definitions below, and highlight them in the reading. Then write them on the correct lines. The line numbers in parentheses will help you find the words.

1. words or categories to describe a person (1–5)　＿＿＿＿＿＿＿＿＿＿＿＿＿

2. inability to accept anything or anyone different (5–10)　＿＿＿＿＿＿＿＿＿＿＿＿＿

3. dead (30–35)　＿＿＿＿＿＿＿＿＿＿＿＿＿

4. abnormally concerned or worried (45–50)　＿＿＿＿＿＿＿＿＿＿＿＿＿

5. controlled; completely influenced (70–75)　＿＿＿＿＿＿＿＿＿＿＿＿＿

6. disease; mental illness (75–80)　＿＿＿＿＿＿＿＿＿＿＿＿＿

7. sudden, powerful expression of emotion (75–80)　＿＿＿＿＿＿＿＿＿＿＿＿＿

8. complete loss of memory (80–85)　＿＿＿＿＿＿＿＿＿＿＿＿＿

Reading Strategy

Understanding Connotation

As you learn new words in English, you need to be aware of **connotation**—the feeling or idea of a word. In some cases, there are several (or many) words that share the same *basic* meaning but have different connotations—in other words, additional ideas or emotions associated with them. The examples below are words that share the basic meaning of *thin*.

Examples:

Positive Connotation	Neutral Connotation	Negative Connotation
slim	thin	skinny
slender		gaunt
svelte		skeletal
		anorexic

My mother always complains that I'm too **skinny**. "You look **anorexic**," she says. On the other hand, my girlfriends compliment me, saying that I am so **slender** and **slim**. In my opinion, I'm just **thin**.

In discussing abnormal psychology, there are many adjectives and nouns to describe abnormal behavior. Some of these words are often used in casual conversation. They are used jokingly among close friends.

Examples:　I think I was **nuts** to volunteer for that committee. There is so much work to do that it's driving me **crazy**!

What?! You want to drop out of college *now*? Are you **insane**? You have only one more semester until graduation.

However, because there is already a negative connotation associated with psychological abnormalities, most of these words are *not polite or appropriate* to use in a psychology class or in referring to a person who truly has such a problem.

C. UNDERSTANDING CONNOTATION Look back at the reading on pages 167–168. Highlight three nouns (one of which is used many times) that mean "psychological abnormality." These words have a neutral—or at least a *clinical*—connotation. They are appropriate to use in a psychology class.

D. FINDING IMPORTANT DETAILS Fill in the chart below with information from the reading on pages 167–168.

Disorder	Symptoms	Culture/Country	Influence of Culture
anorexia nervosa			
dissociative identity (multiple personality)		western culture	seen as a disorder
		India	
		Malaysia and Indonesia	
possession by *jinn*			
		West Africa	
		Latino cultures	

E. SYNTHESIS Which of the disorders in the chart above are similar to each other? In what ways? Discuss your answers with a partner.

BEFORE READING

A. THINKING AHEAD In small groups, look at the photos above and discuss these questions.

1. Which of these people might have psychological problems? What kinds of problems might they have?

2. Can you name any psychological problems? What are their symptoms?

B. VOCABULARY PREPARATION Read the sentences below. What can you guess about the word or phrase in green? Match the definitions in the box with the words in green. Write the correct letters on the lines.

a. attracting

b. going to happen soon

c. high point

d. making religious speeches

e. probability

f. see the difference between

g. serious

h. unavoidable disaster

i. unpleasant feeling that the room is turning around and around

_____ **1.** Bill began **preaching** to groups of people about God.

_____ **2.** Bill is now **drawing** large audiences who come to listen to him.

_____ **3.** It is sometimes difficult to **distinguish** normal from abnormal behavior.

_____ **4.** Some people have mild anxiety, but Jean's is **severe.**

_____ **5.** My worry rose to a **peak,** and then I slowly began to relax.

_____ **6.** Debbie can't seem to escape this terrible feeling of **impending** disaster.

_____ **7.** I'm horribly afraid that this will end in complete **doom.**

_____ **8.** The room was very hot, and I felt a sudden **dizziness.** Then I fainted.

_____ **9.** What is the **likelihood** that this will happen soon?

Now compare your answers with a partner's answers.

READING

Read about abnormal behavior. As you read, highlight the answer to this question:
• What are three ways of defining abnormality?

What Is Abnormal?

A man living in the Ozark Mountains in Missouri has a vision in which God speaks to him. He begins preaching to his relatives and neighbors, and soon he has the whole town in a state of religious fervor. People say that God has "called" him to speak to them. He becomes famous as a prophet and healer, and in time he is drawing large audiences
5 everywhere he goes. However, when he goes into the city of St. Louis and attempts to hold a prayer meeting on a main street at rush hour, blocking traffic, he is arrested. He tells the police officers about his conversations with God, and they hurry him off to the nearest mental hospital.

A housewife is tired all the time, but she has trouble sleeping. Her housework keeps
10 piling up because she has no energy to do it. Applications for adult classes and ads from the newspaper for jobs lie in a drawer, untouched. She goes to her family doctor, but he says she's in perfect health. One night she tells her husband that she's thinking of seeing a psychotherapist. He thinks this is ridiculous—stupid. According to him, all she needs is to get up out of her chair and get busy.

What Is Abnormal Behavior?

15 Who is right? The "prophet" or the policemen? The housewife or her husband? It is often difficult to draw a line between normal and abnormal behavior. Behavior that some people consider normal seems abnormal to others. One approach to abnormality is to say that whatever most people do is normal. Abnormality, then, is any deviation from the average or from the majority. If most people cheat on their income taxes, are honest
20 taxpayers abnormal? If most people are noncreative, was William Shakespeare, the English playwright, abnormal? Because the majority is not always right or best, this approach to defining abnormality is not generally useful.

Another way to distinguish normal from abnormal people is to say that normal people are able to get along in the world—physically, emotionally, and socially. They can feed and clothe
25 themselves, work, find friends, and live by the rules of society. By this definition, abnormal people are the ones who cannot adjust. They may be so unhappy that they refuse to eat or are so sad that they cannot hold a job. They may experience so much anxiety in relationships with others that they end up avoiding people, living in a lonely world of their own.

The terms "mental illness" and "mental health" imply that psychological disturbance or
30 abnormality is like a physical sickness—such as the flu or tuberculosis. Although many psychologists think that "mental illness" is different from physical illness, the idea remains that there is some ideal (perfect) way for people to function psychologically, just as there is an ideal way for people to function physically. The fact that it is difficult to define abnormality does not mean that no such thing exists. It does mean that we should be
35 cautious about judging a person to be "mentally ill" just because he or she acts in a way that we cannot understand. It should also be kept in mind that mild psychological disorders are common. It is only when a psychological problem becomes serious enough to disrupt everyday life that it becomes an "abnormality" or "illness."

Anxiety-Based Disorders

Among adults, 16.4% have symptoms typical of the anxiety-based disorders. People with
40 these disorders are deeply anxious and seem unable to free themselves of worries and fears. When severe anxiety is focused on a particular object, activity, or situation that seems out of

proportion to the real dangers involved, it is called a **phobia.** Phobias may be classified as simple phobias, social phobias, and agoraphobia. A simple phobia can focus on almost anything, including high places (acrophobia), enclosed spaces (claustrophobia), and darkness (nyctophobia). Victims of social phobias fear that they will embarrass themselves in a public place or social setting. People suffering from an extreme fear of crowds (agoraphobia) may stop going to movies or shopping in large, busy stores. Some reach the point where they will not leave their houses at all. Phobias may be mild or extremely severe. Most people deal with their phobias by avoiding the thing that frightens them.

In another type of anxiety disorder, **panic disorder,** panic attacks occur that last from a few seconds to several hours. During an attack, anxiety suddenly—and often without warning—rises to a peak, and the individual feels a sense of impending, unavoidable doom. Although symptoms differ from person to person, they might include an increased heart rate, shortness of breath, unusual amounts of sweating, and dizziness.

Mood Disorders

U.S. President Abraham Lincoln. British Queen Victoria. American writer Mark Twain. The common link among these people? Each suffered from attacks of **major depression,** one of the most common mood disorders.

We all experience mood swings. Sometimes we are happy, while at other times we feel miserable or depressed—sad. Occasional depression is a common experience. When psychologists speak of major depression, they do not mean the sadness that comes from experiencing one of life's disappointments. Some depression is normal following the breakup of a long-term relationship, the death of a loved one, or the loss of a job. In some people, however, these moods are more intense and last longer. These individuals often get the sense that their depression will go on forever and that there is nothing they can do to change it. People who suffer from major depression might feel useless, worthless, lonely, and hopeless about the future. They might experience such feelings for months or even years, and they are at risk for suicide.

Women are twice as likely as men to experience major depression; approximately one-fourth of all females will experience it at some point in their lives. Furthermore, although no one is quite sure why, the rate of depression is going up throughout the world. Results of in-depth interviews in the United States, Puerto Rico, Taiwan, Lebanon, Canada, Italy, Germany, and France indicate that the incidence of depression has increased significantly. In fact, in some countries, the likelihood that individuals will suffer major depression at some point in their lives is three times higher than it was for earlier generations.

A person who alternates between periods of mania (an extended state of intense, wild happiness) and depression has **bipolar disorder.** The swings between highs and lows might occur as frequently as a few days apart or over a period of years.

Schizophrenia

We can understand depression. Most of us have experienced anxiety. However, it is hard to understand an individual with **schizophrenia,** who has lost contact with reality and lives life as an unreal dream. Schizophrenia is not a single problem; rather, it is a collection of symptoms.

• *Delusions.* People with schizophrenia often have delusions, firmly held beliefs with no basis in reality. Most commonly, they believe they are being controlled by someone else.

• *Perceptual disorders.* People with schizophrenia do not perceive the world as most other
85 people do. They might see, hear, or smell things differently than others do.

• *Emotional disturbances.* People with schizophrenia sometimes show a lack of emotional response to the most dramatic events. Or they might display emotion that is inappropriate to a situation.

• *Withdrawal.* People with schizophrenia tend to have little interest in others. They tend
90 not to socialize or hold conversations with others, although they might talk *at* another person.

Psychological disorders are far from rare, and yet the stigma (a negative label that leads people to be seen as different) against people who experience a psychological disorder remains real.

Sources: *Understanding Psychology* (Kasschau) and *Essentials of Understanding Psychology* (Feldman)

AFTER READING

A. CHECK YOUR UNDERSTANDING Use the information that you highlighted to help you answer the question on page 172. Compare your answer with a partner's answer.

B. APPLICATION Read the descriptions of three people below. What might be each person's problem? Use the reading to help you identify each problem.

1. Angie has felt deeply sad for over a month. She finds no pleasure in anything. She's tired all the time and has trouble remembering things. She doesn't want to eat and can't sleep well. She feels that everything she has ever done has been wrong and feels totally hopeless.

   Disorder: _____

2. Maria is no longer able to go to work or carry out daily activities. She hears voices that command her to do things. She believes these voices come from outer space and must be obeyed. She has a strange, illogical use of language. She deeply distrusts all people in uniforms and believes they are trying to kill her.

   Disorder: _____

3. For several days Hong feels great, and he has enormous energy. He talks fast and has many, many ideas for new projects. It is a time of intense creativity. Then, suddenly, he loses all energy, becomes very sad, and feels completely hopeless.

   Disorder: _____

C. DISCUSSION In small groups, discuss these questions.

1. In your opinion, how is a phobia different from a normal fear? What might be some "healthy fears"?

2. What are you afraid of? (High places? Crowds? Snakes? etc.) Can you think of when you first had this fear, and why? How do you deal with this fear?

3. Do you know anyone who is phobic? How does this phobia affect her or his life?

4. Do you know of any famous people who suffered from a psychological disorder? If so, who were they? Do you know what disorder they had?

5. Do you think there are fewer stigmas against people with psychological disorders than in the past? Among whom? Why?

Test-Taking Strategy

Understanding Stems and Affixes

Many standardized exams test your knowledge of stems and affixes—word parts. Most of these come to English from Greek and Latin. They are good to know because you can often guess the meaning of a word that you've never seen if you know its parts. There are many words with such stems and affixes in the three readings in this chapter. Some are on the following list.

Prefixes	Meanings
ab-	not; away; off
an-	without
anti-	against
dis-	apart, separate
im-, in-, ir-	not

Stems	Meanings
acro	high (place)
aero	air
agora	marketplace, place where people gather
aqua, hydro	water
onym	name
orexi	appetite, hunger
phob	fear
psych	mind
therap	treatment
xeno	foreign, strange

D. UNDERSTANDING STEMS AND AFFIXES Choose the best answer to complete each sentence. Circle the letter of the correct answer.

1. A person with **hydrophobia** is probably _____.

    A. afraid of high places

    B. angry or harmful toward society

    C. afraid of water

    D. more anxious than most people

2. People who have **xenophobia** _____.

    A. don't like to be on an elevator

    B. have fear of becoming overweight

    C. are afraid of crowded places

    D. have fear or hatred of foreigners

3. A piece of art labeled **"anonymous"** in the museum _____.

    A. is a painting of a marketplace

    B. was created by an artist whose name is not known

    C. is going to be moved to another museum soon

    D. was created by someone with psychological problems

4. If a person **dissociates** during a horrible experience, he or she _____.

    A. is able to help other people through the experience

    B. might commit suicide

    C. tries to stay close to other people

    D. separates psychologically from the experience

5. People who are **agoraphobic** _____.

    A. are afraid to be out in crowded places

    B. are angry or harmful toward society

    C. have an eating disorder

    D. have a terrible fear of being in high places such as tall buildings

PART ③ ACADEMIC READING
Approaches to Psychological Therapy

BEFORE READING

A. THINKING AHEAD You are going to read about four (of the many) types of therapy for people with psychological disorders. What do you expect to read about? In other words, what kinds of psychotherapy do you already know about? Discuss your answers in small groups.

B. VOCABULARY PREPARATION Read the sentences below. Guess the meaning of each word in green and write your guess on the line. (When you write your guess, be sure to *use the same part of speech* as that of the green word.) Then check with a dictionary to see if your guesses were close.

1. I had a sudden **impulse** to run out of the room, but I stopped myself.

   Guess: _____

   Dictionary Definition: _____

2. His **motive** for robbing the store was to get money to buy drugs.

   Guess: _____

   Dictionary Definition: _____

3. He hopes to **overcome** his fear of flying so that he can begin to travel again.

   Guess: _____

   Dictionary Definition: _____

4. I know that my fear is **irrational;** I can't explain it logically, but it's real to me.

   Guess: _____

   Dictionary Definition: _____

5. Applying to college can be a lengthy **procedure.** There are many steps to go through.

   Guess: _____

   Dictionary Definition: _____

READING

Read about psychological therapy. As you read, highlight the answer to this question:
• There are four types of therapy described in the reading. What happens in each type of therapy?

Approaches to Psychological Therapy

For a long time, **psychoanalysis** was the only formalized psychotherapy practiced in Western society. It was this type of therapy that gave rise to the classic picture of a bearded Viennese doctor seated behind a patient who is lying on a couch. Psychoanalysis is based on the theories of Sigmund Freud. According to Freud's views, psychological disturbances are due to anxiety about hidden conflicts in the unconscious parts of one's personality. One job of the psychoanalyst, therefore, is to help make the patients aware of the unconscious impulses, desires, and fears that are causing the anxiety. Psychoanalysts believe that if patients can understand their unconscious motives, they have taken the first step toward gaining control over their behavior and freeing themselves of their problems. Such understanding is called **insight.**

Psychoanalysis is a slow procedure. It may take years of fifty-minute sessions before the patient is able to make fundamental changes in his life. Throughout this time, the analyst assists her patient in a complete examination of the unconscious motives behind his behavior. This task begins with the analyst telling the patient to relax and talk about everything that comes into his mind. This method is called **free association.**

As the patient lies on the couch, he may describe his dreams, discuss private thoughts, or recall long-forgotten experiences. The psychoanalyst often says nothing for long periods of time. The psychoanalyst also occasionally makes remarks or asks questions that guide the patient, or she may suggest an unconscious motive or factor that explains something the patient has been talking about, but most of the work is done by the patient himself.

Psychoanalysis has sometimes been criticized for being "all talk and no action." In **behavior therapy,** there is much more emphasis on action. Rather than spending a large amount of time going into the patient's past history or the details of his or her dreams, the behavior therapist concentrates on finding out what is specifically wrong with the patient's current life and takes steps to change it.

The idea behind behavior therapy is that a disturbed person is one who has *learned* to behave in the wrong way. The therapist's job, therefore, is to "reeducate" the patient. The reasons for the patient's undesirable behavior are not important; what is important is to change the behavior. To bring about such changes, the therapist uses certain conditioning techniques first discovered in animal laboratories.

One technique used by behavior therapists is **systematic desensitization.** This method is used to overcome irrational fears and anxieties the patient has learned (Smith, 1990). The goal of desensitization therapy is to encourage people to imagine the feared situation while relaxing. For example, suppose a student is terrified of speaking in front of large groups—that, in fact, her fear makes her unable to speak when called on in class. How would desensitization therapy change this person's behavior?

The therapist might have the student make a list of all the aspects of talking to others that she finds frightening. Perhaps the most frightening aspect is actually standing before an audience, and the least frightening is speaking to a single other person. The client lists her fears, from the most frightening on down. Then the therapist begins teaching the patient to relax. The client tries to imagine as clearly as possible the least disturbing scene on her list. As she thinks about speaking to a single stranger, the student may feel a mild anxiety. But because the therapist has taught her how to relax, the patient learns to think about the

45 experience without being afraid. The therapist attempts to replace anxiety with its opposite, relaxation. The procedure is followed step-by-step through the list of anxiety-arousing events.

In the forms of therapy described thus far, the troubled person is usually alone with the therapist. In **group therapy,** however, he is in the company of others. There are several advantages to this situation. Group therapy gives the troubled person practical experience
50 with one of his biggest problems—getting along with other people. A person in group therapy also has a chance to see how other people are struggling with problems similar to his own, and he discovers what other people think of him. He, in turn, can express what he thinks of them, and in this exchange he discovers where he is mistaken in his views of himself and of other people and where he is correct (Drum, 1990).

55 Another advantage to group therapy is the fact that one therapist can help a large number of people. Most group therapy sessions are led by a trained therapist who makes suggestions, clarifies points, and keeps activities from getting out of control. In this way, her training and experience are used to help as many as 20 people at once, although 8–10 is a more comfortable number.

60 Therapists often suggest, after talking to a patient, that the entire family should work at group therapy. This method is particularly useful because the members of the group are all people of great importance in one another's lives. In family therapy, it is possible to work on the complicated relationships that have led one or more members in the family to experience emotional suffering.

65 An increasing number of **self-help groups** have emerged in recent years. These voluntary groups, composed of people who share a particular problem, are often conducted without a professional therapist. During regularly scheduled meetings, members of the group come together to discuss their difficulties and to provide support and possible solutions. Self-help groups have been formed to deal with problems ranging from
70 alcoholism, overeating, and drug addiction, to child abuse, widowhood, single parenting, adjusting to cancer, and gambling. The best known self-help group is Alcoholics Anonymous (AA), which was founded in 1935. Far more people find treatment for their drinking problems through AA than in psychotherapy or treatment centers.

The various "talking" and "learning" therapies described so far have been aimed
75 primarily at patients who are still generally capable of functioning within society. But what of those people who are not capable of clear thinking or who are dangerous to themselves or others? Antipsychotic drugs are used in the treatment of schizophrenia. The most popular of these medicines have been the phenothiazines—including Thorazine and Stelazine. Patients with schizophrenia who take these medications improve in a number of
80 ways: they become less withdrawn, become less confused, have fewer auditory hallucinations, and are less irritable. Although the patient who takes antipsychotic drugs is often improved enough to leave the hospital, he or she may have trouble adjusting to the outside world. Many patients now face the "revolving door" syndrome of going to a mental hospital, being released, returning to the hospital, being released again, and so on.
85 Phenothiazines also have a number of unpleasant side effects, including a dry mouth, blurred vision, sleepiness, and muscle disorders. Another class of drugs, called antidepressants, relieve depression. Interestingly, they do not affect the mood of nondepressed people. It is almost as if these medicines supply a chemical that some depressed people don't naturally have. Some of the antidepressants have severe side effects.

Source: *Understanding Psychology* (Kasschau)

AFTER READING

 A. CHECK YOUR UNDERSTANDING Look back at your highlighted information that explains each kind of therapy. (For some therapies you've probably marked a lot. For others you haven't marked as much.) Compare your markings with a partner's markings. Do you agree about what is important?

Reading Strategy

Finding an Implied Main Idea

Textbook authors don't always state the main idea of a paragraph or section in a clear topic sentence. As the reader, you often need to **infer** this main idea. It is the sum of the details. One way to do this is to highlight the important details and then decide what they have in common.

B. FINDING AN IMPLIED MAIN IDEA The last paragraph of the reading does not have a clear topic sentence. To understand the main idea of this section, discuss these questions with a partner.

1. What are the two topics of the last paragraph?

2. What do these two topics have in common?

3. What does the author say about each of these topics?

4. Write one sentence that includes both topics. Then compare your sentence with that of other students. Your sentences should be similar.

C. MAKING INFERENCES The author clearly states some information directly and **implies** (suggests) other ideas. Answer these questions with a partner.

1. What do you think the author believes about psychoanalysis?

2. Which therapy might be the most expensive? Which might be the least expensive? Explain your answers.

D. MAKING CONNECTIONS In Part 2, you learned about some specific psychological disorders. In Part 3, you learned about various types of therapy. Write the therapy that the author of the reading in Part 3 (179–180) might suggest for each situation.

1. a phobia _____

2. schizophrenia _____

3. alcoholism _____

4. depression _____

E. WORD JOURNAL Go back to the readings in this chapter. Which words are important for you to remember? Put them in your Word Journal.

Critical Thinking Strategy

Using a T-Chart to Analyze Advantages and Disadvantages

A textbook reading frequently explores advantages and disadvantages (good and bad points) of a situation. Finding advantages and disadvantages and highlighting them is a good idea, but the next step—especially when studying for an exam—is to put them in a graphic organizer. This makes them easier to learn because you are actively working with them.

You've used a number of graphic organizers in this book so far. Another specific type of organizer is a **T-chart**. It's called a "T-chart" because of its shape. It is a good tool for organizing advantages and disadvantages. Usually in a T-chart, you put advantages in the left column and disadvantages in the right column.

F. USING A T-CHART TO ANALYZE ADVANTAGES AND DISADVANTAGES Go back to the reading on pages 179–180 and highlight the advantages and disadvantages of each therapy. Some of the advantages and disadvantages are just implied, so they might be harder to find than those that are stated. Then fill in the chart below.

	Advantages	Disadvantages
Psychoanalysis		
Behavior Therapy		
Group Therapy		

 G. DISCUSSION In small groups, discuss this question:
• If you needed help, which type of therapy would you feel most comfortable with? Why?

H. RESPONSE WRITING Choose one of the following questions to answer:
• What is one psychological disorder that interests you? Describe it.
• Do you know anyone who has a psychological disorder? Is this person receiving help?
• In another culture you know, are people generally open to psychological therapy, or do people often deny that they have a problem?

Write about your topic for 10 minutes. Don't worry about grammar and don't use a dictionary.

PART ④ THE MECHANICS OF WRITING

In Part 4, you will practice using the passive voice, relative clauses, and correct sentence structure to express advantages and disadvantages. You will need this grammar in Part 5 to write a paragraph about one method of psychological therapy.

Using the Passive Voice

Writers can choose to use active or passive voice in their writing. In the active voice, the subject of the sentence does the action expressed by the verb. The focus is on the subject and the verb. Writers often use the passive voice to emphasize the person or thing receiving the action.

Example: Psychiatrists **interviewed** the man from the Ozarks. (active voice)
The man from the Ozarks **was interviewed** by psychiatrists. (passive voice)

We use the passive voice in this way (with *by* or another preposition) to emphasize the object (from the active voice) and the verb. In the example above, we use the passive voice if it is more important to know *whom* the psychiatrists interviewed than *who* interviewed the man.

As you learned in Chapter 2, we don't use the *by* phrase at all if the subject (from the active voice) is *obvious, unnecessary,* or *unknown.*

Examples: The man **was arrested**. (It's obvious that he was arrested by the police.)

Ken **was hospitalized** for mental illness. (It's unnecessary to say that he was hospitalized by psychiatrists.)

If Ken had stayed home, he **would have been considered** to be perfectly normal. (We don't know who would have considered him normal–probably people in general in his hometown.)

The passive voice consists of the *be* verb and the past participle of another verb. The *be* verb can be in any tense except present perfect continuous or past perfect continuous, or it can have a modal.

is done	will be done
was done	might be done
has been done	should be done
is being done	would have been done

A. USING THE PASSIVE VOICE Change these active voice sentences to the passive voice. Use the same tense as in the active voice. In some cases, you won't need a *by* phrase.

1. Psychiatrists classify phobias as simple phobias, social phobias, and agoraphobia.

_____

_____

2. We find just four disorders in all cultures of the world.

_____

_____

3. According to traditional beliefs, either demons or gods possessed that person.

_____

_____

4. Cultural factors may influence the specific symptoms of the disorder.

_____

_____

5. People have criticized psychoanalysis for being "all talk and no action."

_____

_____

6. A trained therapist leads group therapy sessions.

_____

_____

7. People have formed self-help groups to deal with problems such as alcoholism.

_____

_____

8. A violent outburst characterizes "amok," a behavior that we find in Malaysia. (**Note:** Change both clauses.)

_____

_____

Writing Definitions with Adjective Clauses

As you learned in Chapter 1, a definition often includes an adjective clause.

Examples: A manic-depressive is a person **who suffers from bipolar disorder**.
Schizophrenia is a serious disorder **in which people lose touch with reality and have hallucinations**.

B. WRITING DEFINITIONS WITH ADJECTIVE CLAUSES   Define the words or expressions below in complete sentences. Use adjective clauses beginning with *who* or *in which*. Look back at the readings in the chapter if necessary.

1. anorexia nervosa

_____

_____

2. a schizophrenic

_____

_____

3. *amok*

_____

_____

4. *marabout*

_____

_____

5. a psychologist

_____

_____

6. panic disorder

_____

_____

Writing about Advantages and Disadvantages

When you write about advantages and disadvantages or drawbacks, it helps to know the following structures.

| *a(n)* *one* *another* | *advantage* *disadvantage* *drawback* | *of* *to* | noun noun phrase + verb *be* gerund | noun noun phrase *(the fact) that* + clause |

Examples: **One advantage to** psychoanalysis **is that** people can become aware of the causes of their disorder.

A disadvantage of going through psychoanalysis **is the fact that** it can take many years of sessions.

Another drawback is the expense.

C. WRITING ABOUT ADVANTAGES AND DISADVANTAGES Choose two topics from the list below. On a separate piece of paper, write three sentences about the advantages and/or disadvantages of each topic.

- a new car
- marriage
- learning a new language
- watching TV
- living in another country
- beginning college in middle age
- having a phobia (hydrophobia, acrophobia, agoraphobia, etc.)

Using Adverbial Conjunctions

In Chapter 2 (page 56), you learned how to use adverbial conjunctions. Here is a brief review of two groups of these transitional words that are common in academic writing.

in addition
moreover
} *and*

however
on the other hand
} *but*

Examples: One advantage to psychoanalysis is that people can become aware of the causes of their disorder. **However,** a disadvantage of going through analysis is the fact that it can take many years of sessions; **in addition,** an implicit drawback is the expense.

Adverbial conjunctions often begin a sentence or independent clause. There is a period or semicolon before the adverbial conjunction. There is a comma after it.

D. SENTENCE COMBINING: ADVERBIAL CONJUNCTIONS Combine each pair of sentences. Use *in addition, moreover, however,* or *on the other hand.*

1. A person who hears voices of the deceased may be considered to be disturbed. In Native American Plains culture, this isn't seen as a disturbance at all.

   _____

   _____

2. People who are agoraphobic usually stop going to movies or crowded stores. Some will not leave their homes at all.

   _____

   _____

3. People with bipolar disorder suffer from deep depression. They also experience intense happiness and have great energy.

   _____

   _____

4. All of us are sometimes depressed, and there is nothing abnormal about this. In some people, the depression is intense and possibly dangerous.

   _____

   _____

E. REVIEW: FINDING ERRORS In the paragraph below, there are at least five errors. These are errors with the passive voice, one adjective clause, two structures for writing about advantages and disadvantages, and an adverbial conjunction of contradiction. Find and correct them.

According to Richard A. Kasschau in *Understanding Psychology,* psychotherapy based on the theories of Sigmund Freud. Freud believed that psychological problems are the result of conflicts in a person's unconscious. The psychoanalyst's task is to guide the patient through perhaps several years of sessions which the patient explores the unconscious motives for her behavior and becomes aware of the causes of her anxiety. One advantage on psychotherapy is that the patient can gain insight, however, a clear disadvantage is the lengthy process. Another implied drawback is the process takes so many years, so it is most certainly expensive.

PART ⑤ ACADEMIC WRITING

WRITING ASSIGNMENT

In Part 5, you will write a paragraph about one approach to therapy. In the first few sentences, summarize the approach. Then in the rest of the paragraph, present the advantages and/or disadvantages to the approach.

STEP A. CHOOSING A TOPIC Choose one of the following approaches to therapy:

- behavior therapy
- group therapy
- drug therapy

Writing Strategy

Paraphrasing and Citing Your Sources

One of the most common types of writing in college is summary. In order to write a good summary, you need to be able to **paraphrase** and **cite your sources**.

Paraphrasing
When you write a paraphrase, you restate information from a reading by using different words. When paraphrasing, you need to be sure you don't change the author's meaning.

When you write a paraphrase:

<u>**Do**</u>
- change words to their synonyms
- change passive to active
- change active to passive
- use different conjunctions with the same meaning
- change sentence structure
- cite your source

<u>**Do Not**</u>
- use quotation marks
- include your own opinion
- change words that have no synonyms
- change specialized or technical vocabulary

Citing Sources
When you use the words or ideas of another person in a paragraph or essay, you *must* cite your source (give credit to that person and say where you found the information). If you don't cite your source, you are **plagiarizing**—i.e., stealing ideas. Here are some ways to cite your source in your paragraph.

Examples: According to Tim Howe in *Health*, . . .

In *Health*, Tim Howe tells us that . . .

Meghan Anderson, in her book *New Horizons in Health*, points out that . . .

In her article, "Depression and Medication" in *Psychology Today*, Julia Pitner states that . . .

Combining Sentences in Paraphrasing

In paraphrasing, you might also combine several short sentences into one—again, without changing the author's meaning. Usually, only the author's last name (surname) is given.

Here is one way to paraphrase the following two sentences, but there are certainly other possible ways.

Example: **Original:** "No human can go through life without being depressed. For people with major depressive disorder, the bouts of depression are extended and interfere with their ability to function in daily life" (Howe, *Health*).

Paraphrase: As Howe points out in *Health*, all humans are depressed from time to time; however, people with major depressive disorder suffer from long periods of depression that hamper their efforts to go about everyday activities.

PARAPHRASING AND CITING YOUR SOURCES Paraphrase the sentences below. Be sure to cite your source. (All of these sentences were written by Richard A. Kasschau in a book called *Understanding Psychology*.)

1. It is often difficult to draw a line between normal and abnormal behavior.

_____

_____

2. The fact that it is difficult to define abnormality does not mean that no such thing exists.

_____

_____

3. We should be very cautious about judging a person to be "mentally ill" just because he or she acts in a way that we cannot understand.

_____

_____

4. People with anxiety-based disorders are deeply anxious and seem unable to free themselves of worries and fears.

_____

_____

5. Their emotions hamper their ability to function effectively. In extreme cases, a mood may cause individuals to lose touch with reality or seriously threaten their health or lives.

_____

_____

Writing Strategy

Writing a Summary Paragraph

When you write a **summary**, you use all of the same techniques that you use in paraphrasing, but a summary is *shorter*. In a summary, include only the main idea(s) and most important details. You might summarize one paragraph in a single sentence; or you might summarize a whole book in a few pages. You will often have to summarize in academic writing.

In writing a summary, you should remember several points:
• Understand the material well before writing your summary.
• Use your own words; e.g., use synonyms, different word forms, different grammatical structures, and different transition words.
• Don't add your own opinion.
• Cite your source (author and title) in the first sentence of the summary.

It is often a great temptation to copy phrases from the original. To avoid the temptation of copying, try these steps:

• Make sure that you read the material several times and understand it very well before beginning your summary.
• Turn the original material upside down or put it away. Do not look at the original as you write your summary.

Example: Here is a summary of the 3 paragraphs (lines 15–38) on page 173 of this chapter:

> In *Understanding Psychology,* Richard A. Kasschau points out that there are three ways to define a person as psychologically abnormal. One is to say that anyone who is different from most other people is abnormal. Another is that an abnormal person cannot get along in everyday life. The third implies that an abnormal person is not psychologically healthy or functioning at some ideal level. However, Kasschau cautions that we ought to be careful before we label someone as "mentally ill."

 Analysis: Compare this summary with the original paragraphs. Answer these questions.

1. What is included in the first sentence of the summary?

2. The summary gives three ways to define abnormal. For each one, find the lines in the reading on page 173 that are paraphrased.

3. How is the language in the summary different from the source?

WRITING A SUMMARY PARAGRAPH Summarize the paragraph about anorexia nervosa on page 167 (lines 44–60). Then compare your summary with a partner's summary.

STEP B. ORGANIZING INFORMATION

1. Look over the main ideas that you marked on pages 179–180 about the approaches to therapy. Make sure that you have a good understanding of the approach that you chose. Take brief notes. Then close your book and write a short summary of the approach you chose.

2. Look over the advantages and disadvantages to your approach on your chart on page 182. Is there one approach for which you have more information than the others? Your topic should be the approach for which you have the clearest summary and several clear advantages (and/or disadvantages).

STEP C. WRITING THE PARAGRAPH In your paragraph, summarize the approach to therapy that you've chosen and present the advantages and/or disadvantages to this approach. Cite the source in the first sentence. Write complete sentences; be sure to use the structures on page 186. As an example, here is a summary of psychoanalysis from page 179, including advantages and disadvantages.

Example:

According to Richard A. Kasschau in *Understanding Psychology,* psychoanalysis is based on the theories of Sigmund Freud. Freud believed that psychological problems are the result of conflicts in a person's unconscious. The psychoanalyst's task is to guide the patient through perhaps several years of sessions in which the patient explores the unconscious motives for her behavior and becomes aware of the causes of her anxiety. One advantage of psychotherapy is that the patient can gain insight. However, a clear disadvantage is the lengthy process. Another implied drawback is that because the process takes so many years, it is most certainly expensive.

STEP D. EDITING Read your paragraph and answer these questions.

1. Is the paragraph form correct (indentation, margins)?

2. Is the source cited in the first sentence?

3. Is the summary in different words from the original?

4. Was opinion avoided?

5. Are the advantages (or disadvantages) presented with the correct grammatical structures?

6. Are transition words of addition or contradiction used correctly?

7. If the passive voice is used, is it used correctly?

STEP E. REWRITING Write your paragraph again. This time, try to write it with no mistakes.

UNIT ③ VOCABULARY WORKSHOP

Review vocabulary that you learned in Chapters 5 and 6.

A. MATCHING Match the words to the definitions. Write the correct letters on the lines.

<u>Words</u>   <u>Definitions</u>

_____ **1.** chaotic   **a.** attract

_____ **2.** draw   **b.** including an opinion

_____ **3.** ill will   **c.** high point

_____ **4.** key   **d.** very important

_____ **5.** likelihood   **e.** fear, anger, or hatred

_____ **6.** objective   **f.** probability

_____ **7.** peak   **g.** including facts but no opinion

_____ **8.** plausible   **h.** in a state of confusion

_____ **9.** spell   **i.** reasonable; possible

_____ **10.** subjective   **j.** magic words

B. TRUE OR FALSE? Which statements are true? Which are false? Write T for *True* or F for *False* on the lines.

_____ **1. Colleagues** are students in their first year of college.

_____ **2. Dizziness** is a feeling that the room is turning around you very fast.

_____ **3.** A person with **amnesia** has lost his or her memory.

_____ **4.** People usually enjoy **nightmares**.

_____ **5.** When a person **preaches**, the topic is usually religion.

_____ **6.** When you have an **impulse** to do something, you've been planning for a long time to do it.

_____ **7.** A **guide** can help you if you don't want to get lost.

_____ **8.** A sense of **doom** is a pleasant feeling that everything will be good in the future.

C. WORDS IN PHRASES: PREPOSITIONS In this activity, fill in the blanks with the correct prepositions that belong in the phrases. To check your answers, turn back to page 146.

The Senoi people of Malaysia are **famous** _____ their art of dream
                                                        1
interpretation, which they practiced until recently. Traditionally, they used their dreams to control their

waking life. Each day, adults used to **meet** _____ **each other** to discuss their
                                                        2
dreams _____ **order to** solve personal and community problems.
                3

_____ **breakfast** every day, children told their dreams to older family members
        4
and learned dream interpretation in the discussion and analysis that followed. Children learned to use

their dreams creatively and **change feelings of ill will**—fear, anger, or hatred—

_____ feelings of good will. For example, if a child had a nightmare about
            5
falling, his elders told him that it was a wonderful dream; it was the quickest way to contact the spirit

world, and there was nothing to **be afraid** _____. In his next falling dream, he
                                                        6
should relax and see where the dream might take him. If a child dreamed that she was attacking

someone, she needed to **apologize** _____ **that person** and share something
                                                        7
good with him. The goal was for dreamers to **gain control** _____ **their dream**
                                                        8
world and then the waking world.

D. VOCABULARY EXPANSION Write the different parts of speech for the words in the chart. Use a dictionary to fill in these blanks.

	Verb	Noun	Adjective
1.			sufficient
2.		sacrifice	
3.	tolerate		
4.			obsessed
5.		vision	
6.	signify		
7.		motive	

E. THE ACADEMIC WORD LIST In the box below are some of the most common academic words in English. Fill in the blanks with words from this box. When you finish, check your answers in the reading on page 179. For more words, see the Academic Word List on pages 259–262.

assists	conflicts	insight	periods	relax
aware	factor	method	procedure	task
classic	fundamental	motives	psychological	theories

For a long time, psychoanalysis was the only formalized psychotherapy practiced in Western society. It was this type of therapy that gave rise to the _____ picture of a

1

bearded Viennese doctor seated behind a patient who is lying on a couch. Psychoanalysis is based

on the _____ of Sigmund Freud. According to Freud's views,

2

_____ disturbances are due to anxiety about hidden

3

_____ in the unconscious parts of one's personality. One job of the

4

psychoanalyst, therefore, is to help make the patients _____ of the

5

unconscious impulses, desires, and fears that are causing the anxiety. Psychoanalysts believe that if

patients can understand their unconscious _____, they have taken the first

6

step toward gaining control over their behavior and freeing themselves of their problems. Such

understanding is called _____.

7

Psychoanalysis is a slow _____. It may take years of fifty-minute

8

sessions several times a week before the patient is able to make _____ changes

9

in his life. Throughout this time, the analyst _____ her patient in a complete

10

examination of the unconscious motives behind his behavior. This _____

11

begins with the analyst telling the patient to _____ and talk about everything

12

that comes into his mind. This _____ is called free association.

13

As the patient lies on the couch, he may describe his dreams, discuss private thoughts, or recall long-forgotten experiences. The psychoanalyst often says nothing for long

_____ of time. The psychoanalyst also occasionally makes remarks or
                14

asks questions that guide the patient, or she may suggest an unconscious motive or

_____ that explains something the patient has been talking about, but
                15

most of the work is done by the patient himself.

UNIT 4

HEALTH

Chapter 7
Medicine and Drugs: Addictive Substances

Chapter 8
The Mind-Body Relationship

CHAPTER 7

Medicine and Drugs:
Addictive Substances

Discuss these questions:
- Look at the picture. What do you think the people are saying to the man?
- What should you do if your friend has an embarrassing personal problem?
- What are the signs that someone has a problem with addiction?

PART ① INTRODUCTION Consequences of Addiction

BEFORE READING

What problems might this baby have? What problems might the baby face in the future?

For growing numbers of women and children in Afghanistan, the world's largest producer of **opium**, the recent war has lasting consequences.

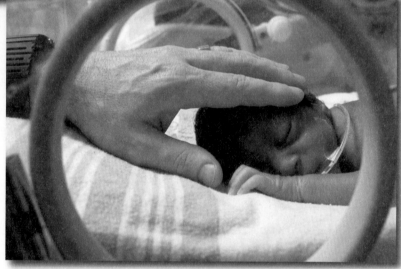

THINKING AHEAD Discuss these questions with a partner.

1. If a pregnant woman is addicted to drugs or alcohol, what might happen to her unborn baby?

2. In your culture, who takes care of the baby of a mother who cannot take care of her child because of her addiction?

3. In your culture, do many people **adopt** a child—in other words, take someone else's child into their home and legally become the child's parents?

4. How might war cause an increase in drug addiction?

READING

Read about addiction. As you read, think about this question:
• What are some problems of children born to mothers who used drugs or drank alcohol during pregnancy?

Consequences of Addiction

Coping with the Legacy of War

Halima first smoked opium to dull the nightmares after her husband's violent death. He was shot in front of her as they tried to flee fighting in Kabul, leaving her a widow at the age of 27 with three young children and a joyless future to look forward to.

"I don't know who fired the shot," she said. "But I couldn't stop playing back my memories of him bleeding to death in the street and nobody to help." In the life of an Afghan widow there was little distraction until a neighbor introduced her to a brown paste.

Soon she needed to smoke opium in the morning, at lunchtime, and at night. "It gives me comfort and helps me forget my sorrows," she said. "It is a shameful thing. If my brother-in-law found out, he would throw me out of his house."

Taking opiates is *haram,* or forbidden, in Islam. Although Afghanistan is the largest grower of poppies and the leading supplier of opium, heroin, and morphine, its use remained mostly medicinal even as the international drug trade moved in during the 1980s, but disapproval nearly always prevented abuse at home.

Finally, however, the opium trade which caused such misery in the West has rebounded in Afghanistan. Kabul now has an estimated 60,000 drug addicts, [and] Afghan women are particularly at risk. The Nejaf Centre knows of around 2,000 female drug abusers and believes there are far more. Most are too ashamed to seek treatment, hiding their habit from their husbands and families. Nearly all have harrowing stories of loss from the war. Most are widows, some are first wives who have suffered the humiliation of their husband taking a second bride. Babies are being born addicted and children working in the carpet trade are allegedly fed opium to numb them through long hours of work; they too become addicts.

Source: "Afghan Women Use Drugs to Cope with Legacy of War" (Meo)

My Son's Devotion Was Total

When I adopted Abel in 1971, I was informed that his birth mother was alcoholic, but at the time not even the medical community was aware of the potential consequences when a woman drank—even moderately—during pregnancy. Now, sadly, I know better. Fetal alcohol syndrome [FAS] could be manifested in a variety of symptoms ranging from the physical (heart, hearing and vision problems, neurological impairments[1], deformation of the brain) to learning deficits[2] affecting abstract thinking and consistent with low I.Q. My son, to one degree or another, had them all.

[1]**neurological impairments:** damage to the brain or nerves
[2]**learning deficits:** not having the same learning abilities as other people of the same age

There is no real cure for the more than 10,000 FAS-afflicted babies born annually in the United States. A majority are Caucasian, but in some Native-American groups, like the one from which I adopted Abel, nearly 25 percent of all infants show some degree of damage from maternal alcohol use.

35   Especially during Abel's childhood, before the full magnitude of his learning block was undeniable, I indulged in the persistent fantasy of his brain as a kind of messy room. If I could somehow get inside his head, straighten up the clutter, turn on the lights, suddenly he would become normal. But the door stayed firmly locked. Finally I gave up, let Abel rest. For me, it was defeat. For him, I'm sure it was a great relief.

Source: "My Son's Devotion Was Total" (Dorris)

AFTER READING

A. CHECK YOUR UNDERSTANDING According to these two articles, how are children affected by their mothers' use of addictive substances? With a partner, write your answers to these questions.

1. In what two ways are Afghan babies and children affected?

_____

2. What are symptoms of children whose mothers drank alcohol during pregnancy?

_____

_____

_____

Reading Strategy

Understanding Metaphors

A metaphor is a phrase that describes one thing by comparing it to something else.

Examples: Max's **round moon face** shone with pleasure.
Liana's **heart, a cold tomb,** would not open for anyone.

B. UNDERSTANDING METAPHORS Highlight the metaphor that Michael Dorris uses in the reading about his son Abel.

C. EXTENSION In small groups, discuss the following question.
• What are some problems for a society that has many babies born to addicted mothers?

PART ② GENERAL INTEREST READING
Drug Use and Abuse Worldwide

BEFORE READING

A. THINKING AHEAD In small groups, discuss your answers to these questions.

1. The next reading discusses several addictive **psychoactive** substances (alcohol, tobacco, and other drugs). What other drugs might these be? Make a list.

2. In what ways can **illicit** (illegal) drugs be **consumed** or **ingested** (taken into the body)? Which drugs are smoked? Which are **injected** (with a needle)?

3. Do you think that certain addictive substances are used more in some countries than in others? Explain your answer.

4. In what countries is **abstinence** (not drinking any alcohol at all) probably important? Which groups of people within a country are abstinent?

B. VOCABULARY PREPARATION Read the sentences below. What can you guess about the words in green? Match the definitions in the box with the words in green. Write the correct letters on the lines.

a. acts of taking (by the police or the government)	f. fact or event in society
b. become steady (less changing)	g. general existence
c. considering	h. serious
d. cooking	i. smelled
e. disease that many people have	j. too unimportant to pay attention to

_____ 1. **Given** the economic rewards of selling drugs, it is not surprising that they are available almost all over the world.

_____ 2. The police have made three **seizures** of illicit drugs and drug money this month.

_____ 3. People take classes or watch cooking shows on TV to learn about new **culinary** ideas.

_____ 4. Health officials are trying to prevent the **epidemic** from spreading to more areas.

_____ 5. The use of cocaine had been rising and falling, but now it seems to have **stabilized**.

_____ 6. The health risks of injecting heroin are **substantial**.

_____ **7.** The **prevalence** of certain diseases is high among people who inject drugs.

_____ **8.** Drug injection in many countries is a relatively new **phenomenon**.

_____ **9.** The cat carefully **sniffed** at the food. It smelled good, so she quickly ate it.

_____ **10.** Problems with drinking used to be **negligible**, but now there are some serious problems related to alcohol.

C. MAKING PREDICTIONS The next reading discusses several addictive substances and their use in different countries. In small groups, discuss how the reading might answer the following questions.

1. Is the use of drugs and alcohol increasing or decreasing in most countries?

2. How does the use of illicit drugs contribute to the **transmission** of disease from one person to another?

3. What illicit drugs are used by **adolescents** (teenagers)?

4. What is the most widely used psychoactive substance? What is the second most widely used one?

READING

Read about drug use around the world. As you read, look for the answers to the questions that you just discussed in Activity C.

Drug Use and Abuse Worldwide

Although alcohol, tobacco, and other drugs differ in many important respects, including their legal status, they share important characteristics: they are all
5 psychoactive substances with the potential for creating dependency, and they can cause very significant public health problems and widespread social harms.

Global Spread of Substance Abuse

Many social, economic, and political
10 factors have contributed to the global spread of alcohol and other drugs. In the nineteenth century, drugs tended to only be available where they were produced, or very close to the source of production.
15 However, the growth of transportation, tourism, and communications has made it possible to transport goods and people quickly to any part of the world. Drugs, too, are being transported to distant places.
20 Given the economic rewards of producing and transporting drugs, it is not surprising that they are available almost all over the world. It has been estimated that the illegal market for drugs is worth between US $100
25 billion and US $500 billion world-wide (Reuters, 1996). There is enough evidence to indicate certain trends in the globalization of drug use and the cyclical nature of drug epidemics.

Cannabis

30   Globally, cannabis [marijuana and hashish] is the most widespread and commonly used illicit drug. The United Nations Office on Drugs and Crime estimated the number of cannabis users

35 worldwide to be 163 million people (UNODC, 2003).

In the United States, approximately one-third of the population over the age of 15 have tried cannabis and 9.3% have used 40 the drug in the previous 12 months (UNODC, 2003). Similarly high rates of use amongst the general population are reported in Canada.

In most countries, rates of cannabis use 45 are generally higher in younger adults, and higher amongst males than females. In western European countries, data suggest that rates of cannabis use are lower than those reported in the United States and 50 Canada.

In some northern and sub-Saharan African countries (e.g. Egypt, Kenya, Morocco, Nigeria, and Tanzania), there is a long tradition of cannabis use for culinary, 55 medicinal, and ceremonial purposes.

Cocaine and Crack

Cocaine and "crack" cocaine[1] provide an example of both the globalization of substance use and the cyclical nature of drug epidemics. Traditionally, coca leaves 60 have been chewed by people in the Andean countries of South America for thousands of years. The main alkaloid of the coca leaf, cocaine, was isolated relatively recently, in about 1860. Cocaine was then 65 used in patent medicines, beverages, and "tonics" in developed countries in Europe, North America, and in Australia until the early 1900s. Laws restricting cocaine saw a decrease in consumption in these countries 70 until the 1960s. From that time, cocaine use became popular among certain groups of young people in some developed countries and in the producer countries of South America. Cocaine became widely available 75 in North America in the 1970s and Europe in the 1980s. Cocaine use is also gaining in popularity in some developing countries outside of the producer countries and in Central and Eastern Europe. In 2001, 56%

80 of countries surveyed showed an increase in rates of cocaine consumption.

The United States remains by far the world's largest single market for cocaine and crack. However, use of the drug has 85 declined in the U.S. even as it increased in the rest of the world. After reaching a peak in the 1980s, cocaine use in the United States dropped dramatically in the final years of the twentieth century, falling by 90 60% from 1985 to 2001. The rate of decrease slowed throughout the 1990s, and by the turn of the century, cocaine use in the U.S. had stabilised at a roughly constant level. This stabilisation may 95 demonstrate the cyclical nature of drug epidemics. Similar cycles of increase, stabilisation, and decline (sometimes followed by further increases often after a period of many years) have been observed 100 for different drugs in many countries.

Heroin

The available evidence shows that there has been a global decrease in the production of heroin (UNODC, 2003). Throughout the 1990s, worldwide cultivation of heroin has 105 decreased 15%.

Nonetheless, use of heroin is causing widespread health and social problems in many countries. In Europe, heroin injectors who regularly consume large amounts of 110 different drugs face a risk of death which may be 20 or 30 times higher than non-drug users in the same age range (EMCDDA, 1996).

Since heroin is commonly used by 115 injecting, the health risks, including that of HIV and hepatitis transmission, are substantial. The shared use of injection equipment has played a critical role in fuelling a number of local, national, and 120 regional HIV-1 epidemics. HIV-1 prevalence is high in drug-injecting populations in southern Europe, the northeast of the United States, parts of Asia, and parts of South America

[1]"crack" cocaine: cocaine that is smoked in a pipe

125 (Donoghoe and Wodak, 1998; Stimson et al., 1998). In the Russian Federation, HIV infection exploded in the first years of the twenty-first century, with about half the new HIV diagnoses caused by injection drug use.

130 Drug injection in many developing countries is a relatively new phenomenon. Reasons for the spread of injecting are complex and differ from country to country. Certain factors are involved,
135 however, including changes in the availability of drugs and the location of countries in relation to drug production and transportation. Drug injection has become widespread in some countries of
140 southeast Asia where earlier patterns of opium smoking have been replaced first by heroin smoking and then by heroin injection (Stimson et al., 1996). In West Africa, the injection of illicit drugs is a
145 relatively new phenomenon in countries which have no tradition of injection.

Inhalants

The use of inhalants occurs in all regions of the world (Kozel, Sloboda, and De La Rosa, 1995). These substances are
150 often used by children and adolescents, especially street children, many of them homeless. In all parts of the developing world, glue is the substance which is most

Why do street children **inhale** (breathe in) glue? What are the dangers of this?

often inhaled. It is cheap, available, and
155 provides a "rapid high" when children sniff it from the container or from a plastic bag.

Alcohol

Next to tobacco, alcohol is the most widely used and abused substance and is
160 available in all but the most isolated areas of the world or in a few countries with strict religious prohibitions. Although alcohol consumption has recently declined in many developed countries (Smart, 1991,
165 Edwards et al., 1994), its use has been increasing in developing countries (Saxena, 1996). This increase is often occurring in countries with no tradition of alcohol use and few methods of prevention, control,
170 or treatment.

China

- China has a long history of beverage-making dating from the Shang Dynasty (B.C.E. 1600–1110). Problems related to drinking were negligible until the end of the 1970s for cultural, economic, and ethnic reasons.

- From the beginning of the 1980s, patterns of alcohol use changed (and increased) rapidly. However, Chinese tradition emphasizes drinking in social situations, which regulates the amount and frequency of drinking. The Chinese almost always drink while they eat. Because of this, alcohol-related problems are less severe than in some countries, but drinking is on the rise.

- Males have a higher rate of drinking than females.

- Reasons for drinking are social (activities for increasing intimacy), psychological (increasing confidence and decreasing negative feelings), and physical.

India

- Traditionally, abstinence was considered the norm. Brahmins [high caste] were forbidden to drink. Other classes were allowed to drink but only on special occasions (like wars, religious events, and festivals). Alcohol use was not a health or social problem.
- The pattern of drinking has changed from ritualistic and occasional to a part of routine social interaction and entertainment.
- Rates of use range between 23% and 74% among males. The abstinence rate among women is above 97%.
- The basic purpose of drinking alcohol is to get drunk.

Mexico

- Traditionally, fermented beverages were consumed in rituals associated with agriculture, religion, and life cycles.
- Today, alcohol is rarely consumed on a daily basis. It is, rather, linked to special occasions, on which high quantities are often ingested.
- Women drink far less than men. Rates of abstinence are high among women. Education plays an important role: the highest numbers of drinkers are among the less educated.
- Reasons for drinking are occasions such as weekends, paydays, and festivities.

Tobacco

Tobacco continues to be the substance causing the maximum health damage globally. According to WHO estimates, there are around 1.1 thousand million
175 smokers in the world, about one-third of the global population aged 15 years and over. Substantially fewer cigarettes are smoked per day per smoker in developing countries than in developed countries;
180 however, the gap in per adult cigarette consumption is narrowing. Unless effective tobacco control measures take place, daily cigarette consumption in developing countries is expected to increase as
185 economic development results in increased real disposable income.

Tobacco is estimated to have caused around three million deaths per year in the early 1990s, and the death toll is increasing.
190 Unless current trends are reversed, that figure is expected to rise to 10 million deaths per year by the 2020s or the early 2030s (by the time the young smokers of today reach middle and older ages), with 70% of those
195 deaths occurring in developing countries. The chief uncertainty is not whether these deaths will occur, but exactly when.

In which countries do you think people are smoking more? How does this harm people's health? Where are they smoking less?

Sources: "Guide to Drug Abuse Epidemiology" and "Surveys of Drinking Patterns and Problems in Seven Developing Countries," World Health Organization and *World Health*

AFTER READING

A. CHECK YOUR UNDERSTANDING Working in small groups, look back at Activity C, Making Predictions, on page 204 and answer the questions. Were your predictions correct?

B. VOCABULARY CHECK: PHRASES Look back at the reading to find two phrases and the meaning of a third phrase.

1. In the paragraph beginning on line 171, what is a phrase that means "money that people can spend"?

2. In the paragraph beginning on line 187, what is a phrase that means "the number of people who die"?

3. Lines 94–100 explain the sometimes "cyclical nature" of drug epidemics. Fill in this graphic organizer, which depicts this phrase.

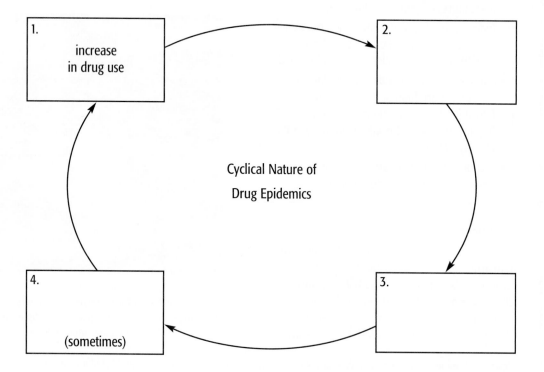

C. FINDING DETAILS: CAUSE AND EFFECT Look back at the reading on pages 204–207 to find causes and effects. Write them in the chart below.

Paragraphs	Causes	Effects
Lines 9–29		It is possible to transport drugs to distant places.
Lines 106–129	the use of heroin	
Lines 130–146		The practice of injection heroin is spreading to many developing countries.
Lines 147–157		Glue is the substance which is most abused by street children.

D. FINDING DETAILS: CHRONOLOGY According to the paragraph beginning on line 130 on page 206, what has been the chronology of heroin injection in some countries of southeast Asia? In other words, what is the history of heroin use there? Fill in this graphic organizer.

heroin injection

Test-Taking Strategy

Finding Sentences with Similar Meaning

In the reading section of some standardized tests, you will need to look in a reading to find sentences that mean almost the same as given sentences. On computerized tests, you will usually highlight the sentences in the reading. To find the correct answers, don't expect to find sentences with the same structure or order. Instead, look for sentences with synonyms.

E. FINDING SENTENCES WITH SIMILAR MEANING For each sentence below, find one or two with a similar meaning in the paragraph lines indicated. Highlight it in the reading on pages 204–207.

1. Widespread use of drugs often goes through cycles. (Paragraph lines 82–100)

2. The serious spread of HIV-1 in various areas is largely due to drug addicts who use each other's needles. (Paragraph lines 114–129)

3. The second most common substance (after cigarettes) is alcohol, which can be found worldwide except for a few countries. (Paragraph lines 158–170)

4. People in wealthy countries smoke much more than people in poor countries do, but this situation is changing. (Paragraph lines 171–186)

F. IN YOUR OWN WORDS: SUMMARIZING For each item below, write the topic of the paragraph(s). Use a noun or noun phrase. Then write the main idea. Use an independent clause.

1. Paragraph lines 9–29 are about _____.

   The author says that _____

   _____

2. Paragraphs lines 106–129 are about _____.

   The author says that _____

   _____

Reading Strategy

Noticing British English

Although British and American English are very similar, there are some differences that probably won't interfere with your understanding of the material. As you read something written in British English, notice these differences, but don't let them worry you.

• Some words are spelled differently (e.g., *center* in American English and *centre* in British English).

• Some nouns (e.g., *family, team, government*) that are singular in American English are plural in British English.

• In both American and British English, 1,000,000 = "one million." However, in American English, 1,000,000,000 is "one billion," but in British English this is "one thousand million."

G. NOTICING BRITISH ENGLISH Look back at the reading on page 204–207 to find these examples of British English.

1. What is the British word for *among*? (lines 40–45)

2. How are the words *stabilized* and *stabilization* spelled in British English? (lines 90–95)

3. Approximately how many smokers are there in the world, according to the reading? How would you say this in American English? (lines 170–175)

H. DISCUSSION In small groups, discuss these questions.

1. What substances do people use (or abuse) in your culture? What reasons can you give for this use (or abuse)?

2. Are there any health problems in your country as a result of drug use?

3. Is there anything that surprises you about the information about China, India, and Mexico in the boxes on pages 206–207? If so, what?

4. If you are *not* from China, India, or Mexico, what information about your country would you give about history, use, gender differences, and reasons for drinking?

PART ③ ACADEMIC READING
Addiction: What Can Be Done About It?

BEFORE READING

👥 **A. THINKING AHEAD** The next reading explains what addiction is and what can be done to help addicts. Before you read the selection, read the box below. Then discuss the questions on page 213 with a partner.

Addiction: The Downward Slide

These steps show the way an addiction to alcohol or other drugs might develop.

Step 1: First use/occasional use
- Takes first drink or uses other drug for the first time
- Likes the way it feels and reduces stress
- Uses the drug in social settings

Step 2: Occasional trouble with drug
- Shows mood swings or personality changes (may happen on the first use)
- Has greater tolerance than others—for example, can outdrink others without seeming drunk
- May cry, get violent, or show high-risk behaviors while drinking and using drugs
- May have blackouts, not remembering what was said or done

Step 3: Regular use of drug
- Finds that tolerance increases—needs more of a drug and may crave it more frequently
- Tries to control drug use but cannot
- Feels guilty after binges, or episodes
- Hangs out with others who drink or use drugs
- Denies problem; gets angry when others suggest a drinking or drug use problem

Step 4: Multiple drug use
- May combine or switch drugs for new and stronger effects or to assure supply
- May become cross-addicted, or hooked on more than one kind of drug

Step 5: Increasing dependency
- Needs drug just to function
- Finds that drug no longer has same effect; needs drug just to stop shaking or feeling sick
- Loses interest in family, friends, school, job, sports—everything but drugs

Step 6: Total dependency
- Suffers major loss because of addiction, such as getting thrown out of school, losing a relationship, causing a car crash, being hospitalized, getting arrested
- Feels physically and emotionally defeated

Source: "Addiction: The Downward Slide" (Merki and Merki)

---

1. Do you think it is possible for people to remain at Step 1 and not move on to the other steps?

2. Can you think of famous people in the news who seem to be at Step 6?

3. In your opinion, what can friends or family of an addict do to prevent this person from "hitting bottom"—reaching Step 6?

4. What is life like for the family of a person at Step 4, 5, or 6?

B. VOCABULARY PREPARATION Read the sentences below. The words and phrases in green are from the next reading. What can you guess about the words and phrases in green? Write your guesses on the lines.

1. When Kim was pregnant, she **craved** strange foods. Once, her husband had to drive to the store at midnight because she had such a strong desire for chocolate ice cream and pickles.

   Guess: _____

2. It's really hard to **cope with** Peter when he's been drinking. I wish he would stay away from alcohol so that we wouldn't have to deal with this problem any longer.

   Guess: _____

3. When Peter's **sober**, he's a wonderful person, but when he's drunk, he changes completely and becomes a kind of monster.

   Guess: _____

4. You can **rely on** Linda to help you. We've depended on her for many years because she's such a responsible person.

   Guess: _____

5. This is **confidential** information, so please don't tell anyone.

   Guess: _____

Compare your answers with a partner's answers.

READING

Read about addiction. As you read, think about these questions:
• What is addiction?
• What are helpful or harmful things that the family of an addict can do?

Addiction: What Can Be Done About It?

An addiction is a physiological or psychological dependence on a substance or activity. One can be addicted to alcohol, drugs, tobacco, gambling—even food. In
5 this passage, we will discuss addiction to alcohol and other drugs. Physiological dependence means that the body has become accustomed to a drug and needs these chemicals just to function. The body
10 of an addict craves these substances. Physiological dependence is determined when a person experiences tolerance and withdrawal. Tolerance means that the body becomes used to the effect of the drug. The
15 body then requires larger doses of the drug to produce the same effect. Withdrawal occurs when the person stops taking a drug on which he or she is physiologically dependent and experiences painful physical
20 symptoms. Psychological dependence means that a person comes to depend on the feeling received from a drug. Psychological dependence often involves denial, in which the addict does not admit
25 or does not realize that he or she is in trouble with alcohol or other drugs. The person believes that he or she can control the use of the drug and is not causing any harm.

Did You Know?

According to *Prevention's Book of Health Facts:*

- About 75% of deaths from lung cancer among women are caused by smoking.

- On average, a cigarette smoker is 10 to 15 times more likely to get lung cancer than a nonsmoker.

Intervention

30 To "wake up" an addicted person from this state of denial, many families rely on a process called intervention. Intervention means interrupting the downward slide before the addict hits bottom. The process
35 begins with meetings of family members and other people important in the life of the addicted person. They usually meet first with a drug and alcohol counselor and someone from a support group such as
40 Alcoholics Anonymous to learn about addiction and discuss how they have been affected by it. Then they have the actual intervention—a surprise meeting with the addict to force this person to see how
45 unmanageable his or her life has become because of the addiction. At this meeting, they present a plan for immediate treatment and let the addict know that it's time to face the consequences of the
50 addiction.

Alcoholism

Alcoholism, or addiction to alcohol, is considered a disease by the American Medical Association (AMA). Since 1987, drug dependence, or drug addiction, has also been considered a disease by the AMA. Both of these diseases are described as **chronic** (happening over a long period), **progressive** (getting worse over time), and potentially **fatal** (possible to die from).

Recovery

Like addiction, recovery—learning to live without alcohol or drugs—is a process that happens over time. The first two steps are (1) to recognize that there is a problem
55 with alcohol or drugs and (2) to make the decision to give them up. The third step is to actually remove these drugs from the body. This process is called detoxification and should take place under medical
60 supervision.

People in recovery describe themselves as "recovering" instead of "recovered." This is because the recovery process is ongoing and lifelong. Alcoholism and drug dependence cannot be cured. They can, however, be prevented from progressing further. And people can begin the recovery process at any point on the downward slide into addiction—even before they suffer major losses.

> ### Did You Know?
>
> Addiction to cocaine is increasing in much of the world. Among those addicted in the U.S., some 200,000 are in drug treatment, 55,000 are homeless, and 1,530,000 were arrested in one recent year.

Most experts in the field of addiction recommend total abstinence for the recovering alcoholic and addict. Total abstinence means not using any mood-altering drugs, including alcohol. Long-term studies show that attempts at controlled drinking and drug use usually fail. Even small amounts of alcohol or other drugs can send an addict back into addiction. Many people in recovery manage to stay drug-free for the rest of their lives. Others may have relapses—periodic returns to drinking and drug use. Yet despite how many times the person relapses, the choice of and chance for recovery are always there.

Treatment Choices

A support group is a group of people who share a common problem and work together to help each other and themselves to cope with and recover from that problem. Regular attendance at such support groups is the most popular form of ongoing treatment for addictions. Support groups such as Alcoholics Anonymous (AA), Narcotics Anonymous, and Cocaine Anonymous have played a major role in helping people to get and stay free of alcohol and drugs. At meetings, which are held frequently all over the world, members provide support and help each other stay sober. Such meetings are confidential; members can remain anonymous because nobody has to give his or her last name. And the meetings are free.

Alcohol and drug treatment centers offer a wide range of services:

- *Detox units* in some hospitals or treatment centers help an addict through detoxification—usually three to seven days. Some people go directly from detox to a support group.

- *Inpatient treatment centers* are facilities where a person stays for a month or more.

- *Outpatient treatment centers* allow a person to live at home during the treatment and spend a few hours each day at the center.

- *Halfway houses* offer housing, counseling, and support meetings for six months to a year to help people learn coping and living skills so that they can return to society.

Codependency

Some people who live with an alcoholic or drug addict become codependent. They are not addicted, but they suffer from a very damaging emotional and social obsession. Codependents try to protect the addict from facing the consequences of the drug problem. They lie for the addict, lend money, make excuses. Such actions, of course, do not help the addict. They just make it possible for him or her to continue in the addiction—and cause a variety of stress-related disorders for the codependent, ranging from depression and eating disorders to high blood pressure.

Source: *Health: A Guide to Wellness* (Merki)

AFTER READING

A. FINDING DETAILS In small groups, discuss these questions.

1. What is addiction?

2. What do codependents do? Do they help an addict?

3. What can the family of an addict do to help him or her stop the downward slide?

4. What are the first two steps that an addict must take to recover from addiction?

B. VOCABULARY CHECK Look back at the reading on pages 214–215. Find words or phrases for the definitions below, and highlight them in the reading. Then write them on the correct lines. Line numbers are in parentheses.

1. a condition in which the body needs chemical drugs just to function (5–10)

   _____

2. a condition in which the body requires larger amounts of a drug to produce the same effect (10–20)

   _____

3. a condition in which a person stops taking a drug and has painful physical symptoms (15–20)

   _____

4. a condition in which a person depends on the feeling that he or she gets from a drug (20–25)

   _____

5. a process of interrupting the downward slide before an addict hits bottom (30–35)

   _____

6. the process of removing drugs from the body (55–60)

   _____

7. periodic returns to drinking or drug use after an addict has quit (80–85)

   _____

C. WORD JOURNAL Go back to the readings in this chapter. Which words are important for you to remember? Put them in your Word Journal.

👥 **D. MAKING CONNECTIONS** In small groups, design a poster and write a short radio commercial to persuade people of the risks of using a psychoactive substance. Target your poster and commercial at a specific group of people. (A sample poster is below.)

Choose one of these substances:
tobacco
alcohol
glue
heroin
crack cocaine
marijuana

Choose one of these groups:
children
pregnant women
teenagers
fathers

Before you begin to write, gather ideas from the readings in Parts 1, 2, and 3. Then consider these questions:

• Why might this group of people be attracted to this substance?
• What arguments might this group of people truly pay attention to?

When you finish, share your group's poster and commercial with the rest of the class.

An Australian poster warns indigenous communities about the risks of alcohol.

E. DISCUSSION In small groups, discuss these questions.

1. There seems to be a lot of drug and alcohol abuse among jazz musicians, rock musicians, and fashion models. What might be some reasons for this? Can you think of other groups of people who have a high rate of substance abuse?

2. In your culture, are there support groups such as the ones in the box?

Alcoholics Anonymous	**Gamblers Anonymous**	**Overeaters Anonymous**
Al Anon Family Groups	**Narcotics Anonymous**	**Smokers Anonymous**

3. What do people in your culture usually do to help a friend or family member who has a problem with addiction?

F. RESPONSE WRITING Choose one of the following questions to answer.

• Should FAS babies be taken away from their mothers? Why or why not?
• What should be the responsibility of the fathers of FAS babies?
• What is one substance that is abused in your country? What is its effect on the society?
• Do you know someone with an addiction? If so, what step (from page 212) is this person at?
• What do you think of groups such as Alcoholics Anonymous?

Write about your topic for 10 minutes. Don't worry about grammar and don't stop writing to use a dictionary.

PART ④ THE MECHANICS OF WRITING

In Part 4, you will practice using the conditional and subordinating conjunctions, and you will learn to identify and avoid sentence fragments. You will need this grammar in Part 5 to write a persuasive paragraph about addiction.

Understanding Subordinating Conjunctions: Review/Extension

In Chapters 3 (page 98), 4 (page 128), and 5 (page 157), you studied subordinating conjunctions of contrast, cause and effect, and time. The list below includes both new conjunctions and those previously learned.

Cause
because
since
as (= because)

Contradiction
although
even though
while (= although)

Condition
if
unless (= if not)

Time
when
while (= when)
as (= while)
before

after
until
whenever (= every time when)
as soon as (= immediately after)

As you've learned, there are two ways to use these conjunctions.

Examples: **Whenever** the child's teacher came near him, he began hurling toys at her.

The child began hurling toys at his teacher **whenever** she came near him.

With subordinating conjunctions of **contradiction,** there is usually a comma before the conjunction when it is in the middle.

Example: To be "one of the crowd," she tried smoking once, **although** she didn't really want to.

A. UNDERSTANDING SUBORDINATING CONJUNCTIONS Often, one word can completely change the meaning of a sentence. What is the difference in meaning between the two sentences in each pair below? Work with a partner to figure this out.

1. **A.** I liked the fruit punch because it didn't have alcohol in it.
   B. I liked the fruit punch, although it didn't have alcohol in it.

2. **A.** He felt sick whenever he had a drink.
   B. He felt sick until he had a drink.

3. **A.** She drank heavily until she found out she was pregnant.
   B. She drank heavily when she found out she was pregnant.

B. SENTENCE COMBINING: SUBORDINATING CONJUNCTIONS Choose a logical subordinating conjunction for each item. Then combine the pairs of sentences in two ways each.

1. We'll ask Kristin to help us with this. She's both knowledgeable and dependable.

   A. _____

   _____

   B. _____

   _____

2. Tom knew a good deal about the danger of addiction. He began to use cocaine. (**Note:** *a good deal* means a lot.)

   A. _____

   _____

   B. _____

   _____

3. Sarah's grades in college suddenly went down. She began taking drugs.

   A. _____

   _____

   B. _____

   _____

4. David adopted the baby. He was informed that the birth mother was alcoholic.

   A. _____

   _____

   B. _____

   _____

5. The baby's mother had smoked crack cocaine. He was born.

   A. _____

   _____

   B. _____

   _____

Identifying and Repairing Fragments

A common mistake in written (but not spoken) English is a fragment. A fragment looks like a complete sentence because it begins with a capital letter and ends with a period, but it is not complete. It is missing something.

Example: **INCORRECT:** He's addicted to drugs. For example, cocaine and heroin.
(The second "sentence" here is not really a sentence. It's a fragment because there is no subject or verb.)

CORRECT: He's addicted to drugs. For example, he takes cocaine and heroin.

Perhaps the most common problem with fragments occurs because of the misuse of a subordinating conjunction. Remember that there must be two clauses in a sentence with a subordinating conjunction.

Example: **INCORRECT:** He can't hold a job. Because he has a problem with drugs.
(The second "sentence" is a fragment because it's missing a main clause.)

CORRECT: He can't hold a job because he has a problem with drugs.
Because he has a problem with drugs, he can't hold a job.

C. IDENTIFYING AND REPAIRING FRAGMENTS Decide which "sentences" that follow are actually fragments. Then correct them. Do not change sentences that are already correct.

1. Arthur was three days old. When his aunt found him.

2. Because of trauma due to the war, opium use in Afghanistan is increasing.

3. He wouldn't let anyone closer than eight feet. Before he began hurling toys at them.

4. Street children in many countries use psychoactive substances. Such as glue or paint thinner.

5. Children sometimes "graduate" from glue to other psychoactive substances. For example, they may later add marijuana, alcohol, cigarettes, or cocaine.

6. Indigenous people are those who were already living on their lands. When settlers came from other countries.

7. In religious ceremonies, Native Americans traditionally used hallucinogens. For example, peyote and certain types of mushrooms that helped them to have visions.

8. Because indigenous people used to have very strict laws and taboos about psychoactive substances. There wasn't such a problem in the past.

9. There wasn't much of a problem. Until indigenous people were exposed to "outside" attitudes and beliefs.

10. Many indigenous cultures are destroyed as global development occurs.

The Present Unreal Conditional

To express a situation that does not actually exist in the present time, you can use the present unreal conditional.

Examples: **If I knew** what to do, **I would help** him.

(This means: I don't know what to do, so I don't help him.)

She **wouldn't have** these problems **if** she **didn't have** fetal alcohol syndrome.

(This means: She has these problems because she has fetal alcohol syndrome.)

In these examples, you see that the conditional is the *opposite* of the real situation. In other words, if the verb in the real situation is negative, it will become affirmative in the conditional. An affirmative verb in the real situation will become negative in the conditional.

In the conditional, the *cause* is in the dependent clause with *if*. The effect or result is in the main clause; it includes *would, could,* or *might* + the simple form of the verb.

In the clause with *if*, the verb is in the past tense, but the meaning is present. If the verb *be* is used in the *if*-clause, use *were*, not *was*.

Example: **If I were** you, I'd try it.

Note: *If* is a subordinating conjunction, so it uses the same punctuation that you use with all subordinating conjunctions (page 220).

D. THE PRESENT UNREAL CONDITIONAL In each sentence that follows, circle the *cause*. Underline the *effect* or *result*. Then change each of these real situations to the conditional. Be sure to keep the cause in the clause with *if*.

1. (Magazine ads link alcohol with the idea of freedom and excitement,) so many teenagers are attracted to drinking.

If magazine ads didn't link alcohol with the idea of freedom and excitement,

many teenagers wouldn't be attracted to drinking.

2. Thousands of babies are born with serious physical and mental problems because their mothers are addicted to crack cocaine.

_____

_____

3. Children sniff glue because it is cheap.

_____

_____

4. Street children don't trust adults, so they don't go to centers for help.

_____

_____

5. There aren't taboos and laws to regulate the use of alcohol because there isn't a tradition of alcohol use in the tribe.

_____

_____

6. Hill tribes in Southeast Asia are now injecting opium instead of smoking it, so there is an increase in the incidence of AIDS.

_____

_____

7. It's especially important to establish treatment centers because the number of addicts is growing.

_____

_____

E. REVIEW: FINDING ERRORS In this paragraph, there are at least five mistakes. There are errors with the present unreal conditional, one subordinating conjunction, and fragments. Find and correct them.

The sale and use of illicit drugs should be legalized in the United States. First, the government cannot collect taxes on income that is made illegally, but if drugs were legalized, they can be taxed. This would be an enormous economic benefit to the country. For example, marijuana in California. The largest cash crop grown in the state of California is marijuana, but the growers must now hide their profits. Because they are breaking the law. The taxes paid on legally grown marijuana, together with the money now spent on enforcing anti-drug laws, could be spent both on education to prevent children from trying drugs and on treatment for the thousands of addicts who want to be free of their addiction. Second, legalization would cause the price of these drugs to drop. As a result, many drug pushers will choose to go out of business because it wouldn't be profitable enough. Not only would some drugs be less available than they are today, but the crime rate in general will drop as crimes associated with drug trafficking become unnecessary.

PART 5 ACADEMIC WRITING

WRITING ASSIGNMENT

In Part 5, you will write a persuasive paragraph about a possible solution to drug, alcohol, or tobacco abuse.

STEP A. CHOOSING A TOPIC Choose one of the following questions to answer in one paragraph:

• What should be done about women who drink alcohol or take drugs when they are pregnant?
• What can be done to persuade children not to begin smoking?
• What can be done to persuade children not to begin taking illicit drugs?
• Should the government be involved in the campaign to stop people from smoking?
• What is one possible solution to the problem of alcoholism?

Writing Strategy

Writing a Good Proposition

In a paragraph of persuasion, the topic sentence is called a **proposition.** A proposition has certain characteristics. It should:

• be arguable—in other words, be an idea that you can support with reasons.
• be an opinion, but not simply a matter of personal taste (that is, an ability to enjoy or judge something).
• not be a fact.
• deal with a single point.
• be limited (specific) enough for one paragraph.

WRITING A GOOD PROPOSITION Which of these are good topic sentences for a paragraph of persuasion? Write *good* on the line. Which are not good? On the lines, write the reason they are not good. (Use the rules in the preceding box to guide you.)

1. I don't like to smoke because it makes my clothes smell terrible.

_____

2. Consumption of heroin in the United States has doubled in the past ten years.

_____

3. Because of the danger to everyone of second-hand smoke, smoking should be banned in public buildings in my city.

_____

4. The government should stay out of people's private lives and let us make our own personal decisions.

_____

5. The government should not have the power to interfere with a person's decision to smoke or not.

_____

6. Banning advertisements for alcohol from TV is a good step toward taking the glamour out of a substance that is dangerous for young people.

_____

7. Children have been experimenting with drugs and alcohol at younger and younger ages.

_____

8. Red wine is better than white wine.

_____

9. The sale of drugs should be legalized so that 1) the government can control the quality of these potentially dangerous substances and 2) the national economy can benefit from the taxation of drugs.

_____

10. In the United States, sales of beer and wine have been increasing, while sales of hard liquor have been decreasing.

_____

STEP B. WRITING YOUR PROPOSITION After you've chosen one question to answer, you will probably need to limit your topic to just one country or perhaps to one group within a country (as in the poster on page 217). Write your proposition below.

_____

_____

_____

Critical Thinking Strategy ⬤⬤⬤⬤

Predicting Opposing Arguments

Before beginning to gather evidence for a piece of persuasive writing, it's important to imagine the opposing arguments. In other words, what would people who *disagree* with your proposition say about it? With these opposing arguments in mind, it will be easier to decide what kind of evidence to include. For example, here is a possible proposition and an argument against it.

Proposition: The sale and use of illicit drugs should be legalized in the United States.

Opposing Argument: If illicit drugs are legalized, rates of drug addiction will increase.

A student who writes a paragraph based on this proposition will have to keep the opposing argument in mind and address it—that is, find evidence to show that it isn't true.

STEP C. GATHERING EVIDENCE Follow these steps.

1. Think about your answers to these questions and then write notes on the lines below.

   A. What do you think about laws or government programs to prevent children and teens from smoking? Should it be illegal to sell cigarettes to anyone under a certain age? Should smoking be illegal for everyone? Should the government stay out of this decision? Give reasons.

   _____

   _____

   B. Do you believe that alcohol should be advertised in magazines or on TV? Why or why not?

   _____

   _____

   C. What should be done about women who drink or take drugs when they're pregnant? Should their children be taken away from them by the courts? (If so, temporarily? Permanently?) Should the women be sent to prison or a treatment center? Should the government stay out of this situation? Give reasons.

   _____

   _____

   D. Who should be responsible for preventing illicit drug use by children? Parents? Teachers? Government? What should they do to prevent drug use?

   _____

   _____

👥 In small groups, discuss your answers. As you listen to other students, take notes on ideas different from yours.

2. On a piece of paper, write your proposition from Step B on page 225. Then write your evidence (support) for your proposition in note form (not sentences). Use your own logic and information from the readings in Parts 1, 2, and 3 of this chapter. For information that you take from the readings, cite your source (give the title and author). If you do not have enough evidence to support your proposition, you may need to change your topic.

3. Write two opposing arguments for your proposition. Does the evidence that you gathered disprove the arguments—that is, does it show that they are not true? If not, try to gather more evidence.

Opposing Argument 1: _____

_____

Opposing Argument 2: _____

_____

Writing Strategy

Writing a Persuasive Paragraph

In a persuasive paragraph, it is important to begin with a proposition (topic sentence) that is arguable and limited. The rest of the paragraph gives evidence to support the opinion in the topic sentence. Your evidence can be in a variety of forms that you have already studied:

analysis	comparison/contrast	cause-effect
narration	summary	

It can be a combination of these forms. It can include examples. Most important is that you must have enough evidence of good quality to support your opinion. Your evidence can be of two kinds:

• facts
• the opinions of experts

If you use ideas from another source, *make sure to cite your source.* The following paragraph is one possible way to answer this question:

What can be done about the problem of drug addiction?

Example:

   For reasons that may appear purely economic but are essentially humane, the sale and use of illicit drugs should be legalized in the United States. First, Smith points out in her article "Should We Tax Marijuana?" that the government cannot collect taxes on income that is made illegally, but if drugs were legalized, they could be taxed. This would be an enormous economic benefit to the country. To give one example, the largest cash crop grown in the state of California is marijuana, but the growers must now hide their profits because they are breaking the law. The taxes paid on legally grown marijuana, together with the money now spent on enforcing anti-drug laws, could be spent both on education to prevent children from trying drugs and on treatment for the thousands of addicts who want to be free of their addiction. Second, according to Choi, author of "The Price of Legalization," legalization would cause the price of these drugs to drop. As a result, many drug pushers would choose to go out of business because it wouldn't be profitable enough. Not only would some drugs be less available than they are today, but the crime rate in general would drop as crimes associated with drug trafficking become unnecessary.

Note in the example:

- The topic sentence presents an arguable idea; it is not a statement of fact.
- The topic sentence limits the topic to just one country.
- The evidence consists of two reasons.

 Analysis: In the sample paragraph, look for the answers to these questions:

1. What example is included?

2. What is similar about the two reasons?

3. Why is the present unreal conditional used?

4. The second reason contains a chain of causes and effects. Create a graphic organizer to depict this chain.

5. Who are the two sources for the writer's information?

STEP D. WRITING THE PARAGRAPH In your paragraph, begin with your proposition. Follow this with evidence that you gathered in Step C. (However, delete any of this evidence that doesn't stay on target.)

STEP E. EDITING Read your paragraph and answer these questions.

1. Is the paragraph form correct (indentation, margins)?

2. Is the proposition arguable? Is the proposition limited enough for one paragraph? Is the proposition an opinion?

3. Is there clearly presented evidence?

4. If there is evidence from one of the readings, was the source cited?

5. Were opposing arguments addressed?

6. Are subordinating conjunctions used correctly?

7. If the present unreal conditional is used, is the grammar correct?

8. Have fragments been avoided?

STEP F. REWRITING Write your paragraph again. This time, try to write it with no mistakes.

CHAPTER 8

The Mind-Body Relationship

Discuss these questions:
- Look at the picture. What is the young woman doing and why is she doing it?
- How does physical exercise affect your mind?
- How does having a calm mind affect your body?

BEFORE READING

How do our daily habits affect our health?

THINKING AHEAD What do you think new research has concluded about each of the questions in the chart below? Move around the room and ask as many classmates as possible for their opinions. Record their answers on the chart, using slashes. For example, 𝄚 = 5 people answered this way.

How much sleep is probably good for us nightly?	2–3 hours	4–5 hours	6–7 hours	8–9 hours
Which of these beverages is especially good for physical health?	wine	green tea	black tea	hot chocolate
Which of these might be good for physical or mental health?	sunshine	television	voting	

READING

Read about new medical research. As you read, think about these questions:
- Which research involves physical health? Which involves mental health? Which involves both physical and mental health?
- In which studies does stress play a role in patients' physical or mental health?

What Does New Research Tell Us?

Sleeping makes you smarter. A German study found that our brains continue working on baffling problems while we sleep, allowing us to awake with new insights. Researchers at the University of Luebeck assigned math problems to volunteers, some of whom were allowed to sleep during a break from their work while the others stayed awake. When the groups returned to their task, the sleepers were three times more likely to figure out a solution than those who had stayed up. The findings, said researchers, "give us good reason to fully respect our periods of sleep . . . "

Sunshine can ease pain. Researchers at Montefiore University Hospital in Pittsburgh found that surgery patients in rooms with lots of natural light required less pain medication than other patients. Those in brighter rooms also had lower stress levels. Sunlight improves moods by triggering the release of "feel good" chemicals like serotonin in the brain, said Russell Portenoy of Beth Israel Medical Center in New York. And when people are in a good mood, they feel less pain.

Hot cocoa keeps you healthy, said Cornell University researchers in New York state. Cocoa contains more of the powerful antioxidants known to fight cancer, heart disease, and aging than other beverages known for their antioxidant content. A mug of cocoa is twice as rich in antioxidants as a glass of wine, three times richer than a cup of green tea, and five times richer than a cup of black tea. A separate study found that chocolate also suppresses coughs—even more effectively than codeine, the top cough medicine.

Television shortens children's attention spans, said researchers at the Children's Hospital and Regional Medical Center in Seattle. They examined the viewing habits of 1,345 children and found that each hour of television watched daily increased the risk of attention problems at age 7 by 10 percent. The scientists suspect that television's rapid-fire pace may affect brain development, even if the show is "educational" in nature. Other studies have linked television watching by young children to obesity and aggressiveness. "The truth is," said Dr. Dimitri Christakis, "there are a lot of reasons for children not to watch television."

Voting is good for your mental health, said University of Virginia researchers—even if your candidate loses. That's because voting makes people feel that they have more control over their lives, and that feeling reduces stress. Stress often results from the feeling that your life is not under your control. The poor, in particular, benefit from the feeling of involvement that voting provides, since the poor are most likely to feel powerless. "Of course it's better if you win," said political scientist Lynn Sanders. "But there is still a positive effect from voting."

Source: *The Week*

AFTER READING

A. VOCABULARY CHECK Look back at the reading on page 231. Find words or phrases for the definitions below, and highlight them in the reading. Then write them on the correct lines. Line numbers are in parentheses.

1. very confusing (1–5) _____

2. sudden understandings (1–5) _____

3. starting (10–15) _____

4. a kind of cup (15–20) _____

5. fast (20–25) _____

6. rate of speed (20–25) _____

7. being very overweight (25–30) _____

8. probable (30–34) _____

B. SUMMARIZING RESEARCH FINDINGS On the chart below, summarize each of the five paragraphs in the reading.

Topic	Where?	Finding (discovery)	Explanation
Sleeping	University of Luebeck, Germany	Sleep is good for problem solving.	Our brains continue to work while we sleep.
Sunshine			
Hot cocoa			
Television			
Voting			

C. DISCUSSION With a partner, briefly discuss these questions about the reading.

1. Which findings in the reading involve the body? Which involve the mind? Which involve both?

2. In which two studies was stress a factor?

3. Did any of these studies surprise you? If so, which ones?

4. With knowledge of these studies, do you think you might change anything in your life?

PART ② GENERAL INTEREST READING
The New Science of Mind and Body

BEFORE READING

What are some possible treatments
that are used in conventional medicine?

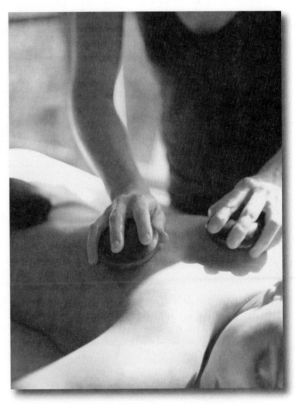

What are some possible treatments
that are used in complementary medicine?

A. THINKING AHEAD In small groups, discuss these questions.

1. Imagine that you are walking alone down a dark street, late at night, in a bad neighborhood. Nobody is around. Suddenly you hear footsteps behind you, and you are certain that someone is going to attack you. At this point, you will probably experience the **fight-or-flight syndrome**. How does your fear affect your body? How do you react to your fear?

2. What are some causes of **chronic** (i.e., long-term) stress in modern life? List them.

3. In **conventional medicine**, there are blood tests, x-rays, and **remedies** such as prescribed medicine, **chemotherapy**, and surgery. In **complementary medicine**, there are **alternative therapies** such as massage and acupuncture. Can you think of other alternative therapies?

4. The chart below shows the mental and physical conditions that are mentioned in the next reading. Which ones do you think might be **physiological** (concerned with the physical body)? Which ones might be emotional states? Check (✓) the box.

Physiological	Emotional	Condition
		alienation (feeling of not belonging to a group)
		anxiety (worry)
		hostility (unfriendliness and anger)
		hypertension (high blood pressure)
		obesity (being very overweight)
		optimism (belief that good things will happen)
		serenity (feeling of peacefulness)

5. Which physiological conditions from the chart above might affect a person emotionally? Which emotional states might affect a person physically?

B. VOCABULARY PREPARATION Read the sentences below. Match the definitions in the box with the words in green. Write the correct letters on the lines. Then compare your answers with a partner's answers.

a. are more important or numerous than	f. reduce the strength of
b. full of	g. require impossible solutions from
c. more reasonable; more sensible	h. similar (in importance) to
d. putting together	i. very modern; up-to-date
e. puzzled; unable to figure something out	j. made worse

_____ **1.** A long-term illness can **wear** the body **down** and leave the person vulnerable to disease.

_____ **2.** Our vision was **impaired** as we drove through heavy fog.

_____ **3.** Modern life is **rife with** stressful situations that didn't exist in the past.

_____ **4.** The doctors have tried everything to cure her illness, but it seems to **defy** conventional remedies.

_____ **5.** The benefits of this remedy **outweigh** its disadvantages, so I think we should try it.

_____ **6.** Some remedies might seem crazy, but others seem **saner.**

_____ **7.** It was a very difficult problem. We were absolutely **stymied** as to how to solve it.

_____ **8.** University hospitals usually practice **state-of-the-art** medical techniques.

_____ **9.** Some clinicians are now **integrating** conventional and alternative medicine.

_____**10.** Stress is a risk factor for heart disease that is **comparable to** obesity.

READING

Read about the science of mind and body. As you read, highlight answers to these questions.

• What seems to be the main way in which the mind can affect physical health?

• How can people **enhance** (improve) their immune system in order to fight off certain diseases?

The New Science of Mind and Body

The relationship between emotions and health is turning out to be more interesting, and more important, than most of us could have imagined. Viewed through the lens of 21st-century science, anxiety, alienation, and hopelessness are not just feelings. Neither are love, serenity, and optimism. All are

5 physiological states that affect our health just as clearly as obesity or physical fitness. And the brain, as the source of such emotional states, offers a potential gateway to countless other

10 tissues and organs—from the heart and blood vessels to the gut and the immune system.

Modern life is rife with potential stressors, and there is now little

15 question that uncontrolled stress can kill. Experts now believe that 60 to 90 percent of all visits to the doctor involve stress-related complaints. As researchers chart the effects of hostility and hopelessness, they're also gaining insights into the mind's power to heal.

20 Can we teach ourselves to be healthier? That is the central question of mind-body medicine[1]. Stress-related illness often defies conventional remedies, and when we try to heal these illnesses with high-tech pills and procedures, the costs of treatment can easily outweigh the benefits. Mind-body medicine offers a saner starting place. It could reduce

> ### Long-Term Effects of Chronic Stress
>
> After years of chronic activation, stress responses can wear the body down. Some of the common symptoms include:
>
> • impaired memory
> • a weakened immune system
> • high blood pressure
> • stomach ulcers
> • skin problems
> • digestive difficulties

[1]**mind-body medicine:** the idea that your mental and physical health are closely connected

medical costs while improving our health and our lives. And whatever its limitations, it has the advantage of doing no harm.

We All Need a Dose of the Doctor

You're the doctor. Your patient feels ill, but you don't have anything curative[2] in your medicine bag[3]. What do you do? That question has long stymied[4] physicians. A founding insight is that patients who have a good and trusting relationship with a clinician are more satisfied—and satisfied patients get better clinical results. They're more motivated to take care of themselves, more comfortable seeking help when problems arise, and more willing to follow advice and take medication as prescribed.

The medical profession is struggling to revive the healing relationship. The medical schools at Harvard, Columbia, Duke, and the University of Arizona have all created programs intended to pull medicine away from an exclusive focus on disease and toward the promotion of wellness, stressing the doctor's role as partner, teacher, and coach. And at least two-thirds of all U.S. medical schools now devote some part of their curriculum to integrating conventional and alternative therapies that patients find more friendly. With the right reorganizing of priorities, the system can cultivate a deeper personal role for physicians.

For a Happy Heart

The Japanese have a word for it—*karoshi*, or "death by overwork." But can stress on the job really do you in[5]?

It should come as no surprise that emotions affect the heart—and not only in metaphorical—symbolic—terms. Suffer a fright, and your heart begins to pound. Get angry, and your blood pressure rises.

In a major study in *The Lancet*, researchers surveyed more than 11,000 heart-attack sufferers from 52 countries and found that in the year before their heart attacks, the patients had been under significantly more stress—from work, family, financial troubles, depression, and other causes—than some 13,000 healthy control subjects. "Severe stress didn't pose as great a risk as smoking," admits Dr. Salim Yusuf of McMaster University, senior investigator on the study. "But it was comparable to risk factors like hypertension[6] and abdominal obesity. That's much greater than we thought before."

If there's a common explanation, it may lie in the stress response. The classic stress condition is the fight-or-flight syndrome, which primes the body to flee from an attacker. The heart shifts into high gear and blood pressure rises. Platelets in the blood become more "sticky" to aid clotting in case of a wound. That's perfect for a zebra sprinting from a lion. But when the body responds the same way to

The body's reaction to a frightening situation is similar to its reaction to stress.

[2]**curative:** helping to stop sickness
[3]**in your medicine bag:** a metaphor for everything the doctor knows
[4]**stymied:** puzzled or confused
[5]**do you in:** kill you
[6]**hypertension:** high blood pressure

Tai chi focuses the mind and relaxes the body.

everyday stressors, the cardiovascular[7] system suffers.

The implications are dramatic—not only for our risks of developing heart disease, but also for treating it. Stress reducers like yoga, meditation, and group sharing have direct effects on cardiac risk, lowering levels of stress hormones and helping to relax arteries[8]. They also have indirect effects. Participants gain a sense of well-being that helps them stick to a diet and exercise plan. And they have each other for support.

Combination Therapy

These days tens of thousands of cancer patients are using mind-body practices like relaxation, talk therapy, music therapy, visualization, tai chi, and prayer to help them deal with their disease. Eighty percent of cancer patients report using some kind of complementary medicine, a category that includes mind-body techniques as well as nutritional supplements and other holistic approaches. And no wonder. Scientists have found that mind-body practices help patients sleep better and cope with the pain, anxiety, and depression often associated with traditional cancer treatments. Recent research has shown that mind-body practices can subtly enhance a cancer patient's immune system, too.

Although many of these techniques have been around for thousands of years, scientists have only recently been exploring how they can be used in the fight against cancer. In a five-year study published in *The New England Journal of Medicine* in 2001, doctors at the University of Toronto found that breast-cancer patients who attended weekly support groups and talk therapy in addition to undergoing conventional chemotherapy[9] reported much less anxiety and pain than patients who went through standard treatment without such help.

Repeated studies have shown that conscious relaxation and meditation can counteract stress by lowering heart rate and blood pressure, and reducing levels of the stress hormones cortisol, epinephrine, and norepinephrine in the bloodstream. They also enhance immune function. In a published study, researchers at the Ohio State University Comprehensive Cancer

Ways to Calm Your Mind

Over the past three decades, many studies have confirmed the benefits of what we call the "relaxation response," a state of mental calm during which your blood pressure drops, your heart and breathing rate slow, and your muscles become less tense. Practicing the relaxation response on your own is simple. Once you're comfortable with it, you can use it to cope better with stresses.

[7]**cardiovascular:** affecting the heart and lungs
[8]**arteries:** the system that carries the blood away from the heart to cells, tissue, and organs
[9]**chemotherapy:** the use of strong chemicals to stop cancer from spreading

Center observed 227 breast-cancer patients for 10 years. Scientists found that the patients who received regular relaxation training and attended therapy in a support group had higher T-cell function than those who didn't participate in mind-body training.

Three simple ways to reduce stress:

- **Meditation:** Choose a short phrase or prayer that is rooted in your belief system, such as "peace." Sit quietly in a comfortable position and close your eyes. Relax your muscles, progressing from your feet to your calves, thighs, abdomen, shoulders, neck, and head. Breathe slowly and naturally, and as you exhale, say your word or phrase silently to yourself. Ideally, you'll continue the exercise for 10 to 20 minutes, but even five minutes of deep relaxation can leave you calm and refreshed.

- **Paced respiration:** Start by inhaling slowly. As you exhale, say the number "five" silently to yourself. Breaths should be deep enough to cause the belly to expand fully. After pausing briefly, take another slow breath, and think "four" as you exhale. Continue at your own pace, counting down to one.

- **Repetitive activities:** You don't always have to sit quietly to evoke the relaxation response. You can do it while walking, jogging, playing a musical instrument, or carrying out simple repetitive tasks such as knitting. Yoga, tai chi, meditation, and repetitive prayer are other ways to put yourself in this healthful frame of mind.

AFTER READING

A. CHECK YOUR UNDERSTANDING In small groups, discuss these questions.

1. What is the central question of mind-body medicine?

2. What does the author mean when she says, "We all need a dose of the doctor"?

3. List as many ways to reduce stress as you can find in the reading.

4. In what ways can mind-body practices help patients? What can mind-body practices enhance?

5. How can relaxation and meditation **counteract** (act against) stress?

Reading Strategy

Scanning for Specific Information

Scanning can save you time when you read textbooks. To scan—find specific information quickly in a chapter or reading passage—follow these steps:

- Decide what the general topic is so that you know which section to look in.
- Have a specific phrase or question in your mind.
- With this phrase or question in mind, **scan** the section for that phrase or the answer to your question. In other words, run your finger down the middle of the passage until the phrase or answer "pops out" at you.

B. SCANNING FOR SPECIFIC INFORMATION Before scanning the reading on pages 235–238, read the questions below. Write the topic and phrase you will scan for to answer the question. Then scan the reading. Highlight the answers in the reading.

1. Why do patients with a "good and trusting relationship" with their doctor seem to do better than those without one?

    Topic: _____

    Phrase: _____

2. Why is severe stress a risk factor for heart attacks?

    Topic: _____

    Phrase: _____

C. MAKING INFERENCES The last paragraph of the reading mentions T-cells but does not explain what they are. What can you infer about T-cells (in general) from this paragraph?

D. VOCABULARY CHECK Look back at the reading and the headings on pages 235–238. Find words or phrases for the definitions below and highlight them in the reading. Then write them on the correct lines. Line numbers are in parentheses.

1. the part of the body through which food moves (10–15) _____

2. doctor (25–30) _____

3. recommended amount (of a medicine) that a person should take at one time (30–35) _____

4. thickening of a liquid into a lump (60–65) _____

5. a damaged place on the body, such as a cut in the skin (60–65) _____

6. a medical practice that combines conventional and alternative techniques (70–75) _____

7. a system in the body that protects the body from disease (85–90) _____

E. IN YOUR OWN WORDS: SUMMARIZING Fill in the first blank with the topic of the reading on pages 235–238. Use a noun or noun phrase. Fill in the second blank with the main idea of the reading. Use an independent clause. (Because there seem to be two main ideas in this reading, you might use two independent clauses connected by *and* or *but*.)

This article is about _____

The author says that _____

F. DISCUSSION In small groups, discuss these questions.

1. What are sources of stress in your life?

2. Do you do something to relieve stress—meditation? yoga? repetitive activities? something else?

PART ③ ACADEMIC READING A Skeptical Look: Placebo Effect

BEFORE READING

A. THINKING AHEAD Discuss this question with a partner:

• In many medical experiments, one group of people is given true medication. The other group of subjects is given a **placebo** that looks the same as the true medication but has no medicine in it. None of the subjects knows who is taking which pills. Frequently, at the end of the experiment, many subjects taking the placebo actually report that they feel better. What might explain this?

Reading Strategy

Guessing the Meaning from Context: Review of Dictionary Use

This book has emphasized guessing the meaning of new words from the context. This skill is important when you are reading large amounts of material. However, there are times when a dictionary is essential.

Don't use a dictionary if:

• you can guess the meaning from the context.
• you can guess something about the meaning but don't understand the word exactly. (You might see the same word later in the reading and be able to understand it better.)
• you can't figure out the meaning at all but can still understand the sentence or paragraph without the word.

Use a dictionary if you can't understand the word at all and can't understand the sentence or paragraph because of this.

To use a dictionary, follow these general guidelines.
1. Figure out from the context what the part of speech is.
2. Look up the word with that part of speech. Do not waste your time looking at other parts of speech for that word.
3. If the word has several definitions (as many words do), look back and forth from the context to the dictionary to choose a definition that fits your context.
4. Be sure to look at the sample sentences in the dictionary, if there are any. These will help you to use the word correctly. Also, it is sometimes easier to understand the example than the definition.

B. GUESSING THE MEANING FROM CONTEXT The sentences below have words that may be new to you. If you can guess the new words from the context (or guess *something* about them), highlight them and write your guess in the chart below. Circle words that you cannot guess. Then look them up in a dictionary and write the definitions in the chart.

1. When someone feels better after using a product or procedure, it is natural to credit whatever was done.

2. Most ailments are self-limiting, and even incurable diseases and disorders can vary from day to day.

3. In certain circumstances, a lactose tablet (sugar pill) may relieve not only anxiety but also pain, nausea, vomiting, palpitations, shortness of breath, and other symptoms.

4. Reassurance from a doctor that no serious disease is involved might be therapeutic by itself.

5. There may be symptoms that the patient attributes to the underlying disease, although they are not related to this disease.

6. If the quack's promises make the patient feel hopeful, the symptoms of depression might improve, and the patient might conclude that the quack's approach has been effective.

7. In double-blind drug trials, healthy volunteers had adverse effects 19% of the time, although they were taking placebos.

8. False responses can obscure the real disease.

9. Devices and physical techniques often have a psychological impact.

10. Because they spent a lot of money on medicine that gave them no relief, it was a financial rip-off.

Words I Guessed

New Words	Definitions

Words I Looked Up

New Words	Definitions

 Now compare your words and meanings with your partner's chart.

READING

Read about the placebo effect. As you read, think about this question:
• What is the placebo effect and what does the author think about it?

A Skeptical Look: Placebo Effect

When someone feels better after using a product or procedure, it is natural to credit whatever was done. However, this is unwise. Most ailments are self-limiting, and even incurable conditions can have sufficient day-to-day variation to enable quack methods to gain large followings. Taking action often produces temporary
5 relief of symptoms (a placebo effect). In addition, many products and services exert physical or psychological effects that users misinterpret as evidence that their problem is being cured. Scientific experimentation is almost always necessary to establish whether health methods are really effective.

What Is It?

The placebo effect is a beneficial response to a substance, device, or procedure
10 that cannot be accounted for on the basis of pharmacologic[1] or other direct physical action. Feeling better when the physician walks into the room is a common example.

A placebo may be used to satisfy a patient that something is being done. The term itself is derived from the Latin word *placebo*, which means "I shall please." By lessening anxiety, placebo action may relieve symptoms caused by the body's
15 reaction to tension (psychosomatic[2] symptoms). In certain circumstances, a lactose tablet (sugar pill) may relieve not only anxiety but also pain, nausea, vomiting, palpitations, shortness of breath, and other symptoms. The patient expects the "medication" to cause improvement, and sometimes it does.

Temporary Relief

Many studies suggest that placebos can relieve a broad range of symptoms. In
20 many disorders, one-third or more of patients will get relief from a placebo. Temporary relief has been demonstrated, for example, in arthritis, hay fever, headache, cough, high blood pressure, premenstrual tension, peptic ulcer, and even cancer. The psychological aspects of many disorders also work to the healer's advantage. A large percentage of symptoms either have a psychological component
25 or do not arise from organic disease. Hence, treatment offering some lessening of tension can often help. A sympathetic ear or reassurance that no serious disease is involved may prove therapeutic by itself.

Confidence in the treatment—on the part of the patient and the practitioner[3]— makes it more likely that a placebo effect will occur. But the power of suggestion
30 may cause even a nonbeliever to respond favorably. The only requirement for a placebo effect is the awareness that something has been done.

People suffering from chronic symptoms are often depressed, and depression often produces symptoms that the patient attributes to the underlying disease. If the

[1]**pharmacologic:** using drugs to cure a disease
[2]**psychosomatic:** a sickness caused by your mind but affecting your body
[3]**practitioner:** a doctor, nurse, or therapist

quack's promises make the patient feel hopeful, the depressive symptoms may
35 resolve, leading the patient to conclude—at least temporarily—that the quack's
approach has been effective against the disease.

Negative Effects

Responses to the treatment setting can also be negative ("nocebo effects"). In one
experiment, for example, some subjects who were warned of possible side effects of
a drug were given injections of a placebo instead. Many of them reported dizziness,
40 nausea, vomiting, and even depression. A recent review of 109 double-blind drug
trials found that the overall incidence of adverse events in healthy volunteers during
placebo administration was 19%.

Placebo responses, such as feeling less pain or more energy, do not affect the
actual course of the disease. Thus, placebo responses can obscure real disease,
45 which can lead to delay in obtaining appropriate diagnosis or treatment.

The placebo effect is not limited to drugs but may also result from procedures.
Devices and physical techniques often have a significant psychologic impact.
Chiropractors, naturopaths, and various other nonmedical practitioners may use
heat, light, . . . hydrotherapy, manipulation, massage, and various gadgets. In
50 addition to any physiologic effects, their use can exert a psychologic force that may
be reinforced by the relationship between the patient and the practitioner. Of course,
devices and procedures used by scientific practitioners can also have placebo effects.

Doctors are confronted by many people who complain of tiredness or a variety of
vague symptoms that are reactions to nervous tension. Far too often, instead of
55 finding out what is bothering them, doctors tell them to take a tonic, a vitamin, or
some other type of placebo.

Quacks who rely on the placebo effect pretend that (a) they know what they are
doing, (b) they can tell what is wrong with you, and (c) their treatment is effective for
just about everything. . . . Medical doctors who use vitamins as placebos may not be
60 as dangerous, but they encourage people to habitually use products they don't need.
Because most people who use placebos do not get relief from them, their use is also
a financial rip-off.

Source: "Alternative Medicine: A Skeptical Look: Placebo Effect" (Barrett)

AFTER READING

A. CHECK YOUR UNDERSTANDING Discuss these questions with a partner.

1. What is a placebo, according to the author?

2. How does a placebo function?

3. What is a "nocebo"?

4. Find all the examples of placebos in the reading.

Determining Topic, Main Point, Purpose, and Tone

Standardized reading tests frequently require you to choose the topic, main point (main idea), purpose, or tone (connotation, "feeling," mood) of a reading selection. There may be multiple-choice questions about a paragraph, section, or entire reading.

You already know how to find the topic and main point.

To determine the **purpose,** it will help if you can figure out what *kind* of reading selection it is:
• cause-effect (reasons, explanations)
• definition (synonyms, classification, function, pure definition)
• comparison/contrast
• analysis
• argument (persuasion)
• description
• narration

To determine the **tone**, look for words that express the opinion of the author. You know that they are opinion words if you can imagine people disagreeing with the author's choice of them.

B. DETERMINING TOPIC, MAIN POINT, PURPOSE, AND TONE Look back at the reading to answer these questions. Circle the correct letter.

1. The purpose of the two paragraphs in lines 9–18 is to _____.
 A. explain how placebos are beneficial
 B. define the term *placebo*
 C. give the history of the word *placebo*
 D. list symptoms that a placebo may relieve

2. The main point of the paragraphs in lines 19–36 is that _____.
 A. people suffering from chronic symptoms are often depressed
 B. one-third or more of patients get relief from placebos
 C. a psychological factor is involved when the patient experiences relief from a placebo
 D. confidence in the doctor is important

3. The topic of the paragraph beginning on line 43 is _____.
 A. placebo responses
 B. pain
 C. diagnosis or treatment of disease
 D. the danger of placebo responses

4. The tone of the paragraph beginning on line 57 is _____.
 A. critical of unethical medical practices
 B. instructive about good medical practices
 C. uncertain
 D. neutral and not expressing an opinion

C. VOCABULARY CHECK Look back at the reading on pages 242–243. Find words or phrases for the definitions below, and highlight them in the reading. Then write them on the correct lines. Line numbers are in parentheses.

1. symptoms caused by the body's reaction to tension (10–15) _____

2. physical conditions such as pain, nausea, and vomiting (15–20) _____

3. mechanical things (45–50) _____

4. unethical doctors or people who pretend that they are doctors but really aren't (55–60) _____

D. WORD JOURNAL Go back to the readings in Parts 1, 2, and 3. Which words are important for you to remember? Put them in your Word Journal.

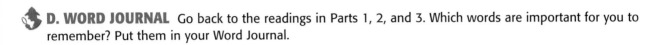

Critical Thinking Strategy

Seeing Two Sides of an Issue

In academic courses, you often need to see an issue from two or more sides. Sometimes you need to make a list of pros and cons—that is, reasons to be in favor of the issue and reasons to be against it. Sometimes you need to compare two or more readings and find the points of agreement and disagreement. You will often be expected to decide which side you agree with and state your reasons.

E. SEEING TWO SIDES OF AN ISSUE Are mind-body practices good for the health or harmful? The following is a list of some of the mind-body activities mentioned in this chapter. How might the authors of the readings in Parts 1 and 2 support their belief in mind-body activities? What do you think **skeptics**—such as Stephen Barrett (the author of "The Placebo Effect: A Skeptical Look," in Part 3)—would say about them? Follow the steps on page 246 to find evidence to support each side of the issue.

being in a bright, sunny room	repetitive activities: yoga, meditation, tai chi
group sharing	talk therapy
having a good relationship with your doctor	visualization
music therapy	voting
prayer	

1. Form small groups for this activity.

2. Half of the groups will find evidence that is critical of the activities in the box on page 245.

3. Half of the groups will find evidence in support of these activities.

4. When you have finished finding evidence, join with a group from the opposite side. Share your evidence. To disagree politely, use some of these expressions:
    - I understand that, but . . .
    - That's true, but . . .
    - I see your point, but . . .
    - That's a good point, but it's also true that . . .

5. After you exchange evidence, decide which evidence is more persuasive. What is your own opinion?

F. DISCUSSION Look over the quotations in the box below. In small groups, discuss these questions.

1. Is there one quotation that you especially like? Why?

2. What might people in favor of mind-body medicine think about them? What might skeptics think about them?

3. Is there a famous proverb about health from your culture? If so, think of how to say it in English and share it with your group.

> Early to bed and early to rise, makes a man healthy, wealthy, and wise.
> —Benjamin Franklin, *Poor Richard's Almanac*
>
> Natural forces within us are the true healers of disease.
> —Hippocrates, *Aphorisms*
>
> Meditation, education, and psychotherapy *can actually change the brain.*
> —Steven Pinker, Harvard University
>
> Keep breathing. [Her answer to the question: What is the key to long life?]
> —Sophie Tucker (American singer)

G. RESPONSE WRITING Choose one of the following questions to answer:
- What do you do in order to relax?
- What kind of relationship do you have with your doctor?
- Is your mood affected by the atmosphere of the room that you're in?
- What do you think is the key to a long, healthy life?

Write about your topic for 10 minutes. Don't worry about grammar and don't stop writing to use a dictionary.

PART ④ THE MECHANICS OF WRITING

In Part 4, you will practice combining ideas by using all three kinds of conjunctions that you learned in previous chapters. You will also practice using expressions of possibility, italics, and quotation marks. You will need this grammar in Part 5 to write a paragraph of persuasion.

Expressing Possibility

There are several ways to express possibility: with the word *possibly, possible,* or *likely* (= possible), the clause *It is possible that* . . . or *It is believed that* . . . , or a modal. The modals of possibility for the present or future are:

may
might } + (not) + the simple form of the verb
could

Example: The quality of light in a room **may affect** mood. (= possibly affects)

In the negative, *couldn't* doesn't mean "maybe not," as the others do. It means "absolutely, for certain not."

A. EXPRESSING POSSIBILITY Write your answer to each question. Use an expression of possibility in each. Numbers in parentheses indicate pages where you can find the answers.

1. How does television shorten children's attention spans? (231)

_____

2. How many doctor visits involve stress-related complaints? (235)

_____

3. What explains the danger of severe stress as a factor in heart attacks? (236)

_____

4. What do conscious relaxation and meditation do? (237)

_____

5. In certain circumstances, what does a lactose tablet—a placebo—relieve? (242)

_____

6. What role does confidence play in the treatment of a patient? (242)

_____

Review of Conjunctions

There are often many ways to express the same idea. Knowing how to connect sentences in several ways can add variety to your writing. In previous chapters, you studied the three types of conjunctions: coordinating, subordinating, and adverbial.

As a review, notice how you can express a relationship of contradiction or cause and effect in various ways.

	Contradiction	**Cause and Effect**
Coordinating	but	so (= that's why) yet (= but) for (= because)
Subordinating	although even though while (= although)	because since (= because) as (= because)
Adverbial	however nevertheless even so	therefore as a result consequently } (= so) for this reason thus

Compare the punctuation in these sentences.

Examples: Many people believe that psychosomatic illnesses are unreal, **but** this is inaccurate.

Although many people believe that psychosomatic illnesses are unreal, this is inaccurate.

Many people believe that psychosomatic illnesses are unreal; **however,** this is inaccurate.

B. SENTENCE COMBINING: CONJUNCTIONS Combine each pair of sentences in three ways—with a coordinating conjunction (C), a subordinating conjunction (S), and an adverbial conjunction (A). In some cases, you will need to change the order of the two clauses.

1. Cocoa is more healthful than tea. It has more antioxidants, which fight cancer, heart disease, and aging.

C: _____

_____

S: _____

_____

A: _____

_____

2. Stress isn't as bad for the health as smoking. It is as bad as high blood pressure.

C: _____

_____

S: _____

_____

A: _____

_____

3. Many symptoms have a psychological component. Treatment that lessens tension can help to reduce the symptoms.

C: _____

_____

S: _____

_____

A: _____

_____

4. Ten to twenty minutes of meditation is ideal. Even five minutes can leave you calm.

C: _____

_____

S: _____

_____

A: _____

_____

5. Placebo responses can be dangerous. They can obscure real disease and lead to delay in treatment.

C: _____

_____

S: _____

_____

A: _____

_____

Using Italics and Quotation Marks

Here are four common ways in which writers use italics in academic writing:
- for the title of a book, movie, newspaper, or magazine
- for emphasis
- for a foreign word used in an English sentence
- when they mean "the word . . ." or "the term . . ."

Examples: A special issue of *Newsweek* is devoted to the mind-body relationship. (title of a magazine)

He lived not only long but *well*. (emphasis)

The Japanese have a word for it–*karoshi*. (foreign word in an English sentence)

Quack means "an unethical doctor." (= the word quack)

Writers also use quotation (quote) marks in academic writing in four ways:
- for a direct quotation of someone's exact words
- for the meaning of a word
- for the title of a short story, short poem, or newspaper or magazine article
- when they are using a term differently from its usual meaning or with the word's opposite meaning

Examples: The findings, said researchers, "give us good reason to fully respect our periods of sleep." (direct quotation)

In Latin, that word means "I shall please." (meaning of a word)

In "A Skeptical Look: Placebo Effect," there is a critical view of placebos. (title of an article)

The patient expects the "medication" to cause improvement. (not really medication)

C. USING ITALICS AND QUOTATION MARKS Write the reason for the use of italics or quotation marks.

1. The root of the word seems to suggest "thoughtful action to establish order."

_____

2. It may affect brain development, even if the show is "educational" in nature.

_____

3. I absolutely *craved* some ice cream. _____

4. People in drug recovery describe themselves as "recovering" instead of "recovered."

_____

5. In the first chapter of *Healing from the Heart,* Mehmet Oz explains the biology of a heart attack.

_____

6. *Psychosomatic* is derived from two Greek words. _____

7. It does not mean "unreal" or "not serious." _____

8. They drank a few glasses of *ouzo*. _____

Using Quotation Marks

Make sure to put quote marks around all words from another source but not around your own words. It is possible to put the **attribution** (i.e., who said this) in the middle of the quote, but if you do this, you need two sets (pairs) of quote marks. If your attribution is at the end of a quoted sentence, a comma comes before the end quote marks. Notice the punctuation in these examples.

Examples: According to Barrett, "Procedures used by scientific practitioners can also have placebo effects."

"The truth is," said Dr. Dimitri Christakis, "there are a lot of reasons for children not to watch television."

"Stress didn't pose as great a risk as smoking," admits Dr. Salim Yusuf.

D. REVIEW: FINDING ERRORS   In this paragraph, there are at least six errors. These are errors with modals of possibility, conjunctions, quotations, and italics. Find and correct them.

Many people are skeptical about attempts to improve health through mind-body medicine. Stephen Barrett, for example, is critical of doctors "who rely on the placebo effect" and calls them quacks. However, mind-body relaxation techniques can be an effective way to reduce stress, which is a serious risk factor for heart disease. In a 2004 study, it was found that stress is "comparable to risk factors like hypertension and abdominal obesity", according to Dr. Salim Yusuf of McMaster University. The problem seems to be chronic stress. Although it may be not possible to escape long-term stressful situations in life, relaxation exercises such as yoga are beneficial to cardiac health. In Newsweek, Anne Underwood explains that this happens by "lowering levels of stress hormones and helping to relax arteries". Relaxation might be just a placebo, nevertheless, even Barrett admits that placebos reduce a patient's anxiety and thereby "may relieve symptoms caused by the body's reaction to tension." When it comes to the prevention of heart attacks, this is a benefit.

PART ⑤ ACADEMIC WRITING

WRITING ASSIGNMENT

In Part 5, you will write a persuasive paragraph about the mind-body relationship.

STEP A. CHOOSING A TOPIC Choose one of these topics (A, B, C, or D) for your paragraph.

Topic A
A benefit of one of the following:
- sleep
- sunshine
- hot cocoa
- mind-body medicine (specify one kind)

Topic B
A problem with one of the following:
- television
- chronic stress
- mind-body medicine

Topic C
A danger of placebos

Topic D
The importance of a patient's relationship with his or her doctor

Writing Strategy

Hedging

In academic writing in English, it is essential to be able to **hedge**. In other words, you need to choose words that allow you to *avoid expressing an opinion that you cannot prove* and to *avoid overstatement and exaggeration.* This is important in the proposition but also elsewhere in a paragraph.

In conversational English, overstatement and exaggeration are common, and the listener understands that it is probably not meant literally.

Examples: The candidate I vote for **never** wins.
This job is **killing** me.
Mind-body medicine is **really** dangerous.

In academic English, you need to stay away from words such as *all, every, always,* and *never,* as well as adverbs such as *extremely, really, strongly,* and *completely.* Instead, academic English makes liberal use of indefinite adverbs such as *often, frequently,* and *almost,* modals of possibility, verbs of uncertainty, and other cautious use of language.

Examples: It **seems** that the candidate I vote for **doesn't usually** win.
This job **tends to be** stressful.
There **can be** dangers in mind-body medicine.

Such sentences are much easier to support than sentences without hedging.

Here are some words that are commonly used in academic writing:

> frequently, often, generally, usually, most of the time
> occasionally, sometimes, from time to time
> rarely, almost never, seldom
> almost
>
> probably, possibly
> It is probable, likely that . . .
> It is possible that . . .
>
> most, many, a great many, a good deal of
> few, not many, little, not much
>
> can, may, might, could
>
> Evidence suggests, indicates, points to, tends to suggest . . .
> It appears, seems that . . .

HEDGING Which sentence in each pair contains hedging and is therefore better to use in academic English? Circle the correct letter.

1. **A.** Stress-related illness defies conventional remedies.
   B. Stress-related illness often defies conventional remedies.

2. **A.** Mind-body medicine could reduce medical costs.
   B. Mind-body medicine reduces medical costs.

3. **A.** The explanation lies in the stress response.
   B. The explanation might lie in the stress response.

4. **A.** A sympathetic ear is therapeutic.
   B. A sympathetic ear may be therapeutic.

5. **A.** Relaxation techniques appear to lower hypertension.
   B. Relaxation techniques lower hypertension.

STEP B. WRITING YOUR PROPOSITION After you've chosen a topic, write your proposition on the following lines. Consider including a hedge in your proposition to make it easier to support.

_____

_____

_____

STEP C. GATHERING EVIDENCE Go back to the readings in Parts 1, 2, and 3 and highlight support for your proposition. On the following lines, write this evidence (support). Make sure to make a note of the source; in other words, what was the name of the author of the reading and/or the magazine from which it came? (If no author is given, just give the source. If no source is given, cite this textbook and its author, Pamela Hartmann.) Also, for any evidence that you copy exactly, use quotation marks, although you might later decide to paraphrase it.

_____

_____

_____

_____

_____

_____

_____

_____

_____

_____

Writing Strategy

Writing a Persuasive Paragraph

Review

In Chapter 7, you learned about the two elements of a persuasive paragraph: a proposition (topic sentence) that is arguable and limited, and evidence to support the opinion in the topic sentence. You also learned of the importance of having enough good quality evidence.

If you have access to source material, it's far better to use factual information or opinions of experts as support than to use your own opinion. However, if you use ideas from another source, make *sure* to cite your source.

New

So far in this text, you have learned to begin a paragraph with the topic sentence. However, it is possible for the topic sentence (or proposition) to appear later in the paragraph. Many persuasive paragraphs begin with the opposing argument. The proposition appears after that.

The example paragraph on the next page is one possible way to explore a benefit of mind-body medicine. Notice where the topic sentence is placed and the use of source material.

Example:

Many people are skeptical about attempts to improve health through mind-body medicine. Stephen Barrett, for example, is critical of doctors "who rely on the placebo effect" and calls them "quacks." However, mind-body relaxation techniques can be an effective way to reduce stress, which is a serious risk factor for heart disease. In a 2004 study, it was found that stress is "comparable to risk factors like hypertension and abdominal obesity," according to Dr. Salim Yusuf of McMaster University. The problem seems to be chronic stress. Although it may not be possible to escape long-term stressful situations in life, relaxation exercises such as yoga are beneficial to cardiac health. In *Newsweek*, Anne Underwood explains that this happens by "lowering levels of stress hormones and helping to relax arteries." Relaxation might be just a placebo. Nevertheless, even Barrett admits that placebos reduce a patient's anxiety and thereby "may relieve symptoms caused by the body's reaction to tension." When it comes to the prevention of heart attacks, this is a benefit.

Analysis: In the sample paragraph, look for the answers to these questions:

1. Which sentence is the topic sentence?
2. Which words indicate that the topic sentence is an opinion?
3. Which mind-body technique is the focus of the paragraph?
4. What is the purpose of the first two sentences?
5. The paragraph contains three adverbial conjunctions and two subordinating conjunctions. What are they? Highlight them and notice the punctuation.
6. How many sources are cited? What is quoted? Highlight this quoted information.
7. What are five examples of hedging?

STEP D. WRITING THE PARAGRAPH In your paragraph, begin with the opposing argument. Follow this with your proposition and then the supporting evidence that you gathered in Step C.

STEP E. EDITING Read your paragraph and answer these questions.

1. Is the paragraph form correct (indentation, margins)?

2. Does the paragraph begin with an opposing view?

3. Is the proposition arguable? Limited enough for one paragraph? An opinion?

4. Is there language of hedging in appropriate places?

5. Is there clearly presented evidence?

6. Were sources cited and either quoted or paraphrased?

7. Are quotation marks and italics used correctly?

8. Are coordinating, subordinating, and adverbial conjunctions used correctly?

STEP F. REWRITING Write your paragraph again. This time, try to write it with no mistakes.

UNIT 4 VOCABULARY WORKSHOP

Review vocabulary that you learned in Chapters 7 and 8.

A. MATCHING Match the words to the definitions. Write the letters on the lines.

Words	Definitions
_____ **1.** chronic	**a.** difference
_____ **2.** epidemic	**b.** rate of speed
_____ **3.** gap	**c.** a condition of being very overweight
_____ **4.** illicit	**d.** not legal
_____ **5.** obesity	**e.** doctor
_____ **6.** outweigh	**f.** be more important than
_____ **7.** pace	**g.** use the nose to smell something
_____ **8.** physician	**h.** lasting a long time
_____ **9.** sniff	**i.** a disease that many, many people have
_____ **10.** subject	**j.** person in a medical research study

B. VOCABULARY EXPANSION Write the different parts of speech for the words in the chart. Use a dictionary to fill in these blanks.

	Verbs	Nouns	Adjectives
1.		withdrawal	
2.			alienated
3.	consume		
4.			comparable
5.		ailment	
6.	impair		
7.			sober
8.	defy		

C. WORDS IN PHRASES Fill in the blanks with nouns, verbs, or prepositions to complete the phrases.

Nouns

1. Children who watch a lot of TV have a shorter **attention** _____ than those who don't.

2. The **rapid-fire** _____ of TV may affect brain development.

3. This is **state-of-the-**_____ technology.

Verbs
What are some ways in which people use illicit drugs?

4. _____

5. _____ } drugs

6. _____

Prepositions

7. It's hard to **cope** _____ a friend or relative who is an addict.

8. You can **rely** _____ **her** to help. She is very dependable.

9. A long-term illness can **wear the body** _____.

10. Modern life is **rife** _____ stressful situations.

D. THE ACADEMIC WORD LIST In the boxes below are some of the most common academic words in English. Fill in the blanks with words from these boxes. When you finish, check your answers in the readings on page 235 (for numbers 1–9) and page 242 (for numbers 10–16). For more words, see the Academic Word List on pages 259–262.

affect	percent	potential	source
involve	physical	researcher	stress

The relationship between emotions and health is turning out to be more interesting, and more important, than most of us could have imagined. Viewed through the lens of 21st-century science, anxiety, alienation, and hopelessness are not just feelings. Neither are love, serenity, and optimism. All are physiological states that _____ our health just as clearly as obesity or
1

_____ fitness. And the brain, as the _____ of such
2   3

states, offers a gateway to countless other tissues and organs—from the heart and blood vessels to the gut and the immune system.

Modern life is rife with _____ 4 stressors, and there is now little question

that uncontrolled _____ 5 can kill. Experts now believe that 60 to 90

_____ 6 of all visits to the doctor _____ 7

stress-related complaints. As _____ 8 chart the effects of hostility and

hopelessness, they're also gaining insights into the mind's power to heal.

Can we teach ourselves to be healthier? That is the central question of mind-body medicine.

| credit | evidence | sufficient | temporary | variation |
| establish | misinterpret | | | |

When someone feels better after using a product or procedure, it is natural to

_____ 9 whatever was done. However, this is unwise. Most ailments are

self-limiting, and even incurable conditions can have _____ 10 day-to-day

_____ 11 to enable quack methods to gain large followings. Taking action

often produces _____ 12 relief of symptoms (a placebo effect). In addition,

many products and services exert physical or psychological effects that users

_____ 13 as _____ 14 that their problem is being

cured. Scientific experimentation is almost always necessary to _____ 15

whether health methods are really effective.

The list on pages 259–262 is Sublist One of the most common words on the Academic World List, a list compiled by Averil Coxhead. To view the entire list, go to Averil Coxhead's AWL website (http://language.massey.ac.nz/staff/awl/index.shtml).

Each word in italics is the most frequently occurring member of the word family in the academic corpus. For example, *analysis* is the most common form of the word family *analyse*.

The Academic Word List includes both British and American spelling.

analyse
  analysed
  analyser
  analysers
  analyses
  analysing
  analysis
  analyst
  analysts
  analytic
  analytical
  analytically
  analyze
  analyzed
  analyzes
  analyzing
approach
  approachable
  approached
  approaches
  approaching
  unapproachable
area
  areas
assess
  assessable
  assessed
  assesses
  assessing

assessment
  assessments
  reassess
  reassessed
  reassessing
  reassessment
  unassessed
assume
  assumed
  assumes
  assuming
  assumption
  assumptions
authority
  authoritative
  authorities
available
  availability
  unavailable
benefit
  beneficial
  beneficiary
  beneficiaries
  benefited
  benefiting
  benefits
concept
  conception
  concepts

conceptual
conceptualisation
conceptualise
conceptualised
conceptualises
conceptualising
conceptually
consist
  consisted
  consistency
  consistent
  consistently
  consisting
  consists
  inconsistencies
  inconsistency
  inconsistent
constitute
  constituencies
  constituency
  constituent
  constituents
  constituted
  constitutes
  constituting
  constitution
  constitutions
  constitutional
  constitutionally

constitutive
unconstitutional
context
  contexts
  contextual
  contextualise
  contextualised
  contextualising
  uncontextualised
  contextualize
  contextualized
  contextualizing
  uncontextualized
contract
  contracted
  contracting
  contractor
  contractors
  contracts
create
  created
  creates
  creating
  creation
  creations
  creative
  creatively
  creativity
  creator
  creators
  recreate
  recreated
  recreates
  recreating
data
define
  definable
  defined
  defines
  defining
  definition

definitions
redefine
redefined
redefines
redefining
undefined
derive
  derivation
  derivations
  derivative
  derivatives
  derived
  derives
  deriving
distribute
  distributed
  distributing
  distribution
  distributional
  distributions
  distributive
  distributor
  distributors
  redistribute
  redistributed
  redistributes
  redistributing
  redistribution
economy
  economic
  economical
  economically
  economics
  economies
  economist
  economists
  uneconomical
environment
  environmental
  environmentalist
  environmentalists

environmentally
environments
establish
  disestablish
  disestablished
  disestablishes
  disestablishing
  disestablishment
  established
  establishes
  establishing
  establishment
  establishments
estimate
  estimated
  estimates
  estimating
  estimation
  estimations
  over-estimate
  overestimate
  overestimated
  overestimates
  overestimating
  underestimate
  underestimated
  underestimates
  underestimating
evident
  evidenced
  evidence
  evidential
  evidently
export
  exported
  exporter
  exporters
  exporting
  exports
factor
  factored

factoring
factors
finance
    financed
    finances
    financial
    financially
    financier
    financiers
    financing
formula
    formulae
    formulas
    formulate
    formulated
    formulating
    formulation
    formulations
    reformulate
    reformulated
    reformulating
    reformulation
    reformulations
function
    functional
    functionally
    functioned
    functioning
    functions
identify
    identifiable
    identification
    identified
    identifies
    identifying
    identities
    identity
    unidentifiable
income
    incomes

indicate
    indicated
    indicates
    indicating
    indication
    indications
    indicative
    indicator
    indicators
individual
    individualised
    individuality
    individualism
    individualist
    individualists
    individualistic
    individually
    individuals
interpret
    interpretation
    interpretations
    interpretative
    interpreted
    interpreting
    interpretive
    interprets
    misinterpret
    misinterpretation
    misinterpretations
    misinterpreted
    misinterpreting
    misinterprets
    reinterpret
    reinterpreted
    reinterprets
    reinterpreting
    reinterpretation
    reinterpretations
involve
    involved
    involvement

involves
involving
uninvolved
issue
    issued
    issues
    issuing
labour
    labor
    labored
    labors
    laboured
    labouring
    labours
legal
    illegal
    illegality
    illegally
    legality
    legally
legislate
    legislated
    legislates
    legislating
    legislation
    legislative
    legislator
    legislators
    legislature
major
    majorities
    majority
method
    methodical
    methodological
    methodologies
    methodology
    methods
occur
    occurred
    occurrence

occurrences
occurring
occurs
reoccur
reoccurred
reoccurring
reoccurs
percent
   percentage
   percentages
period
   periodic
   periodical
   periodically
   periodicals
   periods
policy
   policies
principle
   principled
   principles
   unprincipled
proceed
   procedural
   procedure
   procedures
   proceeded
   proceeding
   proceedings
   proceeds
process
   processed
   processes
   processing
require
   required
   requirement
   requirements
   requires
   requiring

research
   researched
   researcher
   researchers
   researches
   researching
respond
   responded
   respondent
   respondents
   responding
   responds
   response
   responses
   responsive
   responsiveness
   unresponsive
role
   roles
section
   sectioned
   sectioning
   sections
sector
   sectors
significant
   insignificant
   insignificantly
   significance
   significantly
   signified
   signifies
   signify
   signifying
similar
   dissimilar
   similarities
   similarity
   similarly
source
   sourced

sources
sourcing
specific
   specifically
   specification
   specifications
   specificity
   specifics
structure
   restructure
   restructured
   restructures
   restructuring
   structural
   structurally
   structured
   structures
   structuring
   unstructured
theory
   theoretical
   theoretically
   theories
   theorist
   theorists
vary
   invariable
   invariably
   variability
   variable
   variables
   variably
   variance
   variant
   variants
   variation
   variations
   varied
   varies
   varying

VOCABULARY INDEX

SKILLS INDEX

Academic Focus
Art, 69–136
 Egypt, 105–136
 Themes and purposes in art,
  71–104
Business, 1–68
 Global economy, 35–68
International business, 3–34
Health, 197–261
 Medicine and drugs, 199–228
 Mind-body relationship,
  229–258
Psychology, 137–195
 Abnormal psychology,
  165–195
 Consciousness, 139–163

Academic Skills
Charts/graphic organizers, 7, 17,
 19–20, 22–23, 39, 46, 51,
 53, 66, 75, 80, 82,
 101–102, 109, 120, 124,
 135, 143, 148, 154, 160,
 162, 170, 182, 193,
 208–209, 230, 232, 234,
 241, 257
Critical thinking, SEE Critical
 Thinking heading
Dictionaries, 150
Test-taking skills/strategies,
 affixes, 66–67, 176–177
 applying information,
  130–131
 checks (for answers that
  apply), 53–54
 circling (best choice), 9–10,
  72, 111–112, 253
 crossing out (answers that do
  not apply), 135
 defining, 45, 52, 77, 88, 121,
  148, 154, 169, 232, 239,
  245
 details (questions about), 155
 determining main point, 244
 determining purpose, 244
 determining tone, 244

determining topic, 244
editing a test essay, 33–34
fill in the blank, 21, 25–26,
 65–66, 67, 80, 127,
 135–136, 144, 193, 194,
 208, 209, 257, 258, 259
finding errors, 31, 59, 99,
 129, 160, 187, 222, 251
finding sentences with similar
 meaning, 209–210
guessing meaning from context, 44
identifying, 59
idioms, 114–115
main point, 246
matching, 13, 18, 83, 116,
 117, 125, 134, 172, 192,
 203–204, 234–235, 257
multiple choice, 14–15, 31,
 59, 61, 65, 99, 109,
 114–115, 129, 155, 177,
 244
purpose, 246
questions about details, 155
stems, 66–67, 176–177
tone, 244
topic, 244
true/false, 134, 192
understanding idioms,
 114–115
understanding pronouns, 81
understanding stems and
 affixes, 176–177

Critical Thinking
Analysis, 24, 33, 63–64, 124,
 132, 163, 182 (T-chart),
 190, 226, 232, 255
Application, 24, 27, 39, 52–53,
 74, 90–91, 109, 130–131,
 143, 156, 175
Cause and effect, 116, 123
Comparing/contrasting, 81–82,
 170
Determining point of view, 142

Inferences, 6–7, 43, 116, 181,
 239
Making comparisons, 81–82,
 170
Making connections, 13, 23, 53,
 87, 147, 182, 217
Making inferences, 6–7, 43,
 116, 181, 239
Making predictions, 110, 204,
 226–227 (opposing argu-
 ments), 230
Point of view, 142
Predictions, 110, 204, 226–227
 (opposing arguments), 230
Seeing two sides of an issue,
 245–246
Summarizing (research), 232
Synthesis, 52–53, 170

Discussion, 8, 52, 82, 140, 155,
 171, 176, 182, 211, 218,
 233, 240, 246
Chapter introduction discussions, 3, 35, 71, 105, 139,
 165, 199, 229
Extension activities, 24, 202
Surveys, 17, 143
Talking About It, 159–160
 (symbols)
Thinking Ahead, 4, 8, 16, 36,
 40, 47, 72, 76, 83, 106,
 117, 144, 149, 166, 178,
 200, 203, 212–213,
 233–234

Extension, 14–15

Making Connections, 13, 23,
 53, 87, 147, 182, 217

READING
Comprehension
Details, 6, 21, 39, 80, 120, 147,
 175, 181, 202, 208, 216,
 238, 243

266 Skills Index

CREDITS

Text Credits

P. 5: Marketing Translation Mistakes (http://www.i18nguy.com/translations.html); p. 11: "International Culture" by Alan M. Rugman and Richard M. Hodgetts from *International Business: A Strategic Management Approach, International Edition*. Copyright © 1995 by McGraw-Hill, Inc. Reprinted with the permission of the McGraw-Hill Companies. p. 18: Reprinted with permission of the publisher. From *Cultural Intelligence: People Skills for Global Business* by David C. Thomas and Kerr Inkson. Copyright © 2004 by David C. Thomas and Kerr Inkson, Berrett-Koehler Publishers, Inc., San Francisco, CA. All rights reserved. www.bkconnection.com; p. 18: From *Culture's Consequences: Comparing Values, Behaviors, Institutions and Organizations Across Nations* by G. Hofstede, 2001. Reprinted by permission of the author. p. 41: Adapted from "How to Buy a House" from *Bitter Lemons* by Lawrence Durrell. Copyright © 1957 by Lawrence Durrell. p. 43: Definition for "skirt" from *Longman Dictionary of American English*, 2004. p. 49: "Economic Systems" adapted from Roger LeRoy Miller, *Economics: Today and Tomorrow*. Copyright © 1995, 1991 Glencoe/McGraw-Hill. Reprinted with the permission of the McGraw-Hill Companies. Also adapted from Abraham Rosman and Paula G. Rubel, *The Tapestry of Culture: An Introduction to Cultural Anthropology*, 8th edition. Copyright © 2004 by the McGraw-Hill Companies. Reprinted with the permission of the McGraw-Hill Companies. p. 73 "Looking at Art: What's the Story" adapted, in part, from *Art in Focus* by Gene A. Mittler. Copyright © 1994 by Glencoe/McGraw-Hill. Reprinted with the permission of the McGraw-Hill Companies. Also adapted, in part, from *Biblical Archaeology Review*, 22 (July/August 1996). p. 78: "The Sacred Realm of Art" adapted from Rita Gilbert, *Living With Art, Fourth Edition*. Copyright © 1994 by Rita Gilbert. Reprinted with the permission of the McGraw-Hill Companies. Also adapted from Gilbert's *Living with Art, Sixth Edition*, p. 49, by Mark Getlein, copyright © 2002 McGraw-Hill. Reprinted with the permission of the McGraw-Hill Companies. p. 85: "Art as the Mirror of Everyday Life" adapted from Rita Gilbert, *Living With Art, Fourth Edition*, copyright © 1994 by Rita Gilbert. Reprinted with the permission of the McGraw-Hill Companies. Also adapted from Gilbert's *Living with Art, Sixth Edition* by Mark Getlein, copyright © 2002 The McGraw-Hill Companies. p. 107: "Rules of Egyptian Art" adapted, in part, from Gilbert's *Living with Art, Sixth Edition*, by Mark Getlein, copyright © 2002 McGraw-Hill. Reprinted with the permission of the McGraw-Hill Companies. "Rules of Egyptian Art" adapted, in part from Gene A. Mittler, *Art in Focus*. Copyright © 1994 by Glencoe/McGraw-Hill. Reprinted with the permission of the McGraw-Hill Companies. p. 113: "Finds Reveal Much of Life at Pyramids" from *The Star Free Press* (May 31, 1993). p. 118: "Egyptian Civilization: A Brief History" adapted, in part, from Gene A. Mittler, *Art in Focus*. Copyright © 1994 by Glencoe/McGraw-Hill. Reprinted with the permission of the McGraw-Hill Companies. p. 141: From *Our Dreaming Mind*, copyright © 1994 by Robert Van de Castle, Ph.D. Used by permission of Ballantine Books, a division of Random House, Inc. p. 145: *Senoi Dream Theory: Myth, Scientific Method, and the Dreamwork Movement* by G. W. Domhoff, 2003. Retrieved October 17, 2004 from: http://dreamresearch.net/Library/domhoff_2000e.html; *Peoples and Cultures of the World, Part I*, by Edward E. Fisher, 2004. Chantilly, VA: The Teaching Company; *Reader in Comparative Religion: An Anthropological Approach* (2nd ed.) by W.A. Lessa and E.Z. Vogt, 1965, Harper & Row; *The Tapestry of Culture: An Introduction to Cultural Anthropology* (8th ed.) by A. Rosman and P.G. Rubel, 2004, McGraw-Hill; *Religion in Ancient Egypt: Gods, Myths, and Personal Practice* by B.E Shafer (Ed.), 1991, Cornell University Press. p. 150: Definition for "vision" from *Longman Dictionary of American English*, 2004. p. 151: Adapted from *Essentials of Understanding Psychology* (5th ed.) by R.S. Feldman, 2003, McGraw-Hill. Reprinted with the permission of the McGraw-Hill Companies. p. 167: Adapted from R.S. Feldman, *Essentials of Understanding Psychology, Fifth Edition*. Copyright © 2003 by McGraw-Hill, Inc. Reprinted with the permission of the McGraw-Hill Companies. Also adapted from A. Rosman and P.G. Rubel, *The Tapestry of Culture: An Introduction to Cultural Anthropology, Eighth Edition*. Copyright © 2004 by McGraw-Hill, Inc. Reprinted with the permission of the McGraw-Hill Companies. p. 173: "What Is Abnormal?" adapted from Richard A. Kasschau, *Understanding Psychology*. Copyright © 1995 by Glencoe Publishing Company. Reprinted with the permission of the McGraw-Hill Companies. Also adapted from Robert S. Feldman, *Essentials of Understanding Psychology, Fifth Edition*. Copyright © 2003 by McGraw-Hill, Inc. Reprinted with the permission of the McGraw-Hill Companies. p. 179: "Approaches to Psychological Therapy" adapted from Richard A. Kasschau, *Understanding Psychology*. Copyright © 1995 by Glencoe Publishing Company. Reprinted with the permission of the McGraw-Hill Companies. p. 201: "Afghan Women Use Drugs to Cope with Legacy of War," by Nick Meo, from Europe Intelligence Wire, *Belfast Telegraph*, (September 30, 2004). Copyright 2004 by Financial Times Information Ltd., and "My Son's Devotion Was Total," by Michael Dorris from *New Choices for Retirement Living* (December 1993). p. 204: Adapted from

"Guide to Drug Abuse Epidemiology," World Health Organization, 2000. Also from *World Health, 43,* July-August 1995 and from "Surveys of Drinking Patterns and Problems in Seven Developing Countries," World Health Organization, 2001. p. 212: "Addiction: The Downward Slide" from Mary Bronson Merki and Don Merki, *Health: A Guide to Wellness.* Copyright © 1994 by Glencoe/McGraw-Hill. Reprinted with the permission of the McGraw-Hill Companies. p. 214: *Health: A Guide to Wellness.* Copyright © 1994 by Glencoe/McGraw-Hill. Reprinted with the permission of the McGraw-Hill Companies. p. 233: "What Does New Research Tell Us" from *The Week,* January 7, 2005. p. 237: Adapted from *Newsweek,* September 27, 2004: "Brain Check," by Herbert Benson, M.D., Julie Corliss and Geoffrey Cowley; "How the Body Harms Itself," by Josh Ulick; "Ways to Calm Your Mind," by Herbert Benson, M.D., and Julie Corliss; "For a Happy Heart," by Anne Underwood; "We All Need a Dose of the Doctor," by Michael C. Miller, M.D.; "Combination Therapy," by Peg Tyre. p. 244: "A Skeptical Look: Placebo Effect" condensed from "Spontaneous Remission and the Placebo Effect" by Stephen Barrett on Quackwatch website, www.quackwatch.org. Reprinted by permission.

Photo Credits